WHERE THE
GHOSTS WALK

D0522416

WHERE THE GHOSTS WALK

The Gazetteer of Haunted Britain

Peter Underwood

Souvenir Press

This book is for
NIGEL & CINDY
in gratitude for
their many kindnesses
and innumerable
cups of coffee

And for MARLENA who,
dancing and dreaming,
brought the stars to
earth for both of us

Contents

Introduction   1
Illustrations   5

Part 1 Haunted Airfields   9

Biggin Hill – Bircham Newton – Colerne –
Davidstow – Heathrow – Leeming – Montrose – North
Weald – Wittering – Other Haunted Airfields

Part 2 Haunted Ancient Sites   45

Ambresbury Banks – Avebury – Badbury Rings –
Cerne Abbas – Grime's Graves – Rillaton – Royston
Cave – St Nectan's Glen – Shrieking Pits –
Stonehenge – Other Haunted Ancient Sites

Part 3 Haunted Battlefields   77

Culloden – Edgehill – Glencoe – Halidon Hill –
Killiecrankie – Naseby – Poyntington – St Albans –
Sedgemoor – Stamford Hill – Other Haunted
Battlefields

Part 4 Haunted Bridges   109

Ballindallock – Bridge of Orchy – Corfe Castle –
Dryburgh – Durweston – Hever – Potter Heigham –
Slaughter Bridge – Stockbridge – Other Haunted
Bridges

Part 5 Haunted Gardens   131

Baddesley Clinton – Beaulieu – Bellechin – Bordean –
Buriton – Heligan – Nanteos – Sandford Orcas –
Scotney Castle – Sutton Place – Traquair House –
Warleggan – Other Haunted Gardens

Part 6 Haunted Graveyards   163

Abbots Langley – Canewdon – Daniel's Knowle –
Hopwas, Tamworth – Llanfaglan – Ludgvan –
Monyash – Portsmouth – St Osyth – Sanquhar – Other
Haunted Graveyards

Part 7 Haunted Highways and Byways   195

Annan – Aylesford – Bath – Beaminster – Camborne –
Flint – Honiton – Moffram – Upminster –
Whitechapel – Winterbourne Abbas – Other Haunted
Highways and Byways

Part 8 Haunted Open Spaces   225

Bossiney – Brooklands – Canvey Island – Cwndonkin
Park – Dartmoor – Gibbet Hill, Hindhead – Glenshee –
Greenwich – Other Haunted Open Spaces

Part 9 Haunted Railways   251

Brighton – Bury – Darlington – Dunphail – Glasgow –
Hammersmith – Hayling Island – Isfield – Maldon –
Rolleston – Swanage – Other Haunted Railways

Part 10 Haunted Ruins   283

Berwick-upon-Tweed – Caerphilly – Castle Rising –
Colchester – Conwy – Corfe Castle – Hadleigh –
Maiden Castle – Margam – Netley – Porchester –
Tintern Parva – Walsingham – Other Haunted Ruins

Part 11 Haunted Seascapes 313

Beachy Head – Boscastle – Isle of Iona – Lindisfarne –
The Mumbles – Purbeck – Sandwood Bay – Sennen –
Other Haunted Seascapes

Part 12 Haunted Waters 347

Berwick-upon-Tweed – Betws-y-Coed – Brimington –
Edgbaston – Gwithian – Lamberhurst – Laugharne –
Llandaff – Mersea Island – Shere – Somerton – Other
Haunted Waters

Part 13 Haunted Woods and Trees 375

Blandford Forum – Brighouse – Dinnington –
Ganllwyd – Hyde Park – North Benfleet –
Northampton – Pengrugla – Tarrant Gunville –
Watton – Windsor – Wootton Rivers – Other Haunted
Woods and Trees

Select Bibliography 405
Index 407

Introduction

There have been hundreds of books detailing apparent ghostly activity in buildings of every description but this is the first, I think, to look at haunted locations, the places where ghosts are reputed to be seen, and we consider haunted airfields, haunted ancient sites, haunted battlefields, gardens, graveyards, highways and byways, railways, ruins, seascapes, waters and woods and trees. Each has its individual ghosts and ghostly activity, it would seem, and many have been haunted for hundreds of years, a few for just a few years, if that.

As in all aspects of psychic activity the variety is enormous and I have tried to present a representative rather than a comprehensive selection. The wide variety of cases gives some idea of the wealth of paranormal phenomena that is extant throughout Britain; places that feed the imagination. While whole books have been written about disappearing cottages and vanishing landscapes, equally mysterious are scenes of history clearly witnessed before disappearing, as for example, a whole Roman legion in Dorset.

Ancient knowledge is often enshrined in folklore and folk memory. Mutilation of the body to prevent it walking after death goes back more than two thousand years. Is this why we sometimes encounter headless ghosts? Many people believe a life force remains around after the death of the body. Is this why we often feel 'something' is apparent at haunted places but we are not sure what, and why tragic and violent deaths often leave behind ghosts?

As appropriate, I explore the history of a site and ancient stones and other early structures since there is evidence to suggest these places have powers that may affect people today and may well be associated with nearby ghosts; and I look at snippets of history that I think may have a bearing on a haunting in question.

In one or two instances I have sought to follow the probable origin of the haunting, for example in the case of a battlefield, in some detail, seeking to establish some reason why it should be that here battle scenes are re-enacted or reappear, on some occasions to some people.

The problem of anniversary ghosts, such as the phenomena at Killiecrankie, manifesting on the date according to the current calendar when the actual event took place before 1752 (when Britain adopted the Gregorian calendar) is a recurring one but it has always seemed to me that the person or persons seeing a ghost, in all probability, themselves unconsciously contribute to the ghostly appearance and with the original date in their mind it could well be that the key is turned and psychic activity ensues. Whatever the answer, there are many well-authenticated accounts of ghosts appearing on the current, but incorrect, anniversary date. Harry Price (1881–1948) was well aware of this problem and the possibilities and he advised me, back in 1946, to be present not only on the 'correct' date (eleven days later) but also on the date in the current calendar. In psychic matters nothing is certain and all we can do is to expect the unexpected.

In addition to some well-known haunted spots I have included some that are little known or unfrequented but certainly haunted. Of all man's traditions and beliefs, his acceptance of ghosts is perhaps the most strongly rooted. Many cultured, learned and knowledgeable individuals entertain the possibility that the dead may return to the world of the living under certain circumstances, and who are we to disagree. Personal experience is all important. As Longfellow put it:

> The spirit world around this world of sense
> Floats like an atmosphere and everywhere
> Wafts through these earthly mists and vapours dense
> A vital breath of more ethereal air.

A fictional television play called *The Stone Tape* was broadcast one Christmas in the 1970s and the intriguing idea that tragic and dramatic and violent happenings can sometimes be stored in stonework, and on occasions can replay, has come to be regarded as a serious theory for some ghostly activity, and it may be so but it is important to remember that the 'stone tape' theory had its origin in a fictional story.

Music is often regarded as having special powers of exercising a magical sensibility, of enhancing the sense of the supernatural, the transcendent and the ineffable, but sometimes ghostly smells are part of paranormal activity related and it is worth remembering that smells can often transport us back to powerful and emotional memories more effectively than sounds. Marcel Proust (1871–1922) advanced the theory and recent research at Utrecht University has confirmed it, concluding that 'odour is a stronger trigger for arousing detailed memories than music, for example'.

Each of my locations will have its supporters as 'the most haunted', from woods and trees, the oldest living things on the planet that can, perhaps, retain echoes of past events, to airfields, and Bruce Barrymore Halpenny is not alone in believing that airfields 'are the most haunted places in the world; that *every* airfield is haunted'. And ancient stones, can they really secrete power? Gwyneth Lewis's mother, holidaying in Aberystwth in the 1960s, decided to show her daughter the Taliesin stone, named after a sixth-century Welsh poet. Sleep with your head on the stone, it was believed, and you would wake up a poet or mad, possibly both. To look at, it's just a boulder in a field and Gwyneth only touched it. But she became the first National Poet of Wales.

Speaking of Wales, I see that in April, 2011, the Dyfed Powys police were asked to investigate twenty-six ghosts and twenty cases of haunting. It's all happening in Wales, it seems.

Overwhelming evidence suggests that odd happenings, frequently of considerable complexity, do happen. Perhaps we should accept these inexplicable occurrences as part of the basic furniture of the world. It has been suggested that whenever a person is thought of, believed in or imagined, there will be his ghost. Perhaps Browning had the answer: his 'silver answer', not death but love, Now let us journey into the unknown.

Peter Underwood
Savage Club
London SW1A 2HD

I gratefully acknowledge the help and assistance I have received writing and illustrating this volume from many people and especially Ernest Hecht, Michael Williams, Alan C. Wood, Marie Campbell, Janet Joel and John Rackham.

Illustrations

Sandford Orcas, Dorset. A photograph, taken on the lawn, looking towards the gate where a farmer hanged himself. The figure in a white smock, standing in front of the gateway and behind the dog in the centre of the picture is thought to be the ghost. (Photo: Peter Underwood Collection)

The winding road through the haunted Pass of Glenshee, Scotland. (Photo: Peter Underwood Collection)

Battle Abbey, East Sussex, as it was in 1905. (Photo: Peter Underwood Collection)

Slaybrook Hall, Saltwood, Kent has a haunted garden, part of it was once a battlefield. (Photo: J. A. Mackenzie)

Some of the mysterious carvings inside Royston Cave, Hertfordshire, looking north. (Photo: Peter Underwood Collection)

A grave, possibly that of King Arthur himself, just upstream from Slaughter Bridge, the scene of his last battle. (Photo: Michael Williams)

The haunted garden at Sandford Orcas, near Sherborne, Dorset. (Photo: Peter Underwood)

The graveyard at Rye, East Sussex, haunted by the ghost of a man wrongly executed for murder. (Photo: Peter Underwood)

The author at Tintern Abbey where ghost monks still walk. (Photo: Peter Underwood)

The author amid the haunted ruins of Margam Abbey in West Wales. (Photo: Peter Underwood)

The crumbling and haunted ruins of Odiam Castle, Hampshire. (Photo: Peter Underwood)

The graveyard and Bronte Parsonage, Haworth, West Yorkshire where ghosts of the Bronte sisters walk. (Photo: Marie Campbell)

Historic and haunted Hever Castle in Kent. (Photo: Peter Underwood Collection)

Hartley Mauditt in Hampshire where the silent pool is skirted from time to time by a phantom coach-and-four and where the little church has echoed with ghostly music. (Photo: Peter Underwood)

The haunted sands of Lulworth Cove, Dorset, where the ghost of Napoleon has been reported. (Photo: Peter Underwood)

A simulated ghost at haunted Berry Pomeroy, Devon. A postcard that used to be sold at the castle. (Photo: Cox: Peter Underwood Collection)

The haunted pool of vanished Old Bayhall Manor, Pembury, Kent. (Photo: Peter Underwood)

The haunted ruins of Conwy Castle, North Wales. (Photo: Peter Underwood)

The haunted garden at Brede Place near Rye in East Sussex where several ghosts walk. (Photo: Peter Underwood Collection)

Carew Castle, Wales, repeatedly haunted by a ghost known only as the White Lady. (Photo: Peter Underwood)

The author dwarfed by some of the ruins at haunted Berry Pomeroy Castle in Devon. (Photo: Peter Underwood)

The Cloisters, part of the haunted gardens at Beaulieu in Hampshire. (Photo: Lord Montagu of Beaulieu)

Scotney Old Castle and the haunted moat. (Photo: Peter Underwood)

Montrose Airfield, Scotland, where Sir Peter Masefield saw an accident re-enacted fifty years after the day it happened. (Photo: Van Werninck: Peter Underwood Collection)

The strange and beautiful waterfall at haunted St Nectan's Glen, Cornwall. (Photo: Michael Williams)

The Italian Ship *Silvia Onorato* meets its end on the treacherous and haunted Goodwin Sands, off Kent. (Photo: Peter Underwood Collection)

Part 1

HAUNTED AIRFIELDS

Theatres and public houses are often thought of as places that have seen the whole gamut of human emotions: sadness and happiness, love and laughter, ecstasy and suffering, life and death, and that sometimes something of some of these past events may express itself in paranormal activity. So much has been experienced that a chord may be struck when someone is present who has knowledge of something similar.

But what about airfields? Here too there have been strong emotions: partings, meetings, accidents, death, survival, hate and love. Here too all the human emotions have been at play and here too something of past happenings may linger, waiting to be re-awakened by the right person there at the right time. The number of haunted airfields is vast. Let us look in some detail at just a few.

Biggin Hill, Kent

Here, at one of the most famous Battle of Britain airfields, there are substantial tales of haunting, tales that include phantom music, a ghostly Spitfire and a fighter pilot's ghost.

Dating back to its opening in 1917 in the days of the Royal Flying Corps, ghostly activity has been reported here. I once attended a book launch and, recognizing a Royal Flying Corps tie, I talked to the wearer and discovered that he lived in Australia and was over for a visit to his son. We arranged to meet for a longer chat at my London club and there he told me all about his early flying days and how he had himself seen a ghostly RFC officer smoking a pipe. He told me the figure was there one minute, for all the world 'as natural and solid as you are' and the next moment he had disappeared from the face of the earth – but the smell of his tobacco lingered on. Making enquiries he discovered that the officer had been seen by other people on the airfield; always in the same place, always smoking a pipe and always disappearing when approached.

When I was at Biggin Hill in 1988 I was told that the totally unexplained but lingering and unmistakable smell of pipe tobacco was quite often reported together with the individual sound of a Spitfire coming in to land.

When I was researching my *Ghosts of Kent* (1985) I discovered that as recently (then) as 1982 a couple of former RAF officers became interested in the reports of ghosts and ghostly happenings at Biggin Hill and uncovered a surprising amount of good evidence for apparently paranormal activity on and around this iconic aerodrome. In particular, those living nearby repeatedly reported hearing the unmistakable sound of a Spitfire screaming in to land. Some of the witnesses were people who had lived there through the war years and knew well the sound of a Spitfire when they heard it.

Biggin Hill was often visited by the prime minister Winston Churchill on his way home to Chartwell; indeed he became its Hon. Air Commodore, for it was one of the four main Spitfire stations in the Second World War and, indeed, until 1950. During that war Hurricanes and Spitfires operating from Biggin Hill destroyed over 1600 enemy aircraft. From its inception as a wireless research station through to the era of jet aeroplanes, 'Biggin on the Bump' has always been an exciting and haunted place.

It even has a specific day when ghostly sounds are most often heard: January 19. But the significance of that date is unknown. It could well be the date when Biggin Hill was under considerable attack – it was the most bombed station in Fighter Command and it never closed – or perhaps it was the date of some forgotten but formidable 'op' that has become imbued forever in the air at this historic place.

Among reported phenomena are the sound of men's voices singing Second World War songs on cold January nights; ghostly aircrew walking along the old Runway 21 and time and time again the sound of a lone Spitfire, sometimes the engine spluttering and missing but always its Merlin engine at full throttle. On warm summer evenings a ghostly Spitfire has been seen, its unmistakable and familiar shape approaching the airfield and performing a victory roll, before disappearing in the suddenly overwhelming silence.

The sounds of a bombing raid have also been heard. The

sounds of aircraft falling earthwards have been reported, followed by a sickening crashing sound, an explosion and then silence. Aircrew in flying clothing have been seen, walking along a route that led from the landing ground to the de-briefing quarters and in the area where once fighter planes were housed. Witnesses have even noticed silk polka-dot scarves on occasions – these were sometimes used by fighter pilots to prevent 'weaver's neck' caused by the constant turning of the head to prevent their being bounced by opposing enemy aircraft – and the inevitable pipe and scent of tobacco.

A correspondent once informed me that during a visit to Biggin Hill he had been told that the sequence of events of one ghostly episode involved the sound of a Spitfire approaching and landing followed by the sound of running footsteps across the airfield and over the road towards the pub often frequented by 'Biggin boys'. There a former land-lord said he was sometimes awakened at dead of night by the sound of men talking loudly, of glasses clinking and the banging on tables and the sound of laughing, card playing and joking talk. Whenever he got up out of bed he could still hear everything until he entered the bar and then all was quiet; until the next time.

Bircham Newton, Norfolk

In 1971 there was considerable publicity regarding an apparent haunting at Bircham Newton aerodrome in Norfolk. Built in 1916 as a training station, it became the first base of the Handley Page RAF long-range bombers, built to deliver bombs on Berlin in the First World War. The armistice of November 1918 came before the bombers had time to carry out this objective.

Without permanent tarmac runways, it had extensive technical and domestic buildings with a squash court built to Air Ministry specifications of 1918. During the Second World War it saw service as home to Coastal Command, mainly of Group No. 16. It was a substantial station with RAF personnel (including airmen and WAAF) totalling nearly 3000 and with thirty-nine squadrons using the airfield.

Closed in 1962 as an RAF airfield it was taken over by a construction firm who used it as a training centre with many of the old buildings remaining intact, including three aircraft hangars. The place was also used from time to time by film crews for training films for the building industry. And it was during one of their filming sessions that a ghost was reportedly regularly seen.

Denny Densham (1921–92) was a cameraman and in August 1970 he was at the airfield working on a film. The former officers' mess is isolated from the rest of the buildings and at that time was only partly reconstructed. While working there a standard film light slowly toppled over as Densham watched, falling and narrowly missing a technician, Peter Clark.

Behind this building two squash courts were often used by the visitors and one evening the only key to the courts was borrowed by Kevin Day who decided to have a knockabout by himself. For a while he played in the left-hand court and then he changed to the right-hand one. As he played there he became aware of a figure standing on the balcony watching him. When he looked more closely and directly at the figure he saw the man was wearing RAF uniform. For a while he returned to his squash and then, puzzled as to who the chap could be, he looked up towards the balcony again, only to see no sign of the figure.

Still more puzzled, he reported the experience to Denny Densham's assistant Peter Clark and he borrowed a tape recorder. They decided to spend a night in the squash court and see whether they could record anything of interest. Once in the building however they were struck by the extreme cold and suddenly they both felt very nervous alone in the big, dark building at night and, feeling more and more scared by the minute, they eventually left the recording machine and wandered about outside, where it was utterly quiet but not frightening. There was bright moonlight and they were able to ascertain that there was no article, car or person anywhere near the squash court.

Half an hour later they went back inside the building to collect the recorder and they both heard the distinct sound of footsteps from the direction of the balcony – and they fled! The recorder, which they had left running, they retrieved later and found it had recorded the sound of them leaving the building on the first occasion, followed by a variety of sounds, some metallic, some rushing or roaring sounds, some almost human-sounding but all seemingly inexplicable in the apparently deserted building. In particular, there was a human voice, sounding feminine, that seemed to say 'too late, too late'.

A week later they tried again and got nothing. A couple of months later still a local newspaper got hold of the story and checked their files and found there had been an airman named Wiley who had committed suicide on the aerodrome during the Second World War and his ghost was thought to be responsible for typical poltergeist activity that had occurred elsewhere on the airfield. This included interference with bedclothes, curtains being torn down and articles thrown across a room. An engineer claimed he had felt his shoulder tapped three times while working in the haunted areas when no one was anywhere near him; he was so unnerved that he refused to work there again. And the figure of a man in RAF uniform was again seen, this time by a man who was taking part in a course at the former airfield. He was so disturbed by what he saw that he refused to complete his course and left the following day. The RAF man he saw looked completely natural and normal in every way until he disappeared into a solid brick wall; so perhaps the witness's dismay can be understood.

I have discovered many ghost stories associated with Bircham Newton. Soon after the Second World War there were alleged sightings of a car full of happy laughing airmen. The car raced across the airfield and seemed to crash into the rear of a hangar – whereupon it suddenly and completely disappeared; all without a sound.

A WAAF was reputed to have committed suicide in one of the rooms in the WAAF block and there were several reports of ghostly activity in the 'haunted' room and the sound of 'something' being pulled out and dragged about the room and along the corridor; another WAAF who volunteered to spend a night in the 'haunted' room awakened there to feel icy fingers touching her.

In April 1949 ACW Mary Tock was at Bircham Newton as a nursing orderly in the Sick Quarters attached to the former Decontamination Centre. In the August of that year she was required to sleep in the Sick Quarters, accompanied by a WAAF ambulance driver. The outer door was locked on the inside and the keys were kept in the Medical Officer's quarters. The heavy inner swing doors between the Sick Quarters and where they were sleeping Tock and her friend wedged open so they could hear any calls and the telephone. The two women were having a light-hearted game of table tennis at about nine o'clock in the evening when they heard the 'clunk' of the heavy swing doors closing. As they stopped play and faced the glass-topped doors into the wards they could see there was darkness in the wards and no lights. Suddenly they both heard heavy footsteps crossing an adjoining room and approaching them. Fear grabbed them and they ran into the staff Duty Room and telephoned the guardroom while keeping an eye on the corridor and the room they had hurriedly left. In response to their call two RAF policemen arrived and checked the locked doors and then searched the whole area but found no one and nothing to account for the sounds heard by the WAAFs.

Some weeks earlier an aircraft had crashed a few miles away and the unaccompanied pilot's body had been brought into the Sick Quarters. Some people, both service personnel and civilians who were involved, felt that the footsteps – also heard by other people – was the unfortunate pilot coming to collect his flying garments and other belongings which were left there for a while. Soon the reported sounds became less frequent and finally ceased altogether.

The whole story of ghostly activity at Bircham Newton became somewhat confused as time passed and Danny Densham, whom I met and talked with on several occasions, is sometimes stated to have been the one who obtained the mysterious tape recording. I was a guest on the Jack de Manio radio show one morning when an engineer rang in to assert that he could offer no explanation, so it must be ghostly activity. I cannot offer any explanation either but I don't feel that that automatically means the sounds were of paranormal origin.

A team, including two mediums, once spent some time in the squash court and appeared to establish contact with a dead airman who said he and two other crewmen were killed in a crash at Bircham Newton, behind the local church. He further maintained that the three of them used to frequent the squash court and they made a pact that if they were killed in action they would meet again in the squash court.

Whatever the explanation for the strange activity reported at Bircham Newton they cannot but be interesting to anyone with an open mind and an enquiring spirit.

Colerne, Wiltshire

Perched on a plateau, RAF Colerne was opened in 1940, one of the last Expansion Scheme airfields to be completed. It was still under construction at the outbreak of the Second World War in 1939 with many of the planned buildings incomplete; others were quickly modified. It opened in late 1940 as a fighter airfield, still only partially completed but it was soon operational and training new fighter squadrons.

In the years that followed, the airfield, designated by Fighter Command as 10 Group Sector HG, saw considerable activity. Blenheims and Beaufighters patrolled Bristol and the south-west, scoring regularly; a BOAC repair facility moved there in 1941 and the following years saw the assembly of secret special installations, including radar and all sorts of one-off modifications. Soon a Polish Hurricane squadron was carrying out sweeps from Colerne and a string of other squadrons spent time there with Whirlwinds, Defiants and Mosquitoes. Later squadrons of the USAAF brought their Lightnings. Altogether, various squadrons from RAF Colerne roamed nightly over France with great success.

After the war, the airfield was used for test flights and ferrying before being included in those airfields listed as 'no longer required' in the 1975 Defence White Paper and it finally closed in 1976. There was for a time a thriving museum housed there.

Eventually, the station was taken over by the Army in 1980 and named Azimghir Barracks, becoming the home of the Junior Leaders Regiment RCT, before the Ministry of Defence began selling the land on the runway approaches. A good view of the airfield area can be obtained from the adjoining Fosse Way (the old Roman road marked by its fosses or ditches on either side to keep the road drained and dry). Eleventh-century writers refer to the Fosse Way as one of the 'royal roads' in Britain.

RAF Colerne was equipped early on with permanent accommodation for its staff and their families and these buildings continued to be occupied throughout the history of the airfield. In March 1995 Basil Wright of Dartmouth in Devon wrote to me about his personal experiences in one of the houses bordering the airfield. He writes:

'As a First Mate in the Royal Maritime Auxiliary Service, I was posted to their H.Q. in Bath and was allocated a semi-detached house in "officer country" at what had been RAF Colerne. At that time the RAF was withdrawing from the station and the M.O.D. was using the quarters to house staff posted to the area from away. My house was in the middle of a row overlooking the airfield, but apart from me, only the house at each end of the row was occupied.

'One evening, having had a very busy day, I went to bed early, but awoke just after midnight to the sounds of a lot of chattering and laughter. In my sleep-befuddled state I decided that a party must be going on next door. I settled down and eventually went back to sleep.

'In the morning I remembered that the houses on either side of me were empty so I mentioned it to the Military Police who told me that if I heard anything during the night it was probably their patrol checking the empty houses as in the past they had had trouble with squatters.

'I thought no more about it until one night when I had been working late and got home at about midnight. There was quite a storm blowing and, having garaged the car, I was glad to get indoors. Having checked that the doors and windows were secured, I went to bed. I had no sooner turned out the light than I again heard voices with a lot of chattering and laughter. I tried to locate where the sounds were coming from until I realised to my horror, that they were emanating from my own front room downstairs!

'As I wondered what to do, the bedclothes were suddenly and sharply pulled across me, tightly, and the mattress at the side of the bed sank as though someone had sat on the edge of the bed to remove his shoes and socks: but there was no one else in the house! I am not usually a praying man, but that night I prayed. By Gosh I prayed. I have never prayed so hard.

'Then, as I prayed, the pressure on the bed eased, the voices and laughter faded and even the raging storm outside seemed to be stilled and I was overcome by a feeling of all pervading peace.

'A few months later, I was giving a colleague a lift to the office. At the start of our journey, we had to drive along a lane with the air station on our right and thick woodland on our left. Towards the end of the lane we passed on our right the eastern end of the East/West runway and on our left a large gap in the woodland. The trees surrounding the gap were badly scorched, having obviously been subject to a very fierce fire.

'My colleague informed me that he was living on the station when that crash happened. It was the last Hastings on the station and it was taking off for a series of practice "circuits and bumps". Unfortunately, someone had omitted to replace a bolt in one of the tail ailerons and the pilot could not get sufficient lift to clear the trees. The plane ploughed into the woods and, with a full load of fuel on board, it blew up in a fireball killing all the crew.

'He added that the pilot was very popular with his crew and on the evening before any flight he always invited them all to his house where they would discuss and work out the flight plan for the following day. When that was over the drinks would come out and they would get down to yarning and joking.

'"He lived along your road," he added. "Laurel Drive." "Oh?" I said, "Which number?" "Number Ten," he replied. All at once everything seemed to be answered. I lived at Number Ten, Laurel Drive.'

Davidstow, Cornwall

RAF Davidstow Moor opened in October 1942 and closed in 1945. When the 19 Group of Coastal Command declared the station open, the first operational aircraft to arrive were eighteen Liberators of the 93rd and 44th Bomb Groups of the United States Army Air Forces.

These and other USAAF bomb groups operated from Davidstow with Flying Fortresses until the middle of 1943. The Coastal and Bomber Command, Polish, Canadian and United States Navy operated from here as well. Aircraft using Davidstow included Whitleys, Wellingtons, Lancasters. Liberators, Halifaxes, Mosquitoes, Hurricanes and Spitfires. The last operational flight was on 19 September 1944 involved Warwick Air Sea Rescue aircraft.

Operations carried out from Davidstow saw aircraft bombing U-boat installations in French ports in the Bay of

Biscay; airborne lifeboat rescue work; anti-submarine patrols; protective flights covering Atlantic convoys; the demonstrations of captured enemy aircraft; the recording of enemy radio and radar activity; air-sea rescue operations in many different locations; night sorties looking for E-boats and strike operations and valuable work in anti-shipping strikes working right up to the D Day invasion of France.

Today the Davidstow Airfield and Cornwall at War Museum occupy much of the old airfield site and exhibits include a U-boat gun, the RAF Davidstow logbook, the original control tower, weapons from the First World War onwards, a First World War trench display and a tracked Rapier missile.

Prudence Pepper was an ex-Ambulance Driver and Despatch Rider in the London Fire Service during the Second World War and in 1959 moved to a cottage on the edge of Bodmin Moor in Cornwall. She had not been there long before she and a friend noticed unusual and unexplained sounds that were heard repeatedly, usually at dead of night. During the course of exploring the district she came across the old airfield at Davidstow; and here, she immediately thought, might be the answer to the strange and persistent night sounds she and her friend heard.

Next day she arrived at the old airfield just before dusk. Miss Pepper hid her motorcycle and quietly made her way to the top of the old control tower. It was a very clear night and she could easily make out the two runways of Davidstow Moor airfield. She decided to watch and see whether anything happened.

She thought she must have dozed off but she was suddenly wide awake as she heard sounds of activity above her. Her watch told her it was just after 3.30 in the morning and the intermittent droning noise grew louder and louder. To her experienced ear it sounded just like aeroplanes coming in to land yet she could clearly see the runways and their approaches and there was no sign of any plane. Then, judging by the even louder sounds, the invisible aeroplanes seemed to overshoot the runways. There was a weird swishing or loud hissing sound and then the noise of a tremendous crash at the end of the runway. Then Prudence saw flames and heard the sound of skidding and a lot of voices and sounds of activity but nothing was visible. Exactly the same thing happened three or four times and then all was quiet.

Miss Pepper looked at her watch again: it had all lasted only about six or seven minutes. Bewildered and puzzled as to what on earth she had witnessed she stumbled down the old broken steps of the control tower and for the next half-hour or so she wandered up and down the runways looking for tracks, skid marks, evidence of fire, anything that would help her rationalize what she had experienced and heard. She found nothing.

She told no one about her clandestine visit and what she had heard but a week later she had cause to visit Davidstow airfield again. She was giving a lift on her motorcycle to a local man (well-known as a poacher!) and they were on the straight and narrow road that cut through the old airfield.

'We were about halfway across,' she said later. 'When my headlights picked out a car lying sideways across the narrow road. I stopped and we hurried across and immediately we thought how strange it was for all the doors to be wide open and the lights on but not a soul in sight. We wondered whether it had somehow hit some of the cattle wandering freely over the moor.' Her companion, who seemed to know everyone in the vicinity, said the car did not belong to anyone locally and, completely puzzled, they resumed their journey, racing off what had once been the old airfield. Next morning Miss Pepper took her friend to see the car; it had disappeared and there was no sign whatever of it ever having been there. No tyre marks, no skid marks, no oil marks, nothing.

Prudence Pepper and her friend left Cornwall shortly afterwards and have never been back. I asked her whether she had ever felt like going back. 'Yes,' she said. 'I'd love to go back to that haunted airfield – but at my age I cannot run as fast as I used to – so I don't think I will go back!'

During my visits to Davidstow Airfield I heard many stories of seemingly inexplicable happenings: sounds of wartime activity, glimpses of wartime personnel, sensations that are indefinable but all too apparent to the people affected.

Heathrow, London

Sometimes claimed to be the busiest airport in the world, Heathrow still has time, it seems, for ghosts and ghostly activity.

The European Terminal 1 VIP Lounge has the reputation of being haunted and a diplomat from an African High Commission in London is just one of many people who believe they have seen the disappearing ghost of a man in a light-grey suit there. Claire Baker, a catering officer in the VIP suite, reported that the diplomat concerned was 'petrified and ran from the Lounge and refused to use the room again'. He said later he had seen the lower half of a man in grey trousers standing in front of him. Claire believed she had seen the same phantom. She saw the man and wondered whether he needed any help but as she approached him, he suddenly vanished and there was nowhere he could have gone without her seeing him; to leave the Lounge he would have had to pass her. However she did not feel afraid and thought that whatever it was, it was friendly. A policeman, Eric Harris, also experienced a strange 'presence' in the VIP Lounge and said, 'I'm a sceptic about the supernatural but I can't explain this'.

In 1975 a bowler-hatted 'ghost' was repeatedly causing some concern when 'he' seemed to enjoy being run over by police cars and leading them on wild goose chases at the airport. An account of the 'ghost's' activities was published in the Metropolitan police journal *The Job* under the heading 'Airport Ghost is at it again'. It stated that the ghost had been haunting the airport for many years and was first seen after a DC3 crashed there in 1948. The appearance of the apparition had become a common subject of conversation, especially by those who had been fortunate, or unfortunate, enough to have first-hand experience.

Inspector Leslie Alton of the Metropolitan police lived in Hounslow and he had the novel and perplexing experience of running over the mysterious figure on two occasions. One dark evening in 1970 he saw the figure 'walking' on the main runway and it was picked up on the control tower radar. For more than three hours the reports continued and each officer who ventured out to find the 'person' responsible came back empty-handed. Finally, Inspector Alton had permission to go out to the runway with three police cars and, with headlights on and every man on the lookout, the whole of Runway One was searched.

They found nothing. Fire appliances and motor-cyclists were called in to help; Inspector Alton was determined not to let the man get away. 'I thought it was someone giving us the runaround,' he said later. Then the control tower reported by radio to the police car, 'You've just run over him! Now he's behind your car and walking away from you'. All the search vehicles turned and, so he was told, he ran over the 'man' again. 'It was a weird feeling,' said Inspector Alton, an airport policemen for twenty years. 'There was nothing there. During the whole time I saw nothing'.

After the DC3 crashed in a remote part of the airport, a man approached several members of the rescue team and asked each in turn whether they had found his briefcase; yet there were no survivors of the crash and this was confirmed by the passenger list. Is the 'man' still looking for his missing briefcase?

A few months later, after other similar reports, Carmen Rogers, a medium from the Spiritualist Association of Great Britain, was called in and she believed she made contact with the man involved and seemed to establish that he was one of the twenty-two people who died when the DC3 crashed and burst into flames on 2nd March 1948.

She revealed: 'His name was something like Thomas Alperton and he had a wife called Mary and two children. I can see he is about six feet tall, in his late forties and clearly ex-Service, perhaps the Guards. He keeps worrying about losing his briefcase in the crash because it contained details of a deal he had just completed abroad. He is also worried about getting home to his wife and children.'

Mrs Rogers said the man did not realize that he was dead and he would keep reappearing when conditions corresponded to those on the night of the crash; but she thought she had been able to help and after visiting the scene of the crash in the right conditions she believed the mysterious man on the runway would vanish forever – and so he did, it would appear.

In 1974, cleaners at Heathrow became terrified and refused to work on their own at night-time because, they said, a ghost attacked them, holding them down by their throat and shoulders. An airport official at the time stated: 'We have reports about some strange presence on the jumbo jet planes and at present it cannot be explained. Some cleaners have said they have been thrown about by something invisible and afterwards have found they are unable to move.'

A manager for the cleaning company concerned said, 'We have certainly had reports from our night staff and an enquiry is being held. They have said they don't want to work alone at nights.' A foreman for the cleaning company, Mr Parsenal Parmer added: 'It happened to me and I was very frightened. Whatever it is seems to be within the rest room which we have on the jumbo jet piers. It all started when we opened the doors one day and there was a strange smell. It went away but came back again later. When I sat down in my chair for a brief rest I was horrified when I found I could not get up again. My eyes shut tight and I could not open them. It was as if someone was holding me down by my shoulders. I would say it was four or five minutes before I was able to move'.

Soon, however, these reported disturbances ceased and everything returned to normal. But other curious happenings began to be reported from Heathrow including an account of a security officer who said she saw 'a spirit form' at Terminal Three. Carol Hammond said something compelled her to look at a wall under some stairs and she saw what she described as 'a grey mist spinning in a whirlpool'. The mist revolved faster and faster and then began to open up in the middle. Then it came to a stop and she saw a cavalier. She was certain that the image had nothing to do with the pattern of the brick wall or anything like that and the face of the figure 'seemed to stand away' from the wall. Later she saw the same form or figure at Gate 12. Carol described the man she saw as having dark and curly, shoulder-length hair, thinning on top, and to have a long nose, a moustache and a single tuft of beard on his chin. She also said the figure was not fully formed but she could see the top of something like a dress shirt.

The security officer added that the face was very restful, 'almost holy looking; I was not at all afraid when I saw him. I felt completely relaxed. He never moved but just looked down and I never saw his eyes.'

One night, Carol was at Gate 12 with a colleague, Eleanor Deabill, when all the lights suddenly went out. They asked for the emergency lighting to be turned on and while they were waiting they both saw a mist forming, like the one Carol had seen before. 'It was like swirling fog and we were both frightened.' The duty officer came over and decided to close the post for the rest of the night. There are also reports by baggage handlers of lights inexplicably dimming, a mist forming and then dissolving, an escalator moving when it has been switched off. None have ever been satisfactorily explained.

Leeming, North Yorkshire

The airfield at RAF Leeming has been claimed to be 'the most haunted airfield' by Bruce Barrymore Halpenny, the military historian and author. Leeming began life as an airfield in June 1940 when it housed Whitley bombers of Number 10 Squadron. These soon joined by the new Handley Page Halifax bomber. In common with most Second World War airfields it saw many fatal crashes.

In 1941 a Whitley bomber aircraft crashed on Widdale Fell, unable to make it home and two flying officers died. In 1942 the Canadians arrived with their Hampdens and there were Canadian aircraft personnel at Leeming for the remainder of the war. Sadly, many planes, returning from bombing missions and badly shot up, crashed in sight of the airfield, unable to land safely. Today, nearby Harrogate Cemetery contains the remains of many Canadians and other aircrews. In February 1945 a Halifax crashed and its bomb load exploded when a tyre burst; just one of the many wartime tragedies at RAF Leeming.

After the war, the airfield housed an Operations Training Unit and, while conversion work was being carried out by a civil engineering firm, one of its employees, Alan Harridence, encountered more than he had bargained for one warm July evening.

He had been fishing in the stream behind the old and disused personnel wooden huts and while making his way back by the former bomb storage hut he stopped in his tracks as he heard, in the still and silent night, the sound of wheels running on tracks. The sounds, he recalled, were clearly audible. He heard too the sound of men's voices. After a moment the sounds ceased and all was quiet. Then, as he walked round a corner of the old bomb store, he saw the unclear figure of an airman, in full flying gear. The misty figure was sitting on a low concrete wall about twenty feet in front of him. He glanced about him but could see no one else – and when he looked back to where he had seen the figure seconds before, there was nothing to be seen! He walked over to where he had seen the form but there was certainly no one there or anywhere near and no sound whatever, and he thought to himself as he picked his way through the rubble and rubbish, no one could possibly have moved from that position in those circumstances without making some noise.

Back in the cookhouse he told the cook he had had a curious experience near the wooden huts used for personnel and the cook said Leeming was the place for curious experiences and that just a few mornings before, as he arrived at the cookhouse and switched on the lights, he saw an airman in full flying kit sitting at the far end of the mess room. The next moment the mess was deserted.

A week later Harridence met a local man who had lived all his life in the area. He said all the buildings on the old airfield were haunted by airmen from the 'four-engined bomber that crashed on that side of the airfield, killing all the crew'. He said he was on the airfield early one morning during the winter of 1940–41 when he heard this bomber coming in to land. He watched as the aircraft hit the runway and burst into flames.

This witness told Harridence that after the war he had once noticed a kind of glow in the middle of the airfield and he had seen a group of airmen in full flying attire walking towards him out of the glowing background. When a breeze sprang up and there seemed to be airmen talking and jostling all about him, this scared man dropped into the long grass for cover. When he raised his head a couple of moments later the wind had dropped, the glow had disappeared, all was quiet and the airfield was totally deserted.

A few weeks after taking notes of this new phenomenon at Leeming airfield, Harridence made a point of talking with the cook again. He and his wife had moved into one of the huts on the airfield for a short while but they found they could not sleep at night because of the sound of men's voices that seemed to be all around them, the sound coming and going all night. Also, once when he was alone in the mess he had seen a group of airmen apparently playing cards. He had slipped out of the mess to fetch a camera but, when he returned, there was no sign of the airmen in the quiet and deserted mess. He said his contract would soon be up and he and his wife would be pleased to get away from the haunted airfield.

In 1956 Peter Hindley was posted to Leeming as a technician and one night, while locking up the hangar he was working in, he suddenly came 'face to face with an RAF officer whom I didn't recognize'. The man wore flying kit and seemed to greet Hindley before disappearing into the night. Afterwards, Hindley realised that the doors of the hangar where he had seen the man were locked, as were the doors he would have had to go through to leave the hangar and he also recalled that he had not heard a single sound. More and more puzzled, Hindley discussed the odd experiences with other men, especially those who did night duty, and he learned of other similar and totally different examples of apparent psychic activity that practical and down-to-earth men recounted somewhat reluctantly. There really were many workmen who complained of mysterious happenings. Two fitters, for example, working late at night heard voices and glimpsed for a moment an airman fully kitted out for flying, standing close beside them. They refused to work there again after dark.

Maybe RAF Leeming is not the most haunted of all airfields but evidence suggests it could be one candidate for that doubtful honour.

Montrose, Scotland

This ancient airfield began life as a Royal Flying Corps training centre a hundred years ago, in 1912, and the best-known ghost here dates back almost as far.

Early in 1913, Number 2 Squadron of the RFC moved here from Farnborough in Hampshire and on 27th May that same year Lieutenant Desmond Lucius Arthur took off from Montrose in an experimental biplane and climbed to 2,000 feet when the upper starboard wing of the plane broke and the disintegrating aircraft plunged to the earth with the inevitable death of Lieutenant Desmond Arthur. It has to be said that another version of the event has the aircraft crashing on take-off with the Lieutenant dying after declaring that the machine had been tampered with. Whatever the circumstances of his death the ghost of Lieutenant Desmond Arthur reportedly soon began haunting the airfield.

After a service funeral with full military honours, the body was interred in Montrose Cemetery where his 'resting' place is marked by a cross and with the inscription: 'Desmond L. Arthur, Lieutenant, Royal Flying Corps, killed at Montrose 27 May 1913'.

An official enquiry found that the wing had not been properly repaired after an earlier incident, although it was decided that pilot error rather than the faulty maintenance caused the death of Desmond Arthur. At the same time it was rumoured that Arthur was very unpopular with his fellow officers and with the ground crew and that his death was no accident.

Before long, the unexplained figure of a pilot in full flying kit began to be reported. Several responsible airmen on the airfield said they had seen figures, often near the officers' mess, once frequented by Desmond Arthur. In the autumn of 1916 Major Cyril Foggin encountered such a form as he was approaching the mess. He did not recognize a man he took to be a fellow officer on the airfield and when he reached the closed mess door, where the figure had disappeared, Foggin was astonished to find no one anywhere in sight and the mess deserted.

Major Foggin saw the same ghostly form several more times but it always disappeared when he drew close to it. A flying instructor awoke one night to see a man in full flying kit, seemingly sitting on a chair in his bedroom. As he got out of bed the figure suddenly vanished. Subsequently, he found that Lieutenant Desmond Arthur had once occupied the room.

In 1942, another aircraft crashed at Montrose, again killing the pilot, another flight lieutenant, and yet again there was talk of the accident being the result of a fault while others suggested pilot error. At all events a new ghostly pilot, wearing Second World War flying apparel, now began appearing at Montrose. He was allegedly seen by many airmen on the airfield and by new student pilots who had no knowledge of any ghostly figures having been seen on the station.

In 1976 Lord Balfour of Inchrye, Under-Secretary for Air 1935–1944, who served in the old Royal Flying Corps, recounted a slightly different ghostly experience, which dated from 1972. He said a youngster was learning to fly at Montrose and one day his instructor told him he was ready for a solo flight. The young man did not feel he was ready but he was sent up anyway. He had hardly taken off when the machine stalled, there was a crash and the pilot was killed. That night the instructor was startled to see in his room the figure of the young flyer, his leather flying jacket blood-stained and his face cut. After a moment the figure disappeared but left bloodstains on the floor. The instructor changed rooms but the same figure appeared that night to the new occupant and the story spread throughout the station. Finally, the station commander assembled everyone together and told them he had issued orders for the 'haunted' room to be locked and sealed and not used. 'And that was the end of the matter,' said Lord Balfour.

Another instance of haunting here involving an apparent ghost flying officer was reported in 1940 when a fighter pilot, whose squadron was sent to Montrose during the winter to rest a while after extensive contribution to the Battle of Britain, related seeing the ghost of a pilot, a figure in flying kit, that disappeared inexplicably. He had no knowledge at the time that such a figure was sometimes seen in the old Officers' Mess, where he saw it.

As the years passed there were occasional sightings of the ghostly lieutenant or someone similar. In 1949, Eric Simpson was posted to Montrose with his squadron. On arrival, the men all received an 'arrival chit', a printed document welcoming them to the station and telling them that the camp was haunted by the ghost of Flight Lieutenant Arthur who had been killed in a crash there.

During his stay there Simpson said many people reported seeing the ghost. A Scottish clerk had no doubt about what he had seen and was much disturbed by the experience; a duty clerk saw the figure of a flying officer late at night apparently riffling through some papers; he asked the 'person' what he was doing and made to approach the figure which seemed to be solid and natural but as he walked forward the figure disappeared. Before it did so the duty clerk noticed that the figure seemed to be standing on a different floor level. The ghost of Lieutenant Desmond Arthur is unique in as much as he appears to be the only ghost officially recognized by the (then) Air Ministry. I knew Bruce Barrymore Halpenny, a former Royal Air Force security officer and in one of his books he states that the ghost at Montrose was still in the records and 'there have been many sightings on this cold and windswept airfield and even today it holds strange secrets'.

Halpenny reveals that some years ago a Mrs Ann Binnie was on holiday in a caravan on the Tayock Caravan Site in Montrose and she awoke one night to see the figure of a clean-shaven young man wearing a brown leather jacket with a fur collar standing looking down at her. After a few seconds the figure completely disappeared. Mrs Binnie had heard of the Montrose ghosts but had never experienced anything of that kind herself before nor did she afterwards.

There have also been reports of ghost aircraft at Montrose. A Hurricane pilot insisted that a biplane had hindered his landing and forced him to fly around and make a new landing. When he landed, somewhat annoyed, he was told there were no other planes anywhere near the lonely airfield when he had aborted his original fly-in and there were certainly no biplanes anywhere in the vicinity. A number of people have claimed to see a phantom Sopwith Camel aircraft in the vicinity of the airfield. Such a plane crashed not far away many years ago.

There was also an incident at Montrose involving an experienced serviceman who had seen service in France, Belgium, Holland, Germany, Denmark and Japan and he laughed at the ghost story when he was told about it on his arrival, saying he had heard lots of weird and wonderful war stories in his time and he had learned to take them with a pinch of salt. Then, when he was taking part in guard duty, he and his companion were intrigued by the arrival that day of a new aircraft, parked close to the control tower, and they decided to keep a special eye on the interesting machine.

In the middle of their watch, a quiet smoke seemed in order and it was arranged that they would each pop round the corner in turn to smoke a cigarette. The new arrival's mate went first and as the new arrival was left alone the doors of the hangar opposite, (which had been checked and found securely closed) suddenly flew open and a figure emerged, an airman wearing goggles, and a flying suit and helmet. As the experienced serviceman on guard duty stared open-mouthed at the silent but somehow frightening figure, wondering what he should do, the figure suddenly vanished and with a loud bang the doors slammed shut and all was quiet again. His companion, returning a few seconds later, had heard nothing.

Sir Peter Masefield, who held a pilot's licence from 1937 until 1970; was Personal Adviser to the War Cabinet 1934–1945; Chief Executive BEA 1949–1955; Chairman, Board of Trustees, Imperial War Museum 1977–8; Council Member, Royal Aero Club, Guild of Air Pilots, etc. told me when I had lunch with him at the Athenaeum that he had personally seen the whole 1913 accident involving Desmond Arthur at Montrose re-enacted in May, 1963, almost exactly fifty years after it had actually happened.

At one time I was in touch with the Montrose Museum curator who told me he had never ceased to be amazed at the number of people who told him of bizarre and quite inexplicable happenings they had experienced at Montrose airfield. RAF Montrose finally closed as an airfield in 1980 and it is now used by various industrial firms. There have, to my knowledge, been no very recent reports of the so-called Montrose Ghost – or ghosts.

North Weald, Essex

The old RAF station at North Weald Bassett has a long history of haunting. A couple of miles north-east of Epping, the original airfield was opened back in 1916 when the Royal Flying Corps was still operating. In 1940 and throughout the Battle of Britain this airfield was in the front line and the seven fighter squadrons stationed there took on the full might of the German Luftwaffe.

One day in late September 1940 a vicious aerial melee developed over the south coast. Eventually, the Germans retreated and the surviving Spitfires returned to North Weald. One was badly shot up and limped back only to burst into flames on landing. The pilot, severely wounded but conscious, insisted on being debriefed before his wounds were treated. The medical officer on duty himself insisted on doing what he could immediately but all the time the pilot wanted to see the de-briefing officer. As the medical officer hurried away to fetch the officer and explain the circumstances, he heard the sound of dragging footsteps and a loud thump from the room he had just left. He hurried back to the wounded pilot only to find him on the floor, dead, and in his hand the telephone. He had evidently been trying to reach someone with his last remaining ounce of strength.

Since that time many people, including telephone operators on night duty, visiting servicemen and civilians, and regular serving men at the station, on and off duty, have all independently reported hearing the sound of dragging footsteps followed by a crashing sound and a heavy bump, from the deserted room where the wounded pilot had been treated.

In 1946, ex-Sergeant Bernard Hughes heard the sounds and said half the personnel at the camp were scared to go anywhere near that room after dark, especially members of the WRAF who otherwise were completely fearless.

In 1949, Flight Lieutenant John Attrill and a fellow officer decided to investigate. They established that all relevant doors and windows were securely shut and locked and they fixed thread across the doorway and strategically inside the room. For hours all was quiet and then, just when they thought it was all a waste of time, they heard a slight sound from the locked and empty room. A moment later they heard the sound of dragging footsteps, then a crash and then a heavy bump. They gingerly made they way towards the room which they found completely undisturbed, quiet as the grave and entirely deserted. Their threads were as they had left them, not broken or altered in any way.

Later, in March 1968 when the Army took over the deserted airbase, the incoming soldiers scoffed at stories of ghosts and ghostly happenings. Before long, however, Corporal Roderick Broomhead, Lance Corporal Steve Lovatt and other tough, seasoned and professional soldiers were all reporting strange and unexplained happenings that caused Lieutenant-Colonel Patrick Winter, the Commanding Officer to comment: 'It sounds crazy but the entire camp is buzzing with stories about ghosts.' North Weald airfield has a long history and a wealth of enduring ghosts although the ghostly sounds of dragging footsteps and heavy bumps ceased after the appropriate room and block were demolished.

Wittering, Huntingdonshire

The old airfield here has a long history of haunting. It was originally a First World War station, developed in 1924 and opened as a Training Station for the Central Flying School, to be replaced at the outbreak of the Second World War by Number 11 Flying Training School with the customary couple of fighter squadrons taking up residence. Too far north to be actively involved as an airfield during the Battle of Britain, it nevertheless played a significant part in the defence of the Midlands when enhanced by three or four more fighter squadrons, destroying many enemy aircraft.

During 1943 and 1944 Wittering saw Lightnings and Mustangs on its runways when Number 55 Fighter Squadron of the USAAF arrived. These were soon joined by Fulmars, Barracudas and Seafires attached to the Royal Navy.

One ghost story appears to date from this period. According to Bruce Barrymore Halpenny, one Private Easters was on guard duty one beautiful August night in 1944 when he was surprised to hear a sudden swishing sound, almost like the sound of a shell in flight and looking up he saw an enormous bomber coming across the runway at a height of only about thirty feet, it seemed, and it was heading straight towards the control tower! Private Easters stared, rooted to the spot. There was nothing he could do: there was going to be an awful calamity. He was puzzled too by the swishing sound, yet no engine noise – then suddenly the bomber was no longer there. It had completely disappeared and he could see the whole of the deserted runway and the silent and intact tower.

Making enquiries, Private Easters discovered that a bomber returning from a mission in the early days of the war had crashed into the control tower and there had been no survivors.

In the 1970s, Wittering became home to Harriers with Number One Squadron and Hunters with Numbers 45 and 58 Squadrons. One night the Air Traffic Controller, Flight Lieutenant Len Devonshire, was on duty in the control tower together with a WAAF officer. She had just made them both a cup of tea when they looked at each other in surprise as they both distinctly heard footsteps coming up the control tower steps. For security reasons the door into the control tower and the whole operations block was always kept locked.

At first they thought they could not have locked the outside door properly and they both went to the landing to see who was apparently coming up the stairs. A man in Second World War air force uniform was coming up the stairs. They both noted the flying suit he was wearing, the fur lined boots and the leather helmet. He appeared to be completely normal and he passed them without a word, not appearing to notice them. His footsteps echoed as he walked along the landing and into the Senior Air Traffic Controller's office. The astonished officers on duty were about to follow into the office when the airman re-appeared, walking straight by them and down the stairs. After a moment all was quiet. The lieutenant and the WAAF officer decided to have a look at the outside door, to see whether it was locked as it should be; they decided to do so together.

They checked the outside door and it was securely locked as was the control tower door which they had to unlock to get out. 'He looked as solid and real as I am,' Devonshire said afterwards and the WAAF officer agreed. They promptly checked everywhere and everything but all was well. Nothing had been touched and nothing was missing. The problem was who had they seen and how could 'he' outdo and surpass locked doors and closed rooms? It was only later, when they began to relate their combined experience did they learn that a crew returning from a war-time bombing mission had crashed into the control tower with no survivors and that afterwards there had been numerous reports of strange happenings and encounters in the vicinity of the control tower and many accounts of the appearance of a ghost airman.

Other Haunted Airfields

The Royal Air Force is riddled with ghost stories, and haunted airfields are legion; they include the Spittalgate Station near Grantham in Lincolnshire, a former RAF base later taken over by the Royal Corps of Transport. In 1977 there was an outbreak of apparent supernormal activity when staff and visitors became convinced that the haunting entity in the old Officers' Mess was 'Tiny' Harris, a former batman. The chief mess steward at the time, Pat Miller, said staff became used to the disturbances and were in the habit of addressing 'Harris', saying 'Don't worry, Tiny, it's only us.' One visitor, Mrs Miller, said she saw the ghost of Harris in his usual place, something she did not know at the time, but 'he' was a familiar figure and the staff were quite used to seeing 'him' and his appearance was taken for granted and nobody was afraid of 'him'. Workmen doing some painting near the Mess reported seeing a series of 'strange goings-on'.

The old Beehive terminal at Gatwick Airport has long been regarded as haunted by a ghost man with grey, receding hair and a pointed nose, wearing a long dark coat. He has usually been seen in the vicinity of the stores hangar. Once, two workmen wondered what he was up to and followed him into a tool store where he mysteriously disappeared. A British Airport Authority photographer saw the same figure standing beside an office door; he noticed that the temperature dropped suddenly when the figure appeared, then the photographer realized he could see clean through the figure; a door handle and wall-mounted fire extinguisher being plainly visible directly behind the apparition As he watched, the figure slowly faded and disappeared. The haunted hangar previously belonged to a company called Airports Ltd and the story goes that a former employee of this company is the original of the ghost who will not rest.

RAF Burtonwood in Lancashire was one of the airfields where American aircraft landed on arrival in this country. One tragic story tells of an American pilot, having flown across the Atlantic, was preparing to land at Burtonwood when he discovered that the undercarriage of his plane was retracted and stuck. Too late to abort the landing the pilot decided in a split second to eject just before the plane hit the ground. Due to a malfunction the canopy in the cockpit slammed back and decapitated the pilot. His headless ghost has been reported standing at the spot where the plane crashed.

The former RAF airfield at Lichfield in Staffordshire is now an industrial estate; it used to be haunted by the alarming figure of a pilot wearing a flying jacket, at the end of Runway 260. Here a pilot once walked by mistake into a rotating propeller that decapitated him and witnesses have said the ghostly figure of the unfortunate pilot used to be seen listlessly walking along before seeming to stagger and the figure was then seen to be without a head!

The large airfield at Lakenheath in Suffolk has a ghost only seen on clear moonlit nights. An Australian pilot crashed his Shirley bomber here during the Second World War and his ghost has been reported walking across the deserted airfield; clearly visible in the moonlight.

Situated to the north of the village, Bassingbourne airfield in Cambridgeshire has many claims to being haunted. Geoff

Parnell of Higham Ferrers in Northamptonshire first alerted me to the haunting. In an unsolicited letter he informed me that a friend, ex-6th Airborne Division, swore the place was haunted, from personal experience.

Apparently, he and his wife, one foggy November evening, heard the sound of a plane diving, followed by the sound of a crash and they saw the light of an explosion. A fire engine and the police turned out to investigate but found nothing whatever to account for what had been heard and seen.

On a separate visit to the airfield, accompanied by his son, they both heard the sound of distinct footsteps from the floor above them which was deserted and in fact it would have been impossible for any living person to be in the place from where the footsteps originated.

Geoff Parnell went again to Bassingbourne to try to look into the matter. He found nothing substantial but he did unearth a curious story about a Wellington bomber returning to the airfield from a raid in the Second World War; the bomber landed safely but all the crew aboard were dead . . .

There are many other reputedly haunted airfields and former airfields including Bletchley, Boscombe Down, Cardington, Cosford, Croydon, Drem, East Kirby, Hendon, Honington, Kelstern Moor, Mildenhall, Scampton, West Kirby and Wickenby. Many fascinating accounts of haunted airfields are to be found in *Military Ghosts* by Alan C. Wood (2010), *Aviation Ghosts* by Kevin Desmond (1998) and the *Ghost Station* books (1986–1995) by Bruce Barrymore Halpenny.

Part 2

HAUNTED ANCIENT SITES

Wherever you wander throughout Britain, Scotland and Wales you will come across monuments and structures built by our distant ancestors long before the invention of the wheel or of metal tools. These signs and relics from the pre-Christian world still exert a magnetic pull. The mystery feels strongest perhaps among our lonely stone circles and great henges but it can also be evident in the vicinity of hill figures, ancient pits and graves and the like. In Britain we are fortunate in having so many reminders and remnants of the past that often produce echoes of ancient times and forgotten events.

Ambresbury Banks, Essex

Epping Forest contains the remains of an ancient, possibly Iron Age, hill fort known as Ambresbury Banks. Hill forts were in reality hill tops defended by walls of stone, banks of earth and fences of wood, often accompanied by one or more external ditches; they are traditionally associated with the Iron Age although a number of hill forts are known to have been begun in the late Bronze Age, perhaps around the time Stonehenge was completed, and often on sites with an even earlier history of occupation.

The Ambresbury Banks plateau fort is shield-shaped and encloses four and a half hectares. It is surrounded by a single rampart or ditch with traces remaining of a counter-scarp bank; the rampart being between three and a half and seven feet high with a V-shaped ditch shown by excavation to be nearly ten feet deep and nearly twenty feet wide.

There are traces of an original entrance in the centre on the western side; an entry way on the south-east is medieval. A stream rises inside the fort providing it with a convenient water supply.

Now appearing to be little more than some raised mounds among the forest trees, Ambresbury Banks may well have been the site of the last battle of the warrior queen, Boudicca. The widow of the King of the Iceni (who inhabited much of East Anglia, certainly Norfolk and Suffolk) she was a ferocious warrior and, gathering about her a large army and driving her two-horse chariot with knives on the hubs, she is said to have been responsible for the deaths of some 70,000 invading Romans. The place of her defeat and death is problematical, with sites in Leicestershire and Warwickshire vying with Ambresbury Banks as the place but the Essex site must seem most probable and likely. According to a 2011 publication, *Paranormal Essex*, it is claimed that the ghost of Queen Boudicca has been seen wandering through the ruins at Ambresbury Banks.

Her ghost has also been variously reported in the Lincolnshire village of Cammeringham (near the old Roman road, Ermine Street) where some say she has been seen driving her ghostly chariot, with her long hair and voluminous clothing blowing and billowing in the wind. At Ambresbury Banks her ghost has long been reputed to haunt the ancient earthworks together with her daughters. The military historian Alan C. Wood has revealed (as also has Martin Caidin) that the impressive ghost of Queen Boudicca has also been reported driving her chariot through a secret RAF nuclear bomb storage depot in East Anglia, followed by a host of her men-at-arms in full cry on foot.

Avebury, Wiltshire

The huge ancient circular earthworks here – the largest prehistoric monument in Europe – encompass the village with its haunted manor house, the church and the old cottages built of Avebury stone (considered by some to be extremely unlucky to live in) and the remarkable stone circles. There are few more impressive or more haunted archaeological sites in all Europe. The main road swings through this massive bank and immediately one is inside the enormous enclosure.

The material for the bank was derived from an internal ditch that must have been dug by gangs of workmen who built up the spoil into this great bank, a formidable undertaking. Parts of the bank are held in position by an inner wall of chalk. The bank and ditch are open at four entrances at the cardinal points and these seem to have been original features. Inside the henge are the remains of three stone circles, one of them the largest stone circle in Britain. It is all quite astounding and it is no wonder that the place attracts considerable attention as a place of mystery and a magnet for those of pagan persuasion.

Probably built more than 3500 years before Christ, maybe older even than Stonehenge, the large size of the circles here indicate the existence, once upon a time, of a large, well-organised population, probably controlled by priests. There is good evidence to suggest serpent worship (its whole plan suggests a coiled snake) or perhaps it was once a vast open temple where pagan rites were practised. For those interested in such things, Avebury is a meeting place of ley lines from the Cotswolds, the Chilterns, the North and South Downs, Salisbury Plain and the Dorset hills; all meet in the centre of this banked circle raised to forgotten gods. There is some evidence to suggest these circles were erected primarily for healing purposes and there are indications that healing properties may still linger here.

Not a few visitors have found comfort in the stones of Avebury. Joan Forman, author, poet and historian, has told of visiting Avebury on a cold and miserable day but finding, when she experimented by leaning with both hands against one and then another of the stones in one of the avenues leading to the circle, that they 'seemed to exude the sensation of warmth and well-being'. Her impression of the stones within one of the circles however was far less pleasant, being 'one of tension and mild unease'.

Edith Oliver, the folklorist and author, had a remarkable experience at Avebury. Driving through the area one day at dusk she came within sight of the stone circles and was somewhat surprised to see what she took to be a fair erected in and around the stones. There were, she reported, unmistakably lights within the circles and she could hear music drifting towards her from what she took to be festival booths and sideshows. As she drew nearer, taking her eyes off the spectacle only for a second, she was astonished to see, when she was nearer and looked again, that the age-old stones were all completely deserted.

No longer was there any sign of anything like a fair, no longer any music and no longer was the place frequented by the moving figures she had so plainly seen. Nothing and nobody was anywhere in sight and she stopped and looked at the great monoliths, silent and lonely against the darkening sky. Later, after she had returned home and did some research, she learned that although it had once been the custom to hold an annual fair within the Avebury stones, the last one had taken place almost a century earlier. She decided that she must have witnessed a time-slip dislocation and, for a few seconds only perhaps, she had been transplanted back to the nineteenth century.

Another reliable witness, Miss J. M. Dunn, an agricultural teacher, has said that she saw one bright moonlit night, among Avebury's haunted stones, a number of what appeared to be rather small human-like figures moving among the stones; they seemed to hurry from one spot to another and then back again as though preparing some special occasion or festival. The figures were plainly visible one moment and had completely disappeared the next. Miss Dunn went in among the stones and made many enquiries and was satisfied that no living person was responsible. In any case the figures were much smaller than normal people of today – and they disappeared inexplicably – and then she recalled that our prehistoric ancestors were small in stature and she was left wondering whether she too had stepped back in time for a brief moment and had observed something that had happened long, long ago.

There have also been reports of phantom horsemen here, riding wildly in the vicinity of the stones, on horses with their long manes flowing in the wind. And all without a single sound.

Avebury Manor is reputed to harbour several ghosts including a ghost monk and a lady wearing white lace and an unlikely white hood, looking like a nun, who is always seen near an iron gateway; there is also the sound only of a ghostly coach and horses drawing up outside the Red Lion inn where there have been several seemingly paranormal happenings within this delightful hostelry. No more than a little exploration will uncover other hauntings in Avebury.

Nearby is Silbury Hill, site of the largest prehistoric man-made mound in Europe; a 130-foot-high cone of chalk that dates from 2600 BC (according to radiocarbon dating) but the true purpose of which is completely unknown, although several excavations have been carried out.

Tradition has it that Silbury Hill marks the grave of a somewhat mysterious King Sil who lies within, still mounted on his revered and favourite steed. Another tradition has it that the hill contains a human effigy made of solid gold. Extensive excavation has brought nothing to light to support these folk memories, if that is what they are. A few unexplained experiences have been reported from the Silbury Hill area but nothing of great moment. Stories of the sound of marching feet; of a figure resembling a Roman centurian and King Sil riding his horse around the hill on moonlit nights and a headless man being seen hereabouts can all, perhaps, be put down to imagination running wild, but Avebury, to coin a phrase, is another kettle of fish, and there 'ghosts' have, I am certain, been seen and probably will be seen again.

Badbury Rings, Dorset

An ancient hill fort near Wimborne, Badbury Ring (actually within the 8500 acre estate of seventeenth-century Kingston Lacy House) has long been subject to stories of ghostly Roman soldiers, in vast numbers, mysteriously appearing and disappearing, as has been reported elsewhere in Dorset: on the Old Priest Track towards Swanage; on the Sherborne to Dorchester road; at Abbotsbury Hill on the otherwise disused stretch of Roman road running parallel to the A354 at Ridgeway Hill, between Dorchester and Weymouth; and also the Dorchester road close to Winterborne Monkton.

Badbury Rings was captured by the Second Augustan Legion under Vespasian in 43 AD so there are undoubted links and connections with Roman soldiers and with violence and death. It was here, according to tradition, that the legendary King Arthur claimed victory over the Anglo Saxons in 518 AD and where, it is said, the mighty king killed at least a hundred and sixty men single handed. No wonder, some people will say, that sometimes at midnight King Arthur and his knights return to haunt the battlefield.

Rodney Legg, the eccentric but generous lover of Dorset and its mysteries, once told me that at Badbury Rings he was more certain of the presence of ghosts than anywhere in Dorset – or anywhere else for that matter. Legg was firmly of the opinion that ghosts were not the spirits of someone who had died, rather ghost sighting is a picture of them doing something they did frequently over a period of time or undergoing mental torture of some kind which leaves its mark on the atmosphere where the happenings took place. 'A ghost,' he said, 'is a form of shadow or a sloughed skin such as a snake might leave.' He had no shadow of doubt that what we call ghosts do exist.

At Badbury Rings he found the air, the whole atmosphere, so laden, so full of the idea that ghosts were present, and so alive with expectation and the very real like-lihood of the appearance of a ghost or ghosts that on one occasion he returned at midnight and believed that he was present when the terrors that had once pervaded and engulfed the area returned, and he always said he was utterly convinced that the shades of Roman soldiers were there that night and that he almost saw them.

Badbury Rings form a conspicuous tree-clad monument, divided by pathways. There are two strong inner ramparts and a weaker third which together enclose what were obvi-ously massive foundations. There are entrances at the east and west ends. At the former, the inner ramparts turn inwards, while the latter is protected by a rectangular enclo-sure formed by the central rampart turning outwards. Two gateways cut the outer and central ramparts on the western side. There are traces of field systems, Bronze Age barrows and four Roman roads beside the fort. I am endebted to James Dyer, O.G.S. Crawford and A. Keiller for this technical and archaeological information.

Excavation took place here in 1970 when an organized archaeological expedition camped within the ridge and they found rather more than they had expected. One night the researchers were awakened suddenly by the sounds of marching men and the clashing of metal accompanied by the shouts of (seemingly) military orders in a language they did not recognize. In some panic, for they all heard the sounds, the camp was quickly abandoned!

At the end of the 1970s there were a rash of reports here of the appearance of a strange-looking ghostly warrior with a hideously scarred face wandering about the Rings at night. He seems to have been last seen in 1997. It is interesting to note that phantom Roman soldiers have also been reported a few miles south of Badbury Rings at the village of Corfe Mullen.

This village is cut in two by the course of an old Roman road that once ran to Badbury. In 1993 a number of residents of the aptly named Roman Heights Estate claimed to hear the sound of marching soldiers, the clink of metal and the sound of men's voices conversing in a strange language.

A 2009 publication by *Reader's Digest* stated that Badbury Rings has always been a popular place for lovers' trysts and in recent times they have been disturbed by a variety of phantoms and ghostly happenings, including the sounds of soldiers fighting. Now acquired by the National Trust who state the parkland here with its fine herd of North Devon cattle, 'is dominated by the Iron Age fort of Badbury Rings, home to fourteen varieties of orchid'. Badbury Rings, like so many of Britain's ancient sites, harbours, if we are to believe reported assertions from a variety of witnesses, ghosts of the past as surely as these atmospheric places have been known to our ancestors for almost 10,000 years.

Cerne Abbas, Dorset

In the cemetery at Cerne Abbas can be found, shaded by mature lime trees, Dorset's premier sacred well. Its strong flow is restricted by large stones. Until the seventeenth century there was a proper shrine here within a chapel (long since demolished) dedicated to St Augustine who, legend has it, 'fetched out a crystal fountain', a spring of holy water, by striking the ground with his staff, to convince and convert the heathen inhabitants hereabouts. Newly born babies used to be brought to St Augustine's Well at sunrise to be dipped into the water and the sick would drink the water to obtain a divine cure. As recently as Victorian times the well was reputed to work 'wondrous cures'. Apparitions were regularly reported seen here.

The nearby Wishing Stone, a pillar carved with the wheel of St Catherine, that may have been a charm or talisman or a sacred wheel of protection, has also long been a place of pilgrimage. At dawn on May Day, Midsummer Day, and on St Catherine's Day (25th November) unmarried girls wanting a husband would go alone and in a state of nudity and there kneel and place their hands on the Wishing Stone and wish they 'may not die an old maid'.

The village is also associated with St Augustine and the Kentish long tails legend. St Augustine, known as 'the apostle of the English', was the first Archbishop of Canterbury – sent to Britain with forty monks by Pope Gregory in 596 – and having converted Kent to the Christian faith, they travelled far and wide over the English provinces as far as Ethlebert's dominions extended, and they visited Cerne Abbas. There St Augustine destroyed their heathen idols and gave tails to the wicked non-believers of Cerne Abbas.

However these early Wessex men had their revenge for, according to William of Malmesbury, the inhabitants, incensed by what St Augustine had done, fastened the tails of cows to the garments of St Augustine and his companions and drove them out of the village! Years later the monks returned and the well became a shrine and a place of baptism and healing, renowned for its apparitions, although no details are extant. Baptism was of course a pagan custom adopted by the Christians, like so many other heathen habits and festivals, and here, in close proximity to the Cerne Abbas giant hill figure, one can suspect an older and more primitive religion. There have been many reports over the years of ghostly figures being seen in the vicinity of St Augustine's Well, especially at sunrise on May Day and Midsummer Day. Villagers and others have long believed that unspecified apparitions could sometimes be seen in the waters of the well, especially around Easter.

There are, or were for many, many years, two bare spots in the grass on the bank of the mill-stream to the west of Abbey Street and these were said to be the last footsteps of a man who had thrown himself into the water here and drowned. His ghost, looking drenched with water, returns from time to time.

Just north of Cerne Abbas village is the 180-foot-high figure of the Cerne Abbas giant, cut into Giant Hill and reputedly haunted: perhaps the oldest man-made object that is haunted. Strange, primitive figures have been reportedly seen on and around the massive hill-figure depicting a man wielding a club and wearing nothing but a belt and exhibiting an impressive member; seemingly human figures that disappear when anyone gets near them. There have also been reports of guttural sounds, frightening and dreadful in the circumstances – the whole area being obviously completely deserted. Once when I was there a young couple were also exploring the place and when I said the whole region around the giant had a curious 'feel' about it, they told me that the previous week, when they had made their first visit to the Cerne Abbas Giant, they saw four figures on the giant, one on each of his feet and one on each hand. They were totally absorbed in some sort of ritual, their eyes closed and they mumbled unintelligible sounds while lifting their hands to the sky in unison. My informants watched them for a few moments, not wishing to interfere with any ceremony but then, when they ceased muttering and lowered their hands to their sides and looked earthwards, the couple thought they would have a closer look at the giant: as soon as they reached the ancient hill carving the figures were no longer there. One moment, they said, the four figures were in front of them, distinct, natural and seemingly solid individuals and the next moment they had completely disappeared. There was certainly nowhere they could possibly be hiding or anywhere they could have gone without being seen. My newfound friends said they had a careful look at the whole of the carving since they were there but they both felt increasingly unwelcome and uneasy with the growing feeling that they were not alone although they patently were. When my wife suggested we all meet up for a drink and a chat the following evening they said they were returning home the next day. I gave them my card and asked them to get in touch and said I would send them one of my books, but I never heard from them.

How the giant came to be at Cerne Abbas, who he repre-sents and who was responsible for carving the well-proportioned and enormous figure is a mystery. He may represent a once real giant who terrorised Cerne Abbas, as an old legend has it, eating the cattle and even devouring children. One day the villagers are said to have found him asleep on the hill and they managed to kill him and then cut his outline in the chalk to commemorate their success. Historians, in general, think he is an ancient god such as Hercules or Gog or Magog or even the native deity Cernunnos while others think it is more likely that he represents a Celtic fertility god. The Celts were undeniably head hunters and it is thought that his left hand once held a severed head.

Above the giant figure there is a rectangular earthwork called the Trendle or Frying Pan which appears to date from the Iron Age and, although that sort of date can be ruled out for the Giant, the Trendle was, say the experts, the scene of maypole dancing, significantly connected with phallic worship which the Cerne Abbas giant shows every sign of representing.

Grime's Graves, Weeting, Norfolk

The intriguing name of the largest and best known group of Neolithic flint mines in Britain and the only prehistoric flint mines so far north of the Thames – and flint knapping is still carried on in the area of Weeting by a few craftsmen. The pits probably date from about 2330 BC to about 1740 BC.

Lying on gentle slopes of a dry valley in the Brecklands of north-west Norfolk, surrounded by Forestry Commission woodland, the cup-shaped depressions mark the shafts of the mines that were called simply 'The Holes'. The suffix 'Graves' has no connection with burials, meaning merely 'hollows' or 'workings'.

Roughly semi-circular in conformation they cover some

twelve acres of the rising ground and encompass fifteen large pits, a Black Hole, and Canon Greenwell's Pit. The large pits are joined in a regular manner, one near to another, the largest seeming to be in the centre, from where commands were probably issued. The pits are dug so deep and are so numerous that it has been suggested that the site had a military significance for they are capable not only of receiving a great army, but also of covering and concealing them in such a manner that they could not be discerned by travellers or passers-by.

In 1852 excavators thought it had once been a fortified settlement of the Iceni, an Iron Age village perhaps, but then later exploration, including the discovery of a female chalk figurine and Neolithic altar, now on view at the British Museum, suggested the commencement of mining here took place in Upper Palaeolithic times and had its cessation in Early Neolithic times.

Flint mines are the first remains of organized industry in Great Britain; such mines have been identified in many parts of the country, some as ancient as 6000 years old. The depth of the shafts depended on the depth of the layer of fine flint that was being sought; at Grime's Graves one climbs down a thirty-foot ladder as the miners must have done, into a darkness once lit by torches and lamps using animal fat.

Grime's Graves are known locally as Grimmer's Graves, suggesting they are anciently attributed to Odin, the Scandinavian counterpart of Woden, who was also called Grim, the Masked One, and high god of the Anglo-Saxons before their conversion to the Christian god in the seventh century.

The long-standing haunting associated with Grime's Graves is a grim and humourless giant demon-like figure known as 'Old Grim'. Grim or Woden or the Devil was popularly held responsible for ancient earthworks, or the word may derive from gruma, a boundary. The same name is found for similar earthworks in Buckinghamshire, Hertfordshire and Wiltshire. In Scandinavia Grim was also the name of a supernatural giant who guarded treasure, and sometimes ravaged human kind with fire and sword.

When I was in the area in 1990 investigating another haunting, my wife and I visited Grime's Graves and made a number of enquiries, both from other visitors and local residents in addition to some Ghost Club members who lived nearby. The overwhelming opinion was that the place was indeed haunted although any sort of identification of the haunting entity or in fact any detailed description was not forthcoming. The general consensus was that the 'ghost' at Grime's Graves was unpleasant, huge, frightening and infrequent.

Rillaton, Cornwall

A burial mound at Rillaton on Bodmin Moor has long been plagued by a ghostly Druidic priest – who must be one of Britain's older ghosts.

There are many stories of passing travellers being waylaid by the phantom and offered a drink from a golden cup that can never be emptied. One story has it that a weary traveller tried to drain the cup and, when he found it impossible to do so, much to the amusement of the ghost Druid, he threw the contents of the cup in the spectre's face, remounted his horse and resumed his journey. Shortly afterwards the bodies of both traveller and horse were found dead at the bottom of a ravine.

This all sounds very unlikely but oddly enough in 1837, when Rillaton Barrow was excavated, a stone-lined vault was found that contained a single human skeleton and a golden cup. The beautiful cup, claimed as treasure trove by the Crown, remained in use by the royal household, I understand, until the death of George V in 1936. Then, the Rillaton Cup, as it became known, was loaned to the British Museum where it is still on display. It is thought to date from 1700 to 1500 BC when Druidism could have been rife in the British Isles.

Nearby to the east, in the church at Linkinhorne, with its holy well to St Melor, there is a rare example of Christ of the Trade, a medieval painting on the church wall where he is surrounded by such things as hammers, axes, saws, scales, scissors and sickles and showing the wounded hands and feet and side of Christ; warning parishioners who refused to rest on Sundays of the sorrow they inflicted on Christ: their tools in effect keeping open his wounds. There are those who have discovered Druidic symbols in the painting.

Royston Cave, Hertfordshire

Situated at the intersection of two ancient roads, Icknield Way and Ermine Street, Royston in north Hertfordshire gets its name from a lady named something like Rohesia; the daughter of William the Conqueror's steward Eudo Dapifer, owner of the local manor house. Remains of the base of a cross once erected to her memory at the junction of the two important roads is still in existence and the area that became known as Rohesia Cross became Rohesia town and eventually Royston.

Over the years, many unexplained sounds and curious events have been reported from nearby Royston Cave, a unique, mysterious, atmospheric and fascinating place, entered from an alley off Melbourne Street; an entrance that is comparatively modern with entry originally being gained by means of a tunnel which can still be spotted from inside the cave, high up on the north-east side.

The cave was discovered by accident in 1742 when a post was being fixed in the ground as part of a bench at the cross-roads. Just below the surface, workmen unearthed a millstone which they found concealed a shaft, some two feet in diameter. A boy was lowered down the shaft which had holes cut into the sides like foot-holds. When the boy reported that the shaft led into another cavity, a slender man carrying a candle entered the shaft, returning with the news that lower down there was a large cave, containing a great deal of earth.

This loose earth was eventually removed, together with a human skull, some human bones, fragments of a drinking cup and miscellaneous other objects. Thinking they might be on the track of buried treasure, the men continued working apace and eventually the remarkable cave was completely excavated, examined and a report submitted to the Royal Society of Antiquaries. No treasure was found.

The cave is bell-shaped, from the floor to the top of the dome measuring about twenty-six feet; the base is almost exactly circular with a diameter of seventeen and a half feet. A broad step or shelf surrounds the cave, eight inches wide and three feet above floor level. About eight feet above the floor a cornice runs round the walls in a reticulated pattern two feet wide, and almost all the space between the step and the cornice is occupied with sculpture that includes crucifixes, saints, martyrs and subjects not easily distinguisable or discernible. There are traces of colour – red, blue and yellow in various places – and the relief of the figures is heightened by a dark pigment.

High up, two dates are cut in the chalk in Arabic numerals, thought at one time to be 1347 and 1350 but now considered to be 1547 and 1550. The carvings, say the experts, are not all by the same hand. The cave may originally have been merely a shaft for burial or for rubbish, but in medieval times it appears that the cave was occupied by a hermit. The cave was in all probability filled in with earth in 1547 and 1550 when the inscribed dates were added. Afterwards the cave seems to have been forgotten and a dwelling was erected over it.

The rudely carved figures appear to date from the time of the Crusades. In 1877 it was suggested that the cavity may have been made at a period before the Christian era and that it was later used as a Roman sepulchre and later still as a Christian oratory and that it was filled in at the time of the Reformation when the entrances were closed and its locality forgotten. The groups of figures have been recognized as representing such subjects as the legend of St Catherine the Martyr; the shrines of St John the Baptist and St Thomas à Becket; St Christopher; Queen Eleanor; King Henry II and Richard Coeur de Lion. Many distinguished visitors have inspected the cave, including Louis XVIII of France. There are those who ascribe the construction of the cave to the Knights Templar, who had a base at nearby Baldock and were famous for their enormous wealth and notorious for their secret rituals.

Royston Cave, certainly two thousand years old, is very impressive and affects different people in different ways. When I was first there I found it oppressive and unwelcoming and perhaps a little alive psychically. I had been exploring reports of supernormal activity at Royston Community Centre, formerly the Old Post Office and I thought it interesting that the cellars of that building adjoined Royston Cave and that perhaps the various odd sounds, also reported from the Cave itself, might be transmitted with alarming clarity through the medium of the chalk sub-soil, resulting in the many unexplained sounds reported by various people over the years at the Old Post Office and later at the Community Centre where, interestingly enough, alterations were being carried out. Psychic activity is often found to be active during structural alterations.

I have spoken to three people who, visiting Royston Cave independently, have been convinced that there is someone standing beside them while they have been alone in the cave and two of these witnesses told me that as they left, glancing back, they are convinced they caught a glimpse of 'someone' standing watching them; a figure that in both instances, disappeared as they watched.

Damien O'Dell, who has enjoyed a lifelong interest in the paranormal, is founder of the Anglian Paranormal Investigation Society (of which I have the honour to be President) and also an author of renown, tells me that on his first visit to the cave he strongly felt a 'mystic, other-world quality' that he had only felt at one other place, the top of Glastonbury Tor. Damien has continued to be 'profoundly impressed' by Royston Cave and is convinced that it is a 'special place'. He too had the distinct impression that he was not alone when he had the rare experience of ascending scaffolding to the roof of the cave. On the same occasion a psychic friend experienced 'strange feelings' inside the cave and saw something like an orb of light and she picked up the impression that human sacrifice had been carried out there and also she had the distinct feeling that someone was hanging suspended from the roof while their life blood slowly dripped into a chalice on the floor of the cave. Two other friends had heard unaccountable screams, as of a child. Perhaps Royston Cave has seen both good and evil practices in its long history. Whether that is so or not the cave exudes the very essence of 'something' and that something has been described by many people as a haunting or a haunting presence.

St Nectan's Glen, Cornwall

I have always remembered the first time I explored atmospheric St Nectan's Glen, often regarded as one of the most beautiful corners of North Cornwall. 'Full of poetry and coloured by legend' said Robert Hunt. Suddenly I felt I had stepped out of this world and was very close to the next, or some other world frequented by 'other' people. As I progressed, the feeling grew stronger and at St Nectan's Waterfall the feeling was almost overwhelming. I tried to relax and welcome whatever was there and although I saw nothing untoward the feeling has stayed with me for well over half a century.

Further along the glen you reach the Rocky Valley Mazes, which are almost certainly prehistoric symbols. This place has a magic all its own. Mazes were, of course, part of an ancient ritual for a way of entering the Underworld.

St Nectan, we are told, was 'one of the most important figures in the ancient Kingdom of Dumnonia' and reputed, in common with many Cornish saints, to have been the offspring of King Brychan of Wales (after whom Breconshire was named). Legend has it that he was beheaded by bandits in the seventh century. The tiny and remote chapel of St Nectan, possibly dating from 1281 and occupying the site of a much earlier building dedicated to the saint, can be found not far from Boscastle, seat of the ancient Bottreaux family who gave Boscastle its name.

St Nectan, who will always be associated with this glen or kieve (stone bowl in Cornish) and spectacular waterfall, is renowned for prophesying on his deathbed that the older, simpler faith of his forebears would one day return to these islands. It has been suggested that there could be a direct link between Nectan and Nudd, the old Celtic river god whose name is rendered as Nathanus in Latin and perhaps Nectan in Cornish. Nudd's son Gwyn ap Nudd is likely to have acquired ancient knowledge from his father, a master astronomer, and it is interesting that an old chapel nearby carries his dedication. The river god is reputed to have made his sanctuary above the mystic waterfall in this remarkably secluded spot, in about the sixth century. Here he is supposed to have built a tower in which hung a silver bell with which he communicated with the monks of Tintagel.

A glance at the Ordnance Survey map will, interestingly, reveal that St Nectan's Waterfall, Bossiney Mound and Tintagel Castle are all in direct alignment, with both the waterfall and the castle being exactly a mile from the mound. There are those who aver that these qualities, straightness and measurement, relate to rulers and hence to the concept of rulership. At all events the atmosphere of St Nectan's Glen and its waterfall is captivating and very special as Arthurian scholar Paul Broadhurst has pointed out.

In his eruditical volume *The Secret Land* (2009) Broadhurst states 'As we stand there, lost in the roaring sound of the rushing waters resonating throughout the rocky chasm ... its roaring created by the river that cascades over the waterfall into the ravine that amplifies the sound, and then runs down through the haunted valley ... Its roaring is perfectly in synchrony with its environment, for as the Goddess of the Earth it is governed by the weather pattern of the atmosphere. On a wild stormy day it can be intimidating, such is the sound that echoes so powerfully through the gorge. On a gentler summer's day it can be mesmerisingly peaceful, with a gentle stream whispering out of the hole in the rocky curtain.'

After his death, Nectan is said to have been interred in an oak chest underneath the waterfall, along with the silver bell, which can still be heard to ring on occasions, it would appear. I have certainly spoken to upwards of a dozen people who, on different occasions, have heard a bell chiming most beautifully but sounding far off, tinkling in a memorable way.

Paul Broadhurst admits too that St Nectan's Glen is 'a place of otherworldly manifestations' and certainly it is by no means uncommon for visitors to report strange happenings including odd light effects that can sometimes be photographed or, occasionally, are only made manifest by the camera. Sometimes these bright globes of light contain 'spirit faces' in them when enlarged; hooded human figures are frequently reported and a multitude of other extraordinary happenings: bell-ringing, voices, lights, human and sub-human figures and forms; sights, sounds and even smells that cannot be easily explained. The glen also has the growing reputation of being a place with healing powers. Paul Broadhurst from his Other World headquarters at Boscastle has reminded us all that such a natural shrine 'should be treated with the utmost reverence and respect', for old Cornish legends remind us that to do otherwise is to 'invite the displeasure (and perhaps ever worse) of the unseen realms'. There are ancient and even recent accounts of miracles attributed to St Nectan.

Interestingly Paul Broadhurst has also suggested that the

spectacular waterfall – seemingly having cut its way through a wall of solid rock – could well be some sort of Druidic sculpture, deliberately created to enhance the dramatic effect of this already stunning natural locale.

There are many stories of inexplicable happenings hereabouts. One writer, who lived nearby, claimed he often heard the sound of chanting monks at night-time; a visitor, working at Bossiney House, told Michael Williams that one evening he heard the sound of sobbing in the deserted glen and when he investigated he was rewarded for some moments by the sound of weird and mocking laughter; Kathleen Everard, who also lived nearby, talked repeatedly of beautiful music; another local person reported seeing, several times, the figure of a woman, a figure that unaccountably and suddenly vanished; other visitors have seen a ghostly monk-like figure in a grey habit with blue lining to the hood, 'very kind-looking' and not at all frightening. A visiting soldier, knowing nothing of any legends or alleged sightings of unexplained forms and figures, met three monks in the glen. 'They looked cheerful fellows,' he declared. They vanished. And of course there is an indefinable atmosphere that is experienced by almost everyone, a feeling that 'something' has happened there and that 'something' may happen again, at any moment. There are also numerous reports of the distinct sound of footsteps when no visible person is present.

Ghost Club member Betty Puttick told me she had first visited St Nectan's Glen when she was in her teens, accompanied by a friend, and she saw the figure of a monk in a long robe on the opposite side of the stream; she wasn't really frightened, more curious, and she said he was certainly there for some time, not moving, but watchful – and then, suddenly, he wasn't there any more.

Peaceful and haunted, this gem of a place affects

different people in different ways. For most visitors it is a place unlike anywhere else on earth, strangely attractive, inviting, alluring and tantalizing with a unique atmosphere that sometimes produces unusual wonders and unexplained happenings; for others the originality of the place was uppermost in their minds. Sir Henry Irving had a particular liking for St Nectan and his glen and the remarkable waterfall inspired him to use something similar in one of his London theatre productions.

Shrieking Pits, Aylmerton, Norfolk

Three miles from Cromer, on wooded slopes overlooking the village, locally called the Roman Camp, the Shrieking Pits consist merely of a number of circular depressions, all that remain of 2000 such hollows which were, in all probability, the work of Stone Age men.

Widely known as the Shrieking Pits on account of the ghostly tall figure of a woman long seen here, peering into the pits. She wrings her hands and utters piercing cries; an arresting vocal and visual appearance that seems to have been occurring for many, many years.

Not only, if she is from the Stone Age, is she one of the oldest reported phantom figures in existence, but, if reports are to be believed, she is also one of the most frequent. There appears to be no set pattern to her appearances and she has been reported in daylight, at dusk and at night-time – just about any time in fact. Visitors to these particular pits, part of a large number of circular pits around

Aylmerton, Weybourne and Beeston Regis, all thought to be remains of prehistoric settlements, might become aware, suddenly and without warning, of a tall, whitish figure around a pit, followed by unearthly, alarming and piercing screams that linger in the memory long after the figure has disappeared.

Sceptics have suggested that mist and bird-noises may account for some reported accounts of the appearance of the ghostly white figure but its frequent appearances to a variety of good witnesses seem to me to make this an unlikely explanation.

A story handed down from generation to generation has it that someone was murdered here and the mysterious female figure that is seen at the opening of one pit had some connection with that event of long, long ago; almost before human memory

Eric Maple, researching his volume *Supernatural England* (1977) told me he was satisfied that the female ghost of the Shrieking Pits was mostly seen at night, peering into the pits and crying as if her heart would break. He regarded this ghost as one of the better authenticated ghosts from ancient times and said there was no denying that her dismal moans and frantic groans had been reported for centuries in this part of Norfolk and he talked with local people, as I have, who are convinced that the place is haunted and that many of them had personal knowledge of the ghost and her ghostly activity. On the other hand, Andrew Green came to believe that the ghost dated only from Victorian times and was that of a woman searching for her baby, murdered and buried in one of the pits by her husband in a fit of jealous rage.

Many folklorists and authors, including Eric Maple, Christina Hole, Peter Haining, Joan Forman and Betty Puttick, have all looked into the mystery of the haunted

Shrieking Pits and they have all told me they are impressed by the evidence. Shrieks echoing from these pits, all that remain of nearly 2000 such hollows, have undoubtedly terrified local residents on many occasions.

Stonehenge, Wiltshire

Stonehenge, one of the oldest man-made structures in existence, with its emotionally named separate stones and puzzling Stone Holes, mounds and ditches, is a place of mystery and enchantment, of wonder and fascination. So too are the unexplained human-like forms and figures seen here for centuries.

Originally, this Sarsen Circle consisted of thirty standing stones with lintels. Sixteen remain standing today, but only six with lintels. Over recent years several stones have fallen and been re-erected. The design once consisted of two circles enclosing two series of standing stones, each the shape of a horseshoe. There is also the leaning Heelstone or Sunstone, 256 feet from the centre of the circle with its top very nearly level with the horizon and near whose peak the sun rises on the longest day. There are also two trilithons, part of a Bluestone horseshoe and a so-called Slaughter Stone. In addition there are mysterious holes, including one regularly spaced set originally comprising fifty-six. Most once contained evidence of human cremation. There are also several banks and mounds and an almost unique ditch outside the whole circle.

In his exhaustive exploration of the Arthurian legend (*The Secret Land*, 2009) Paul Broadhurst has convincingly demonstrated geodatic connections between major prehistoric

sites that link Stonehenge with Arbor Low in Derbyshire,
Bryn Celli Ddu in Anglesey and Morte Point on the north
Devon coast; an alignment that is of considerable interest
and could even explain why the Bluestones were taken to
Stonehenge.

There are theories and tales to suggest Stonehenge was
the work of long departed giants who may have once
roamed the earth, or the work of King Arthur's magician
Merlin – or even that of the Devil himself!

The actual location of Stonehenge is itself a great
mystery, compounded by the enormous labour involved: the
gigantic Bluestones came from Wales and had to travel
more than two hundred miles, presumably without the
benefit of any wheels and there is no river here to assist the
transportation. It must have taken whole communities years
of labour. Perhaps the site was a place of worship, or even
of great political significance. There is evidence of human
activity going back some 7000 years before Christ; long
before the first stone was erected here. Was Stonehenge a
monument to the living or to the ancestral dead? Do the
stones represent or embody the spirits of kings and the elite
from a long departed age? Can stone imprison and impart
something of the past that can occasionally be revealed or
made visible again after all these years? Stonehenge is full
of questions.

The earliest of the stones were erected thousands of years
before Christ and the circle in its present form was probably
constructed several hundred years after that first activity.
There are great stone circles all over north-western Europe
that have caused considerable debate and been the subject
of many theories but unquestionably Stonehenge is the
finest example.

I have in my records three accounts, each some twenty
years apart, of what are described as indistinct and small

human figures being seen among the stones at Stonehenge, especially on nights of the full moon. One couple watched the figures through binoculars and insisted that what they saw was objective and not figments of their imagination or tricks of the moonlight; and they described to me in some detail the meanderings of the various figures and how they could see the different figures seemingly making preparations for some important event. I have also an account of the first-hand sighting and subsequent disappearance of a cowled figure on Midsummer Eve that, in the circumstances related, is quite inexplicable.

Although the general public is no longer able to wander among these vast stones, as they were when I first visited, everyone should spend some time at this remarkable stone circle, full of mystery and wonder, full of awe and majesty, even after more than 5000 years and there is always the possibility of glimpsing one or more of the primitive ghosts still haunting this ancient place, one of the oldest locations on the planet.

Other Haunted Ancient Sites

Bossiney Mound, Cornwall, is reputed to be the burial place of Arthur's Round Table which reappears on Midsummer night, illuminating the sky for a second before disappearing for another year. In recent times strange and completely inexplicable lights have been seen in the windows of the chapel here on Midsummer Eve.

Cadbury Hillfort, Somerset, with its links to Arthur and Camelot and where the fabled King may lie after his last battle, is haunted by a man on horseback, a fifth century warrior – who has reportedly been seen quite recently.

Carlton in Nottinghamshire, has a Devil Stone with many superstitions attached to it, including the appearance of a white lady and impressions of human sacrifice.

Warminster, Wiltshire where Cley Hill was once known as the home of the King of the Fairies from the frequency with which unexplained small figures were seen in the vicinity. There are legends of treasure being buried here, of pagan rites and of underground tunnels and reports of ghostly forms persist.

Creswell Crags, Derbyshire has twenty caves, some dating from thousands of years before Christ, which have been the scene of repeated appearances of witch-like figures and a dark, apparently headless figure. There may have been a mass graveyard here.

The King's Mound at Stirling Castle may hide Arthur's Round Table. Among several reportedly active ghosts here some appear to be Arthurian knights.

Margate Grotto, Kent, has whispering voices, mysterious music and unexplained lights among other ghostly appurtenances.

Roche Rock, Cornwall, where the little chapel set high in the rocky outcrop above a hermit cell is haunted by a shadowy figure, resembling a man, that has been seen glaring angrily from his lofty perch or hurrying about among the rocks.

Ryedale Windy Pits, North Yorkshire boasts eleven species of bats and also unidentified phantoms from another age.

Ghostly thundering hoof-beats have been reported along the ridge above the ancient hill carving of The White Horse at Westbury, Wiltshire. This is one of seventeen white horses cut in the chalk downlands of southern England; not all are ancient but almost all of them have been associated with mysterious happenings.

Wookey Hole, Somerset, once regarded with Stonehenge as one of the wonders of medieval Britain, is haunted by sounds of regular tapping and a percolating sound, flashing lights and noises of someone crawling through a blocked-up tunnel and by a 'black-cloaked apparition'.

On the Island of Vallay in the Outer Hebrides of Scotland there is a haunted pit. The story goes that it can never be filled in because a witch was buried alive there and her ghost still haunts the place. She was buried up to her neck at the entrance to a cattle field and remained there until the cattle passing over her crushed her skull. Her despairing ghost has been seen many times.

Part 3

HAUNTED BATTLEFIELDS

Brigadier Peter Young once said to me: 'Battles and battlefields have a fascination for most people and this is hardly surprising when we reflect that battles are significant events in human affairs which bring out the characters of the participants and reveal their true natures. That such crises sometimes leave behind traces of those battles and the human efforts involved can hardly be surprising.'

Eric Maple once pointed out that 'Every great battlefield in history has echoed the tragedy of the warriors sacrificed there. It is a belief as old as time that lives foreshortened by violence may be doomed by the laws of the spirit to remain earthbound for ever.'

And so we have battlefield sites all over Britain and many of them are haunted.

Culloden Moor, Inverness, Scotland

A few miles east of Inverness on the still bleak and windswept moor (known to Highlanders as Drummossie Muir) a large stone cairn commemorates the 1746 battle that sounded the death knell to the Jacobite forces under Bonnie Prince Charlie when they were utterly crushed by the Hanoverian army under the Duke of Cumberland. The victors cruelly massacred the wounded men who had bravely fought for the Young Pretender. Green mounds still mark some of the soldiers' burial places.

In that year of destiny the Highlanders had besieged Stirling Castle, had defeated Lieutenant-General Henry Hawley at Falkirk and had progressed to Inverness and thence to Culloden, with the Stones of Clava from the Bronze Age nearby. It was all a dramatic and in some ways a romantic affair, since the leading actors were young princes of the rival houses of Hanover and Stuart.

History and legend has transformed Bonnie Prince Charlie into a figure of romance but objective research, exemplified by Brigadier Peter Young, shows Prince Charles Edward to have been something of an arrogant and even stupid young man whose chief assets were a strong constitution and overwhelming optimism.

His opponent – and eventual victor – Lieutenant-General William Augustus, Duke of Cumberland, Knight of the

Garter, and familiarly called 'Billy the Martial Boy' or 'Butcher' according to political preference, was nevertheless an efficient officer, commanding the pick of the British army.

By 1746 the Highlanders were not at their peak; the Prince had been forced to retreat from Derby and the English, grown prosperous under Walpole's leadership, no longer desired with any passion the restoration of the House of Stewart; in fact by 1746 the ever-hopeful Prince was practically the only one of the Jacobite hierarchy who wished to carry on. Things did not look good for the Highland army. The men were unpaid, the food and catering were inadequate and desertion was rife. Furthermore there was disagreement among the leaders and all they really had going for them was the memory of past British Army defeats and its possible indiscipline. But with Cumberland in charge the Highlanders had much to fear.

The eventual battle was fought on 16th April 1746 and on the 8th the Jacobites moved towards the British. However, following disputes, disappointments and disillusion, early on the morning of the 15th, as the Highland army began to take up battle positions on the uneven ground they had chosen, there was much desertion, including some of the usually staunch MacDonalds and the MacPhersons, leaving the army much weaker, possibly no more than five thousand strong. They were prepared in battle formation and awaited the expected advance of the British but that did not materialize. Then the supply services, such as they were, broke down completely and, as time passed, more and more men left their companions to seek food and drink – and few returned. Meanwhile the officers, at headquarters, such as it was, argued, wrangled and disagreed with one another to an alarming degree.

Lord George Murray, perhaps Prince Charlie's most able

general, thought the ground chosen was disadvantageous for the Highlanders and he proved to be right; it was favourable for cavalry in which Cumberland was superior and the open moor gave his artillery the advantage. Following a rare Council of War the Highlanders decided to make a surprise attack on the Cumberland camp, to the aversion of the Duke of Perth and most of the Irish officers who felt it was nothing more than a 'desperate attempt' but Lord George Murray said it was preferable to fighting on the open moor and he won the day. From the beginning things went badly. At the time of the surprise attack officers found almost a third of the men were away foraging and flatly refused to rejoin their comrades until they were fed, whereupon the Prince, ever optimistic, said he would face Cumberland with one thousand men if necessary. And he added that 15th April was Cumberland's birthday so he and his men would probably be drunk anyway. Exhausted and almost starving, the Highlanders eventually trailed back to Culloden where many of them threw themselves on the ground and slept. Others continued the search for food.

Suddenly the call came that Cumberland was marching towards them and the order was given to rendezvous on Drummossie Muir. As they marched forward, the British saw that the Highlanders seemed to be in some disarray and Cumberland's men moved forward in good order, soon out-flanking the Highlanders. As the Prince and his retinue sought to move out of the line of fire the ground he left was soon strewn with the bodies of his men.

Now Cumberland's cannon caused havoc and tore great gaps in the six-deep ranks of the Highlanders who found themselves confused and distracted, some throwing themselves on the ground in frustration while others took to their heels and fled. The Prince ordered his men to attack but by no means all of them followed the command although those who did, courageously led by Murray, made a spirited advance and caused a lot of damage before the dense mass of Highlanders made an excellent target and soon the musketry of the British resulted in awful slaughter; line after line of the Highlanders being mown down to a man and eventually the defeat of the Highland army turned into a rout. Such sporadic fighting and attempted charges as there were met volley after volley of devastating fire and the entire Highland army was on the point of disintegration.

The battle was over and as Cumberland's victorious men pursued the beaten army, they cut down man after man and an estimate of the Prince's loss is 2,000 men. Cumberland's losses we put at about 300.

This last major battle fought on British soil saw the end of Bonnie Prince Charlie's hopes and ambitions. After months of wandering in the Highlands he escaped to France where he endured many years on the run before, a bibulous and unattractive old man, he died, a French pensioner, in Rome.

It has been necessary to explore the Battle of Culloden Moor in great detail in order to appreciate the violence, the despair, the elation, the surge of power, victory, defeat and subjugation and the overall air of anxiety and suffering and death to understand the significance of these emotions that have all left their mark on the battlefield at Culloden.

So to the ghosts: many phantoms of those who died at Culloden have been reported, especially around the anniversary of the slaughter. Marching Highlanders, bleeding men, corpses – all are said to have been seen here by different people on different occasions. And the sounds of fighting, the clashing of swords, the gunfire, the shouts of men in battle, the cries of the wounded, the expiring gasps of the dying; all have been reported from time to time. In particular, there has been seen the ghostly form of a single

Highlander, a tall but dejected and forlorn figure wandering about the place, and sometimes whispered words that sound like 'defeated ... defeated' have been heard. There have even been reports of snatches of the battle being re-enacted; usually viewed in the vicinity of the Wells of the Dead or the Clan Memorials.

Edgehill, Kineton, Warwickshire

South-east of Kineton with its one striking motte and bailey castle, is the site of the 1642 Battle of Edgehill, the first great battle of the Civil War which took place on the hilly ridge above the Vale of the Red Horse, named after the figure of a horse formerly cut in the ironstone of the hillside. This major military action, which took place on 23rd October, was hard-fought and important but of no significance to the sheep grazing on the battlefield at Christmas but it was their shepherds, some farm workers and others who, on the deserted battlefield, were suddenly startled to hear the crash of cannon, the ring of steel on steel, the sound of terrified horses and the shouts and screams of fighting men. Taken by surprise at the fearful noises that seemed to come from nowhere, they were about to flee the area when they were transfixed by the sight of phantom armies in the sky. Petrified, they watched a re-enactment of the Battle of Edgehill.

Eventually, they made their way to Kineton where they related what they had seen and heard to magistrates and clergymen who next night visited the battle site for themselves and saw the same arresting spectral conflict. And again a few days later, for a matter of four hours, they watched the amazing spectacle. The story quickly spread far and wide and when it reached the ears of the King, who had himself commanded his army in the battle, he despatched six of his worthy officers from Oxford to look into the matter. They too reported that they had themselves seen the phantom battle and even claimed to recognize some of the combatants as their fallen comrades.

The battle itself saw a struggle between two armies of fairly equal strength that probably lasted little more than two hours but in that time some 5000 of the 28000 combatants lay on the battlefield, dead or badly wounded. Strategically speaking, King Charles I had the better of the battle but the tactical honours could be claimed by Robert Devereux, 3rd Earl of Essex, with Sir William Balfour and the Parliamentarians. The result was hardly conclusive in any sense of the term but it has become perhaps the most famous ghostly battlefield.

Within a year of the battle and its phantom re-enactment a pamphlet documenting the events was published in January 1643 with the lengthy title: 'A Great Wonder in Heaven, shewing the late Apparitions and Prodigious Noyses of War and Battles, seen at Edgehill, near Keinton, in Northamptonshire – Certified under the Hands of William Wood Esquire and Justice of the Peace in the said Countie, Samuel Marshall, Preacher of God's Word in Keinton, and other Persons of Quality'. It was based on the findings of the commission set up by the King who was anxious to have a 'report upon these prodigies, and to tranquillise and disabuse the alarms of a country town ...'

In 1860 the tract was reprinted as an appendix to Lord Nugent's 'Memorials of John Hampden, his Party, and his Times'. Lord Nugent comments: 'A wild and windy night among the Warwickshire hills, might possibly have influenced the minds of a peasantry in whose memory lingered terrors of battle; but this hardly explained how the minds of certain officers, sent there expressly to correct the illusion, could have been affected in this way.'

Today the battlefield is Ministry of Defence property but permission to visit the site is usually granted. And it cannot but be interesting to record that the phantoms haunting the battlefield at Edgehill are the only ones which the Public Records Office accept as authentic. 'Ghosts of the combatants have frequently been sighted,' wrote Raymond Lamont Brown in 1974. Anne Bradford, writing in 2006 says 'Every year strange experiences come to light' and she mentions various people seeing the whole battle or Prince Rupert on his white charger and people who have heard the noise of battle and she quotes in particular a milk roundsman who encountered a horse and rider dressed like a Cavalier.

In his book *Edgehill, 1642* (1968) Brigadier Peter Young comments that the name of one important character is missing from the lists of personnel in the Edgehill campaign – that of 'Boye', Prince Rupert's famous 'dooge', which, if contemporary comment is to be believed, was in league with the Devil and struck terror into the hearts of the Roundheads. He surely played his part, not only as his master's beloved companion but in the effect his presence had on the morale of the troops.

No wonder that a strange psychic aura hangs over the battlefield where such intense and varied emotions were aroused and so much suffering was inflicted and endured. At Edgehill it seems to me there is little doubt that the past sometimes penetrates the present and sights and sounds long gone return.

Historian Dorothea St Hill Bourne said to me on one occasion when we were discussing Edgehill and its ghosts,

'From the time of the battle up to the present day strange things have been seen and heard at this haunted spot – not uncommon on battlefields.'

As an intriguing afterthought I might mention that an experienced and practical zoologist once pointed out to me, regarding the Edgehill manifestations in particular but perhaps relevant to other fantastic 'ghost' sightings, that the solution may be more mundane than at first appears to be the case. He suggested that the original genuine sighting was the result of ergot poisoning. 'It's certainly possible everybody in the village at that time would have eaten the same flour in bread or the same brew of beer, and when Captain Dudley arrived from Oxford to report on matters for Charles I – well, I'm quite sure he'd have been offered refreshment after his ride so it's small wonder he agreed that there were strange goings-on there.'

Glencoe, Argyll, Scotland

Glencoe is not so much a battlefield, it has been suggested, as the scene of slaughter, a massacre. This wild and gloomy valley in north Argyll with mountains rising steeply on both sides and the bed swept by the 'dark torrent of Cona', as Ossian, the semi-mythical Gaelic bard has it. Some still call it the Valley of Death. Among the places of interest today are the Devil's Staircase; the Cave of Ossian where tradition has it the bard was born; the Signal Rock where the signal was given to begin the massacre; and the Iona Cross created in 1883 by a MacDonald in memory of his many clansmen who perished in 1692.

Always to be remembered on account of its treachery, the

Massacre of Glencoe can never be condoned. A rising by the Highlanders on behalf of James II of England, who fled when William of Orange arrived in 1688, was settled when the clans agreed to take the oath of allegiance by 1st January 1692.

In the far north of Argyllshire the chief of the MacDonalds of Glencoe was late in making his submission and Sir John Dalrymple was determined to make an example of the clan.

He secured an order against the clansmen without revealing that the chief had eventually taken the oath. Led by two Campbells, traditional enemies of the MacDonalds, a hundred and twenty soldiers arrived in Glencoe and were entertained for a fortnight. Then, at five o'clock one morning, they fell upon the MacDonalds after shooting the chief and his wife. Although some escaped at least thirty-eight were killed, including women and children. The wretched deed has never been forgotten.

The massacre has given rise to a number of enduring legends. To this day the nine of diamonds is known as the Curse of Scotland, the pips on the card having, to many Scotsmen, some profound resemblance to the arms of the Master of the Stairs, who bore a great deal of responsibility for the slaughter.

There are, even today, tales of phantom pipes leading any Campbells astray in the mountains where they had once marched on their way back to Fort William. There are also persistent stories, all dating from that long ago event, such as the Campbell who, sickened by an order to murder a woman and her child hiding in the snow, killed a wolf instead and showed his blood-stained sword as proof of his obedience to murder. His ghost has occasionally been seen.

Ghostly MacDonalds also haunt the glen. Various writers and researchers over the years have told of eye-witness accounts of paranormal activity and appearances associated with the dreadful atrocity committed all those years ago, in this vale of misery, especially blood-stained and weary highland soldiers appearing suddenly at some hidden corner and then as suddenly disappearing, and of the cries of the wounded and frightened. There are also many reports of sightings of terrified women hugging children to them, glimpsed for a moment in some secluded spot.

The days and weeks around the anniversary of the event, 13th February, are said to be when phenomena are most likely at Glencoe. Then the weather is at its bleakest but the chill has been incidental for many visitors when they have encountered the silent forms of dead men, sometimes exhibiting the terrible wounds that killed them.

Glencoe is beautiful, spectacular, majestic yet cold, awesome, frightening and atmospheric in the extreme, and its grim history is a fitting background to what is now one of the most popular rock-climbing centres in Scotland.

Halidon Hill, Berwick-upon-Tweed, Northumberland

An eminence called Halidon Hill is situated a couple of miles west of Berwick and there was fought the battle of Halidon Hill. Berwick, a border town with a stormy history, has many reported ghosts.

The capture and subjection of Berwick was among the first objectives of Edward III (1312–77) when he became king in 1327. He made peace with France in order to turn his attention to Scotland where in the early years of his reign he fought three campaigns in which he defeated the Scots but his most notable victory was at Halidon Hill on 19th July 1333.

The English were so positioned that they could not be attacked by cavalry so the Scottish knights (some 1150 altogether) dismounted, committed their horses to their pages, and prepared to fight on foot. As they drew near they were severely punished by the English archers and they were forced to retreat to marshy ground and there the disasters of the day really began. Impeded by the spongy nature of the ground, their ranks were broken and from the crest of the hill the English archers poured down volley after volley with devastating effect. One writer says, 'The arrows flew as thick as motes in a sunbeam' and every moment hundreds were wounded or slain.

After a brief but terrible struggle the English carried the day and the bloody pursuit that ensued continued for several miles. In the end, four thousand Scots lay dead on the field, among them Malcolm, Earl of Lennox, one of the earliest adherents of Robert Bruce. While there was an enormous loss of life and many wounded on the Scots side, the victory was won with little loss by the English; one authority has it that England lost one knight, one esquire and twelve foot-soldiers. Nor would this appear incredible when it is remembered that the English ranks were never broken and that their archers, at a secure distance, incessantly dominated the Scottish infantry.

None the less, as with so many allegedly haunted battle-fields there have been persistent reports over the years of the inexplicable sounds of battle: the clash of weapons, the noise of straining and struggling men and horses, the cries and exclamations of wounded and the dying men and the overall clatter and hubbub of fighting and conflict. Here, where bits and pieces of ancient combative objects are still found from time to time, together with crumbling human bones, there has been talk of the occasional appearance of the apparition of a soldier in long out-of-date uniform running aimlessly about the battlefield at dusk.

Killiecrankie, Perthshire, Scotland

Three miles north of Pitlochry in some of the most beautiful wooded countryside anywhere you come across the atmospheric Pass of Killiecrankie (Wood of Aspens in Gaelic), the actual battle site of the first significant engagement of the 1689 Rising.

Here you can visit the Trooper's Den, the scene of an example of second sight by Cameron of Lochiel (who reputedly killed with his bare hands the last wolf in Perthshire). He said, 'That side will win which first sheds blood' whereupon the Laird of Glemoreston ordered a deer-stalker to shoot a Government officer who had come into sight; when the man fell the Jacobites knew they would have victory.

Here also is The Soldier's Leap where, as the Government troops fled in panic, one soldier performed a superhuman leap across the River Garry; the Claverhouse's Stone, reputed to be the spot where 'Bonnie Dundee' fell from a fatal shot, but this is unlikely and what is probably a Bronze Age standing stone was here several thousand years before the Battle of Killiecrankie.

The Revolution of 1688, which placed William of Orange on the throne was opposed in Scotland, especially by the majority of the Highland chiefs and their clans. Their new commander, however, was not a Highlander, although he won the confidence of the clans, but a follower of the House of the Marquis of Montrose. He had marched to London with the Scottish forces and King James made him a peer of Scotland with the title of Viscount Dundee. The handsome and brave Dundee was among the dead when the battle was over, one of the two or three thousand men slain. At one time the Pass was choked by dying men, horses and the bodies of dead men. On the morning following the battle, the Pass and the River Garry presented the dreadful spectacle of hundreds of dead bodies fearfully mutilated by sword wounds, interspersed with plumed hats, grenadier caps, drums, broken pikes and swords which had been broken by axe and claymore and, as if they had been torn off by cannon-shot, heads, hands, legs and arms lay about everywhere.

The victorious Highlanders owed much to the skill, activity and leadership of Dundee. Without his decisive command the Jacobites faltered and were finally halted at Dunkeld. The day after he died the ghost of the famous general appeared to Lord Balcarres at Colinburgh Castle, promptly vanishing when Balcarres addressed him, and only later learning that he had been visited by the ghost of his friend at the time of his death.

The paranormal activity reported from the Pass of Killiecrankie is varied and unusual. Dundee was said by many to have had a 'strange light' about him. Certainly he had glamour and personal magic. Before the battle his sleep was disturbed on no less than three occasions – by an apparition dripping blood. On the third occasion the spectre seemed to say 'Remember Brown of Priesthill'. Brown was a Covenanter and Dundee justifiably shot him dead but always regretted the act. A 'strange light' or grim red glow has often been reported here around the anniversary of the battle. And there are reports of groups of phantom forms in old-fashioned clothes and carrying lanterns; of phantom armies; bloodied and weary soldiers; the sounds of battle; and of marching; a terrified Highland girl; and miscellaneous phantoms often frightening to see.

During one visit to the spectacular Pass, I spoke to a visitor and a Pitlochry man who told me they had, independently, on 27th July, a date around the anniversary of the battle, seen the forms of Highlanders charging down the gorge in some disarray while the sound of battle and raised voices filled the air. On other occasions, I traced witnesses who had heard similar sounds but had seen nothing. Reports of a strange red glow at times in the Pass continue and Stewart Walker of Dundee had a different experience to recount.

He and a friend were astonished to suddenly encounter four or five people wearing ancient cloaks and three-pointed hats, when they were walking through the Pass one summer day. They both sensed, rather than heard, words that sounded like 'Where do we go now?' issuing from one of the party yet the group did not respond to the visitors' greetings or questions and the strangely attired group wandered off, seemingly oblivious to Stewart Walker and his friend. Later, making enquiries at the Visitor Centre, they were unable to find any natural explanation for what they had seen but they learned that there had been other similar reports of unexplained figures.

Elliott O'Donnell claimed to have spoken to people who had seen phantom armies and there have been a few later accounts that suggest there is substance in the earlier statements.

Recent reported examples of unexplained psychic activity include the sound of marching and other noises that suggest that echoes of the Battle of Killiecrankie still resurface occasionally.

Naseby, Northamptonshire

The site of the final defeat of the Royalists in the Civil War on 14th June 1645 certainly was at one time, and may still be, haunted. After Hastings and the Battle of Britain, Naseby was undoubtedly the most important and decisive battle ever fought in England.

Following the Second Battle of Newbury in October 1644 and the relief of Basing House (a battle I remember seeing vividly re-created by a battle re-enactment society) and a battle that has left its own ghosts; the Parliamentarians profited as a direct result of the quarrels that followed that encounter and they reorganized their forces into the New Model Army and made the formidable Sir Thomas Fairfax its general.

Prince Rupert commanded one wing of the Royalist cavalry and quickly routed the forces opposing him, led by General Ireton, who was married to Cromwell's daughter and a considerable and influential figure in the Parliamentary party. Immediately afterwards the infantry at the centre were on the point of overpowering the formidable army led by Sir Thomas Fairfax, Commander-in-Chief of the Parliamentary army which comprised 14,000 foot soldiers and 7,000 horse, when Cromwell, having put to flight the left wing of the Royalist army, hurried to the assistance of his loyal Commander.

This movement decided the battle, with Rupert losing his advantage by pursuing the fugitives too far. The Royalists were totally routed and the spoils included the King's baggage and his letters to the Queen, his correspondence with the French and with the Irish, which proved that while negotiating with the Parliamentary forces he had no intention of coming to terms with them. The three-hour battle saw enormous loss of life and nearly 5,000 prisoners. In their pursuit Cromwell's troops cruelly killed a hundred soldiers' wives and other women of quality. Is it any wonder the site of this decisive and inhuman battle is haunted by sights and scenes of the conflict?

There is considerable evidence that for years afterwards there were times when people witnessed the struggle being re-enacted accompanied by all the harrowing sounds of mortal combat and vicious fighting. Indeed, for nearly a hundred years, generations of local people from miles around gathered at the battle site on the anniversary of the battle and were sometimes rewarded by seeing elements of the conflict re-enacted in the skies over the battlefield and, whether or not this visual phenomenon manifested, they heard the din of guns, the clash of steel and the cries and groans of the wounded and the dying.

The ghosts at Naseby have even merited a serious mention in the House of Lords. In January 1989, during the course of a debate concerning the building of a link road across the battlefield, Baroness Strange, wife of the 17th Baron Strange, remarked 'The battlefield is known to be haunted.'

Before the battle, King Charles I was staying at the Wheatsheaf Hotel in Daventry and persistent tradition has it that there he was visited by the ghost of a former supporter, the Earl of Strafford, who urged him to continue his march northwards and not to confront the Parliamentary forces.

The King felt inclined to accept the ghost's warning, even more so when the following night the apparition returned with the same message. In the event the King allowed Prince Rupert and other leaders of his cause to convince him that he had every chance of success and the decisive Battle of Naseby took place. An illustration that appeared on a broadsheet of 1651 provides an early representation of a ghost or apparition.

Eddie Burks, a consulting engineer who enjoyed a remarkable career during his later life as a spiritual healer and 'releaser of earth-bound spirits', talked with me after visiting Naseby battlefield where he had met people who had witnessed the ghostly battles on or around the anniversary of the conflict and others who had encountered ghostly troops of soldiers and single figures wandering about the fields amid the sounds of battle.

A retired schoolteacher, living in a sixteenth-century cottage at Naseby asked Eddie whether he could rid the place of bangs and crashing noises that had interrupted his sleep for years. Eddie seemed to make contact with a Roundhead soldier from the Civil War conflict at Naseby who had died in considerable pain. The story that unfolded involved a King's Messenger staying at the affected cottage, who had in his care an important document. The Roundhead arrived at the cottage and was shot while trying to detain the royal servant. In some mysterious way the dead Roundhead seemingly inflicted his fatal wounds on the then owner of the cottage as well as making known his presence by thumping and bumping sounds. Afterwards, Eddie apparently contacted King Charles himself who confirmed much of what Eddie had discovered at the Naseby cottage and later, visiting the battlefield again, Eddie believed he was accompanied by the King. The Wheatsheaf Hotel became a nursing home and there Eddie learned there was a ghostly

tall man with a wide-brimmed hat who had been seen in
some of the bedrooms, a form thought to be a Cavalier, but
not the Earl of Strafford whose ghost had warned the King
before the battle.

Naseby is indeed a haunted battlefield: here phantoms of
the past, sometimes visible, more often invisible, sometimes
audible, more often inaudible, frequent this place of fierce
conflict at all times of the day or night but perhaps
especially during the summer months, around the middle of
June, where the awful and haunting happenings here have
left their mark forever.

Poyntington, Dorset

An insignificant affray during the Civil War has left an
impression so vivid at this isolated Dorset hamlet 'that the
story was perpetuated in local lore for centuries,' Rodney
Legg, the Dorset historian and campaigner once told me. He
could have added, since he was well aware of the fact, that
ghostly remnants of the skirmish continue to this day, if we
are to believe repeated reports from various sources.

In June 1646 Parliamentary forces marched towards
Wincanton. At the small village of Poyntington, just north
of Sherborne, the few Royalist sympathizers rallied the
peasants into something of an ambush. They were led by an
excited twenty-year-old by the name of Baldwin Malet,
who suddenly faced the marching soldiers and commanded
them to halt 'in the name of the King'.

The surprised Parliamentary soldiers, better armed and
organized than their would-be ambushers, promptly gave
battle. Metal glinted and clashed in the meadow by the mill

stream as the arrogant and over-confident Malet led the abortive trap and swept his sword through a score of the foe before he was killed and his bloody corpse was carried to his father's house nearby.

This was a time when the fear of plague was ever-present and next morning while the victorious Parliamentarians continued on their way, Baldwin Malet was hurriedly buried with other victims of the inequal conflict from both sides and their grave mounds can still be seen, haunted from time to time, it seems, by silent but bloody figures of fighting men who are seen wandering about in the vicinity, especially during the summer months.

For centuries after the minor battle so intense was the memory of the conflict here that no villager would approach the 'battle meadow' for dread of a ghostly troop of men, some headless, and at least one female figure that occasionally still haunt the immediate area. What part, if any, the female participant played is no longer known. The comparatively small battle here left a depopulated village that never recovered its pre-calamity stature.

In the church here a heraldic painting bears the arms of the Malet family and carries the inscription: 'Baldwin Malet, second sonne of Sir Thomas Malet, dyed in the King's service, the 3rd day of June AD 1646 in the Twentieth Yeare of his age'. His ghost has been recognized among those haunting this poignant place.

St Albans, Hertfordshire

For many psychic researchers the First Battle of St Albans is the earliest properly reported haunted battlefield in

Britain. Taking place on 22nd May 1455 it was the first battle in the War of the Roses and if we are to believe reports from responsible people, psychic echoes of the battle remain to this day.

St Albans can claim to be one of the oldest towns in England and the clock tower (some very old and interesting houses can be found nearby) has dominated the scene for well over five hundred years. I spent my early years in Hertfordshire and always approach the town of St Albans with great respect. This is the successor to the Roman town of Verulamium, with its remains of a Roman theatre, the enormous abbey church or cathedral with one of the longest naves in Europe and its tower built of thin Roman bricks taken from the ruined buildings of Verulamium, the place that saw the martyrdom of St Alban, a Roman convert and the first Christian martyr in England. And some of the streets are little changed since 1455 as are some of the houses, behind modern fronts.

Since time immemorial an old house called Battlefield was haunted periodically by the sound of galloping horses and the noise of primitive battle. Years ago the then city librarian told me that battlefield was in fact Number 2 Chequer Street, an Elizabethan half-timbered property (with modern shop front) built on part of the site of the battle of St Albans. Apparently it was altered to its later state in 1901; before that it was a private house and earlier still a school. The librarian had taken the trouble to locate a previous owner who stated that when shops were first built in London Road, adjoining Chequer Street, excavations were carried out at the back of Battlefield House which revealed the foundations of a very early building made from flint and stone as used for the Abbey. Indeed the building probably belonged to the Abbey originally. The librarian also asked the previous owner whether he found the place haunted when he lived there and he admitted that occasionally he and his wife felt conscious of someone watching them and instinctively they would look round to see who it was – but there was never anybody there. They knew the house was long reputed to be haunted but they had never been able to trace the origin of that reputation. He added that while he and his wife were comfortable in the house, their guests were not always so and some complained of the eeriness of the place and the noises. The owners before them had plenty of tales to tell about their experiences with ghosts in the house, and particularly with two ghostly survivors of the battle. There was certainly a very long standing tradition that the house was haunted; there was the noise of armoured men and fighting, but the unexplained chanting of monks had also been repeatedly reported.

My friend of many years, Tony Broughall says in his ghost companion to Bedfordshire and Hertfordshire: *Two Haunted Counties* (2000): 'In the mid 1970s the building known as Battlefield House ... was demolished and a row of modern shops built on the site but since then the ghostly noises have still been heard occasionally.'

My late wife and I spent a couple of nights in a haunted establishment in St Albans not far from where the battle may have taken place and our nights were certainly disturbed by sounds and noises best described as sounds of battle, and another occupant at the time complained of the presence of a phantom who appeared to be dressed in very old-fashioned clothing and he succeeded in obtaining a recorded tape of some of the very strange sounds.

St Albans undoubtedly has many reported ghosts and many haunted properties but it is the ghostly echoes from the early battle there that has long been of absorbing interest to psychical researchers.

Sedgemoor, Westonzoyland, Somerset

The Battle of Sedgemoor in 1685 was the last battle fought on English soil and it was between a Roman Catholic king, James II, brother of the recently dead Charles II, and an illegitimate son, the charming James Scott, Duke of Monmouth, who was a Protestant like his father who was very fond of him.

When Charles died in February 1685, Monmouth was in exile at The Hague and enjoying life with his lovely mistress Lady Henrietta Wentworth but his companions in exile included unscrupulous adventurers who were determined that he try for the crown of England.

Eventually he decided to go for it. Lady Wentworth sold her jewels to help and the almost pathetic expedition set out. The plan was for the Duke of Argyll to land in Scotland and raise a loyal army while Monmouth would land in the West Country where he was still popular. It was all to end in tears: at Bridgwater Castle, of which only a solitary archway remains, Monmouth crowned himself king; after his disastrous defeat at the battle of Sedgemoor, he was discovered cowering in a ditch and he met his end with six blows of the axe by public executioner Jack Ketch on Tower Hill.

Monmouth landed at Lyme Regis intending to raise a Protestant insurrection against James II who, on hearing the news, sent a force to the West Country, comprising dragoons and foot soldiers, to keep Monmouth under observation, but in the first skirmish with the Duke's men they came off worse and many of them joined Monmouth who was then collecting supporters all the time.

Still working his way east, Monmouth reached Taunton where he was enthusiastically received and recruits to his cause flooded in and his force was soon a hundred times what it had been when he landed at Lyme Regis but they were poorly armed, badly mounted, untrained and altogether ill-prepared for battle.

After an attempt to capture Bristol, then the second city in England, he seems to have been shocked and surprised when he was greeted by a 'great sound' of men, horses, trumpets and drums and he retreated to Bridgwater where the King's men awaited him. Receiving news that the Royalist army kept poor guard, Monmouth decided on a night attack but they were detected and the ensuing Battle of Sedgemoor showed the real efficiency of the small Royalist army and the inefficiency of Monmouth's leadership. To put it another way, Monmouth's undisciplined forces were hopelessly routed, but the battle has left its mark on this marshy area.

In 1994 a resident of Langport contacted the Ghost Club Society about the possibility of carrying out an investigative visit to the nearby site of the Battle of Sedgemoor. Some attempt was made, preliminary to any visit, to evaluate the available evidence pertaining to the haunting of the battle area. Among the reported psychic activity around the anniversary of the battle, 5th and 6th July, were a variety of unexplained noises, including loud reports of musketry in the early hours, followed by the sound of drumming, bangs and crashing sounds of considerable volume, the noise of steel clashing on steel, hoofbeats, cries and groaning; in short all the sounds one might associate with a seventeenth-century battle. Also reported were sudden lights in the sky, lights on the moor and other mysterious phenomena. There were also the occasional reports of the partial re-enactment of the battle, men and horses in a struggling melee appearing for a moment on the battlefield.

There were also some extremely interesting individual reports; especially of the sound of a woman crying, often about dawn; of lights drifting over the moor; of phantom horses, bearing men in period costume, riding over the dark and damp moor.

During a preliminary visit to the battlefield the then Ghost Club Society Administrator Trevor Kenward together with member Stephen Cleaves found the battle area extremely impressive and at the same time depressing. Employing thermometers, cameras, tape recorders and 'control objects' the investigators carried out an initial study. Their results are not without interest.

At ten minutes after midnight they heard a dull banging sound; an hour later the battlefield ground vibrated for two or three minutes and a feeling of depression was experienced by both men. Forty-five minutes later one of them felt an overwhelming feeling of evil, centred on a tree a little distance away. Just after three o'clock in the morning both observers heard a cry that they likened to a girl's voice that seemed to come from the west of them.

On another occasion, sounds resembling a motorcycle were heard; and later, a dull banging sound followed by what sounded like shots in the distance. Later still, drum beats were heard and also the sound of horses' hooves.

The battlefield at Sedgemoor has seen the awful sight and sound of conflict and more than three hundred years after the event similar sights and sounds have been reported from this place of destiny.

Stamford Hill, Cornwall

The interesting village of Stratton near Bude in Cornwall, was once home to Anthony Payne, a Cornish giant well over seven feet in height and large-bodied with it. An idea of his size can be judged from the reproduction of a painting in the courtyard of The Tree Inn there. The ancient church has a Norman font, an old 'clink' door from the former court-house, a memorial brass to Sir John Arundel of Trerice who died in 1561, and some outstanding relics of the Battle of Stamford Hill.

The battle took place on 16th May 1643 (exactly two-hundred-and-eighty years before I was born!) when the whole county was torn apart by the Civil War. The Parliamentarians, commanded by the Earl of Stamford, arrived hotfoot from Exeter planning a pincer movement into Cornwall. There were already 1,200 cavalry at Bodmin under Sir George Chudleigh and his son Sir John Chudleigh entered Stratton with 200 horse and 5,400 foot soldiers in addition to cannon, mortar, and plenty of provisions and ammunition.

The Royalist Cornish Army, some 2,400 men, was at Launceston and they reached Bude on 15th May and decided to attack without delay before the enemy could be reinforced with cavalry from the south. Consequently, at daybreak on 16th May 1643 the attack began, the Royalists advancing on a broad front, from the present day Bude golf course on Summerleaze Downs, coming up from the south and being joined all the time by local men, spent much of the day pressing on up the hill against the persistent enemy. By three o'clock in the afternoon the ammunition of the Cornish Army was almost spent and they were then charged with pikes causing them to retreat, but a ferocious counter-attack forced the Roundheads back and finally they gave way completely, leaving behind their cannon and other equipment. The Royalist commanders met near the top of the hill where they embraced and celebrated their victory. About three hundred Parliamentarians were killed and some 1,700 taken prisoner. The success of the Cornish Army that day travelled far and wide and it is still considered to be a great day in Cornish history. It is said the field where the battle was fought was so fertilized with the trodden-in blood of men and horses that it produced sixty bushels of barley to the acre.

The battlefield, scene of brutal fighting and stubborn resistance, still somehow exudes a portion of that conflict to this day. There are stories of dark forms being glimpsed in various parts of the battlefield site and of the sounds of battle being heard again and again. I talked with one witness who was crossing the field one day in May 2010 when she found herself in the middle of fighting men. She saw nothing, but all around her there was the sound of violent conflict, the clashing of steel and the groans and curses of fighting and dying men. After perhaps five minutes all was silent.

When I was there in 2011 I felt it was almost as though there was a psychic blanket hanging over the whole area, that might descend at any moment. I find it very difficult to describe my feelings objectively, perhaps the most honest way is for me to say I 'almost' saw something of the conflict more than three hundred years earlier in that quiet meadow and I 'almost' heard the inevitable clash and clamour of war. It is something I shall not forget in a hurry.

I am much indebted to my good friend of many years standing, Michael Williams, Cornishman, for the following account. Michael is President of Cornwall's Paranormal

Investigation, an organization that includes among its members gifted sensitives, mediums and dowsers.

THE STAMFORD HILL BATTLEFIELD

Paranormal Investigation made its first visit to a battlefield in May 2009. We were drawn there by the sheer history of the place and there have been odd comments about a strange figure or figures seen in the area – and the occasional claim of battle sounds heard. The evidence therefore is fairly slight. Nevertheless we decided to make a serious investigation. Our party was not a large one but our experience is that the smaller the group, the better the results.

Our whole approach to this scene of bloody conflict during the Civil War was based on the dictionary definition of paranormal as beyond normal expectation. Membership of Paranormal Investigation is by invitation only because we believe the best results are often achieved by a small unit. But, as one Council Member has put it, we hope our influence will go far beyond the south-west.

Standing on this sloping field was a curious experience: it was a balmy May afternoon, birds creating a symphony of beautiful sound, cattle grazing contentedly in a neighbouring field; an idyllic country scene with a distant view of the sea. Yet beyond the grandeur there was the realization that carnage had taken place there. We know hundreds of men died on this field, many others were wounded and no doubt horses were among the casualties. Here you cannot but be reminded of the futility of war, perhaps especially the Civil War, a struggle for control between King and Parliament, even splitting families. We can picture R. S. Hawker, the Vicar of Morwenstow, not far away, coming here and savouring the remnants of history. In his day, it would have been a more remote spot, reached by lanes rather than by roads. He would have been able to hear the Atlantic breakers at Bude.

Interestingly, three of our members caught something of the spirit of the conflict, all three insisting they had felt they had been wounded physically, briefly but quite startlingly. Moreover, these experiences were in different parts of the field.

We had been warned that the current planetary formations would not make this an easy day for picking up paranormal information but, as a result of our two mediums, Pamela Smith-Rawnsley of St Austell and Maggie Francis of Devoran, using their pendulums, and members responding to the atmosphere, certain interesting facts emerged.

We learned that Sir Bevill Grenville's valour and inspiration were big factors in the Royalists' victory and that Antony Payne, yeoman of Stratton, was a tower of strength. There was also clarification about the location of the Royalists' headquarters – not at The Tree Inn, Stratton, as is sometimes said, then the Grenvilles' own home, but at Ebbingford Manor in Bude.

The Royalist Council of War had decided their strategy on the night before the battle; their men would be divided into four columns and placed along the south and west of the hill. The battle raged for several hours, the Parliamentarians' resistance finally collapsing after repeated and determined attacks by the Royalists under the command of Sir Ralph Hopton. A remarkable victory for the Royalists, heavily outnumbered. They had a force of less than 3,000 against the Earl of Stamford's 5,600 and were short of food and ammunition.

Maggie Francis said her pendulum went 'berserk when tuned in and connected with the spirit of a man who had been wounded in the battle and died of his injuries. The whole area has a strong atmosphere so much so it's possibly on a ley line and curiously I and two others found our attention being drawn to a property nearby. Obviously that house would not have been there in 1643 but the site was probably significant ... as was the lower area of the battlefield. It's interesting to speculate what people would pick up if they didn't know what had happened here. Michael Williams says: 'On the evidence of our visit to Stratton we came away aware of rich heritage, an area soaked in colourful characters, that can sometimes be tapped.'

Other Haunted Battlefields

Lichfield, Staffordshire where, once upon a time, a small group of Saxons took on a contingent of Roman soldiers and in a short battle all the Saxons were slain. The site of a funeral pile of the dead became Lichfield, the Field of the Dead, and here there have been occasional reports of phantom Roman soldiers in the vicinity of the cathedral, the site of the actual battle.

Loch Ashie, Scottish Highlands, saw a battle involving, some say, the Irish hero Fionn mac Cumhaill and the ghosts of various combatants have been reported. Local people, shepherds, men fishing, passersby – all have seen ancient forms and figures. American and English visitors have said they have seen re-enactments of the conflict.

At Lostwithiel, the ancient capital of Cornwall, 'there is history in every stone' said John Betjeman and nearby at Braddock Down there are still echoes of a 1644 battle when

Cromwell suffered a somewhat surprising defeat. The area is haunted by the occasional glimpse of war-weary Civil War soldiers and the sound of galloping horses, as I can confirm from personal experience.

A bloody battle dating from 43 AD featured the Roman Second Legion and involved the siege of Maiden Castle near Dorchester. A ghostly appearance of the battle has reputedly been re-played here on occasions, one in the early 1980s being particularly impressive.

Nechtanesmere, Angus, Scotland where echoes of a late seventh-century battle between the Picts and the Northumbrians, in the early days of Scottish history, saw the Picts victorious. In the 1950s a woman saw flickering lights on the old battlefield here and men in ancient garb wandering about the site among bodies of victims of the battle. Another witness reported seeing the same in 2009 and in 2011 faint lights were reported on the battlefield and the forlorn figure of a solitary old-fashioned-looking soldier who disappeared when approached.

There are also haunted battlefields at Marston Moor, near York; Howley, Yorkshire, where a siege took place in 1643; Woodcroft, Peterborough, also the site of a siege during the Civil War; at Woolmanton, Wiltshire where the tramping of invisible marching soldiers echo an early battle between the Romans and the British; Souter Fell in the Lake District has ghostly marching soldiers from a forgotten battle; and Cadbury Fort in Somerset also has a phantom army from a forgotten battle of long ago.

Part 4

HAUNTED BRIDGES

Bridges come in many forms: old stone bridges, clapper bridges, primitive packhorse bridges, military bridges, very early narrow bridges, pointed arch bridges, eighteenth-century semicircular arched bridges – but all bridges, including stepping-stones and foot bridges, are the means of communication from one place to another; something that takes us somewhere else so perhaps it is not surprising that bridges often have a strange fascination for some people.

Bridges where many drownings or deaths have taken place used to be marked by a cristelmael or Christ sign or crucifix. On Dartmoor the dead were carried miles to burial in a churchyard along well-worn stepping-stones that were known as The Lickway ('cross-way') and ghostly likenesses of such processions are still reported occasionally.

The bridge is the link between two places, sometimes it seems, between two dimensions or between this world and the next.

Ballindallock Castle, Scotland

The sixteenth-century castle here and its fine gardens have long had the reputation of being haunted. There is reported to be a ghostly Green Lady in the Dining Room and a Pink Lady, very appropriately, in the Pink Tower. The ghost of General James Grant, a member of the family who has owned this noble edifice since 1499, was always proud of his achievements and he has been seen in the house and in the grounds where he is mounted on his favourite charger.

Another ghost at Ballindallock is that of an unidentified girl, always seen nearby at the Bridge of Avon, and thought to be an appearance resulting from unhappiness. Research suggests that a one-time member of the family owning the castle fell deeply in love but this was not reciprocated, indeed it was spurned. She tried all ways she could think of to interest the object of her desire but she was unsuccessful and, finding no happiness or prospect of it, she decided she did not wish to live and she brought it all to an end by drowning herself in the river by the Bridge of Avon.

She is thought to be the pathetic figure seen on numerous occasions, sometimes on the bridge, perhaps trying to make up her mind, sometimes in the water beneath the bridge after she has thrown herself into the river, sometimes beside the bridge still hoping perhaps and sometimes running over the bridge, maybe in a hurry to finish things in the only way she can understand.

Interestingly enough, not very long ago the old bridge was bypassed by a new one and workmen engaged in the construction of the new bridge complained on several occasions of seeing the figure of a young woman on the bridge, a figure that always disappeared unaccountably. One of the workmen said he had never seen such sadness as he saw on the face of the girl on the bridge. Ballindalloch Castle is situated off the A95 below Marypark, Moray.

Bridge of Orchy, Scotland

Situated at the north end of Glen Orchy on the god-forsaken road across Rannoch Moor there is a little bridge over a stream that has long been haunted by the figure of an old man.

He sits on a parapet of the bridge and is most often to be encountered there on bright moonlit nights; some witnesses have described him as looking like a gamekeeper. He is quite oblivious to the presence of any human being and seems deeply occupied by his own thoughts.

One tourist set out to walk from The Kingshouse Hotel, not far from Glencoe, the twelve miles to the Bridge of Orchy totally unaware of the treacherous nature of the ground he would be traversing. By the time he was at the far end of Loch Laidon he was very weary and aching all over. He was also conscious of the fact that he had not met a single person all afternoon and he was really tired of concentrating on keeping safe on the narrow and twisting path.

As he squeezed round a large boulder, with boggy ground on both sides, he became aware of the sound of footsteps coming up behind him and he began to look forward to some sort of company in the unwelcoming countryside he was passing through when, as the footsteps came nearer, he heard also a rattle, as of a chain. Now a cool wind began to blow on his back and he decided to give in to his inclination to look behind him and see who was following in his tracks. When the footsteps sounded as though they were almost upon him he did look round and saw the somewhat disturbing sight of a tall and elderly man with a large and misshapen head who slid past him without a word. As our walker stumbled on, the strange form in front of him disappeared from view behind a large rock.

At length, having seen nothing further of the singular man who had passed him, the weary walker, thinking to himself that night was fast approaching, reached the little bridge over the stream and there, sitting sideways on the parapet of the bridge, he saw an old man. At first the thought crossed his mind that it was the strange man who had pushed past him without a word but then he quickly saw that this was someone else entirely, a man who looked like a gamekeeper of some kind.

Now, more or less desperate for company of any sort, he began to look forward to having company on the rest of his outward journey. Having decided on a direct approach, he went straight up to the man on the bridge and was soon relating his story of the day's events in the dim light that was fading fast as the moon disappeared behind a cloud. Did the old gentleman know who the mysterious man was who had just passed him without a word; a man with a rather large and misshapen head?

The old man seemed to be listening but remained strangely quiet. Then the moon reappeared from behind the cloud and the old man turned to face him – displaying his huge and misshapen head! Our traveller remembered nothing more until he woke up in his bed at The Kingshouse

Hotel. His first thought was that it had all been a dream, but he was told that he had been found collapsed on a little bridge out on the moor. He was found to be quite alone. Terence Whitaker told me he had obtained this story from an impeccable source and subsequently he had been fortunate in tracing other witnesses who had encountered a silent old man on the little bridge in question. My own enquiries, including discussing the matter with the knowledgeable and always helpful Norman Adams, elicited the fact that stories about the bridge being haunted were rife in the area and my notes showed me that some twenty years ago the erudite and delightful Donald Ross had once had a somewhat similar experience at that small but haunted bridge.

Corfe Castle, Dorset

Corfe Castle ruins, occupying a commanding position overlooking a gap in the Purbeck Hills, was once defended by a woman, Lady Bankes, wife of the Lord Chief Justice, who held it for the King in 1643, successfully holding it against several attacks by Parliamentarians. It was one of the last places to hold out for King Charles and was finally taken only through treachery. An officer of the castle betrayed it in return for a promise of protection. He managed to smuggle in fifty Roundheads and Lady Mary Bankes had no choice but to surrender. She was permitted to leave with her children and dependants and she lived to see the Restoration, only dying in the year after the return of Charles II.

The main ghost of the bridge is a vague white shape resembling, according to numerous witnesses, a headless woman. It is overall a vague shape but distinctly something that is opaque and mysterious and inexplicable. A local resident who saw the form several times, while alone and while accompanied, wondered whether the form had any connection with a nearby manor house and a secret tunnel long said to lead into the castle. Various visitors over the years have reported seeing something that has no definite shape, in the same place. Some years ago three visitors saw the shape and felt a sudden coldness at the same time but whether the latter was an actual lowering of the temperature or a psychological impression has not been determined.

What is interesting is that the witnesses of this 'vague but distinct' form have, somewhat hesitatingly, added that the form or figure seemed to be almost dancing. They would, perhaps, be unlikely to know that Corfe had once been owned by Elizabethan Sir Christopher Hatton, who was known as the Queen's 'dancing Chancellor'.

Sir Christopher attracted much attention at court by his nimble performances of the sprightly galliard, a lively dance consisting in the main of five steps and a leap into the air, a performance which came to be much favoured by Queen Elizabeth herself. He continued as her devoted dancing bachelor for some years and then, about 1571, she gave Corfe Castle to her dancing Chancellor who was one of fifty Gentlemen Pensioners, instituted by Elizabeth's father Henry VIII, and their primary duty was to perform at tournaments which were always heartily enjoyed by the Queen. At Corfe Castle he was responsible for dealing with pirates and smugglers in the vicinity and he was allowed to hunt red deer and had a right to all the wreckage washed up on the nearby seashore. It is not difficult to imagine him executing his sprightly dance from time to time on the bridge at Corfe Castle and perhaps he is the indistinct form that is still seen occasionally on that bridge.

For a time, unexplained lights were also reported in the vicinity of Corfe Castle bridge but after a gang of smugglers were caught there the 'ghostly lights' disappeared for good!

Dryburgh Abbey Hotel, near Melrose, Scottish Borders

Formerly known as Mantle House this castellated mansion mostly dates from 1892 although it occupies the site of a much earlier edifice. It stands a few miles from Dryburgh Abbey which shares associations with ghost monks and a Grey Lady.

At the Abbey itself there is a legend that many years ago a local laird, a religious and good man, was nearing the end of his life and having no son or anyone to inherit his property and fortune, some of the Abbey monks decided to see whether he would be prepared to leave his estates to the Abbey. He was quite willing and said he would draw up a will to that effect but he died without doing so and the monks decided on a devious plan. They would surreptitiously replace the laird's body with that of Thomas Dickson, a poor man of the parish who bore some resemblance to the dead laird and he would, seemingly, with his dying breath, bequeath everything to the Abbey.

The exchange having been accomplished successfully a lawyer was brought in together with two clerks and the man purporting to be the dying laird asserted in front of everyone present that he wished to bequeath his lands and estate in its entirety to a local man, Thomas Dickson, with a small legacy to the Abbey and he then signed with a shaking hand the 'last will and testament' of the laird; and then gave a great groan, sank back in the bed and closed his eyes tight shut.

The lawyers, the clerks and everyone present were satisfied and they all hurried from the room as the monks said they must hurry and summon the man's doctor. In fact they were furious that Dickson had betrayed them and gained the estate for himself, but if they denounced him they would face the full force of the law and, while Dickson would be punished and deprived of the legacy, the Abbey would face scandal and no financial advantage. So, the less said the better,

Dickson took possession and lived for years in comfort, paying the monks the legacy promised. But the ghosts of the artful man and the deceitful monks of Dryburgh Abbey are sometimes seen to this day and heard saying Mass.

Meanwhile the chain bridge at Dryburgh Abbey Hotel is reportedly haunted by a Grey Lady, She is said to have been the earthly love of one of the monks from the nearby Abbey who had been involved in the deception. After the Abbey learned of his association with the lady in grey, that monk was found drowned and the girl, devastated at her loss, drowned herself by jumping off the bridge where her ghost still walks.

Durweston Bridge, Stourpaine, Dorset

Here a ghostly horseman has haunted the bridge for years and apparently occasioned accidents and damage, even causing a stone parapet to fall into the River Stour flowing below. Time and time again the drivers involved in accidents would assert that they had swerved to avoid a man on horse-back – but of the offending man and animal there was never a sign to be seen.

Rodney Legg told me this ghost horseman has been seen for many years. The story was that some time in the long forgotten past a noted local horseman made a wager with another horseman of renown as to who could first reach Durweston Bridge from Blandford, a distance of some three miles. They galloped neck to neck all the way and arrived at the bridge at such a pace that they were unable to pull up with the result that both horses and their riders jumped the parapet and plunged into the River Stour where men and horses were all drowned.

There have long been stories of the ghost horses and their riders appearing in the vicinity but especially on the bridge, usually in broad daylight on sunny summer afternoons when, presumably, the fatal race was run.

Stourpaine village square is reputedly haunted by one of the county's phantom Black Dogs. This one runs through the village to Hod Hill, a broken chain still tethered around its neck. At Hod Hill the ghost dog disappears. The story goes that the hound was accidentally killed by a horse and cart, after escaping from a cruel master.

The bells at Stourpaine's Holy Trinity church sometimes ring of their own volition, it is said.

Hever Castle, Kent

Hever Castle must be one of the most spectacular and impressive castles in Britain and one of the most historically interesting and one of the most haunted.

Here, if persistent reports are to be believed, the ghost of Anne Boleyn herself has been seen many times gliding swiftly over a bridge that spans the splendid River Eden here in the castle grounds, especially it seems, each Christmas Eve or thereabouts.

It was here that King Henry VIII caught his first glimpse of Anne when visiting her father Sir Thomas Boleyn and it was here that, while still married to his first wife, Catherine of Aragon, he fell into the habit of paying clandestine visits to Anne who nevertheless became the first of his wives to lose her head.

But that sad day was way in the future when Harry and Anne walked here hand in hand through these gardens and chased each other through these rooms.

Almost anywhere inside wonderful Hever Castle and in the courtyards and the spacious and varied gardens and grounds, you can imagine the young and carefree couple strolling together and planning a future together. It is not only tragic and violent happenings that sometimes become recorded in the atmosphere and play themselves back when least expected; moments of great joy and happiness also sometimes become impregnated in the same mysterious way and also become visible again without warning and when totally unexpected.

The haunted bridge in the castle grounds is not a particularly well known haunting but my records contain several interesting accounts of personal experiences there of the phantom Anne. One couple, on a personal invitation visit over the Christmas season, were having a morning walk when they both saw a figure on the bridge. The girl they saw 'with the wit of an angel and worthy of a crown' (as Henry described her to Wolsey) may have had the distinct signs of a sixth finger on one hand and an extra tiny breast, but she was a lissom, lively, dark-haired beauty with bewitching black eyes that sparkled and twinkled like stars. They saw the figure quite close-up and both simultaneously knew it was Anne; they immediately knew, they told me, it could not be anyone else. They stood and watched as the slender young girl threw back her hair that sunny winter day and, seemingly without a care in the world, skipped and danced over the bridge – and then completely disappeared. They hurried to the spot but could find no trace of the silent figure they had both seen or anything that might account for what they had seen.

Another witness, also on a Christmas Eve as it happens, mistook the young girl he saw on the bridge for a fellow guest and hurried forward to accompany her back to the house. He had a very close-up view of her and said he almost felt as though she was flirting with him, flashing her beautiful eyes and then drawing away – but when he was within a few feet of her she completely and utterly disappeared. It was only when he returned to the house and related his experience that he learned of the many reported appearances of the ghost of Anne Boleyn on that bridge over the river and always around Christmas time. He visited again at Christmas, several times, and went to the bridge on many occasions but he never saw the figure again.

The last time I was at Hever, in 2009 with a friend, I made some discreet enquiries and we learned that a member of the household had seen the ghost at the Christmas just past, but they did not wish to publicize the fact unduly.

Potter Heigham, Norfolk

We have here what might be described as a classic case of a haunted bridge in the interesting, if true, and quite remarkable story of the haunting of Potter Heigham Bridge, a recurring and spectacular visual occurrence.

The late Dr Charles Simpson brought the case to the attention of the general public when he highlighted it in his very readable and much-reprinted volume *Ghosts of the Broads* (1931, 1973, 1976, 1979, 1982). Since the value of personal testimony must rely on the integrity, trustworthiness, status and standing of the individual concerned it is worth taking a quick look at Dr Simpson, a Ghost Club member for some years.

Dr Charles Simpson lived at 48 Harley Street, London in 1931 and his name appears in the Medical Directory until 1940, so presumably he died around that year. He published a number of important medical books and papers and held several appointments of consequence including Licentiate of the Society of Apothecaries.

His account of the Potter Heigham phenomenon is vivid, if somewhat flowery, and I amend it accordingly. Each 31st May, he says, a remarkable event takes place and he precedes his description of the cyclic manifestation by recounting what he says is the origin of the event, which I confine to the essentials.

In 1741 the local manor, Bastwick Place, was occupied by the wealthy Sir Godfrey Haslitt who seemed able to resist the charms of all the girls who crossed his path until, one day at Windsor, the King himself introduced Haslitt to Lady Evelyn Montefiore Carew and within a short time the couple were more or less betrothed. Soon the marriage took place, on 31st May, 1741 at Norwich Cathedral and afterwards there was a great feast at Bastwick Place followed by a gathering of the entire assembly in the huge hall there to await the arrival of the bishop who was to conduct an episcopal benediction; however he was late and a mysterious fire broke out that practically destroyed the great house and many of the people inside, although the bride and bridegroom escaped and were driven at breakneck speed away towards Heigham Bridge.

Swaying from side to side at the speed it was travelling the coach reached the bridge where it struck the stonework, smashed itself to pieces and was flung, coach, horses and passengers over the parapet and into the River Thurne below. And then there was complete silence.

Dr Simpson claimed to have seen the striking ghostly manifestation of the re-enactment of the crash himself, accompanied by two companions, just after midnight on 31st May 1930. He also says he talked with George Hallness who saw it in 1926 and with Matthew Denham who saw it in 1929. Simpson also claimed to have photographs, films and sound recordings of some of the remarkable psychic manifestations he had witnessed. For myself I can say I have traced and talked with several people who claim to have seen the arresting spectacle although several visits that I made with other investigators, photographers and sound recordists, proved abortive.

One interesting witness I talked with was the writer and broadcaster of acclaim, A. J. Alan and his wife who lived at Potter Heigham. He told me, swearing me to silence as long as he lived, that on 31st May 1937 he and three companions had, partly by chance and partly on purpose, been in the vicinity of the old bridge around midnight and they had all heard the sound of galloping horses' hooves, the grind of carriage wheels on gravel, faint screams and a shuddering and crashing sound from the direction of the deserted bridge itself, followed by a loud splash and then silence.

None of the shocked watchers saw anything untoward that bright and starry night but the sounds they heard haunted them for the rest of their lives. A. J. Alan died sometime in the late 1940s and his wife followed him not long afterwards. I feel I am now entitled to reveal what he told me about this strange affair.

I also traced other good witnesses for this spectacular phenomenon and it may be that the witnesses themselves in some way contribute to the appearance but, sadly, nothing would convince A. J. Alan to accompany me on another ghost watch at Potter Heigham Bridge, at midnight at the end of May, when the place has a brooding, expectant and poignant atmosphere that reeks with psychic energy.

Slaughter Bridge, Cornwall

The traditional site of King Arthur's last battle and convincingly portrayed as part of the Great Bear of Tintagel by Paul Broadhurst.

Around 800 AD the Welsh chronicler, Nennius, spoke of Arthur as a god-like folk hero and called him 'the Bear of Britain'. Considerable research and dedication to the subject has resulted in Broadhurst being able to reveal, as he puts it, 'an extraordinary and ancient truth'. Set out in the landscape around Tintagel, Arthur's birthplace, he traces with startling reality, the image of a great bear, formed in the landscape around Tintagel. The ancient roads, ancient earthworks, ruins, rivers, holy places and the rest – and Slaughter Bridge forms part of the animal's great shaggy leg and close by a megalithic stone engraved in Latin commemorating a Roman general but known locally and far and wide as King Arthur's Stone. The medieval bridge over the 'crooked River Alan', as it is called in some old Arthurian literature, has long been regarded as haunted.

Writing more than thirty years ago, I said in my *Ghosts of Cornwall*, 'Slaughter Bridge, traditionally the scene of King Arthur's last battle, has a strange atmosphere to this day. Upstream from the bridge, on a bank close to the water, an oblong slab of moss-covered granite is regarded by some as King Arthur's Gravestone.' It is certainly excessively large for a gravestone of a Roman soldier, which the indistinct inscription asserts to be the case.

'Experts are divided on whether in 537 the Battle of Camlam, in which Arthur and the treacherous Mordred fell, took place here but some bloody battle must have been fought hereabouts for the name to be perpetuated in the name of the bridge. Perhaps it has something to do with the misty and unexplained figures that have been seen occasionally crossing this bridge and disappearing into the history-laden air which surrounds this strange place.'

Broadhurst reminds us that Slaughter Bridge has long been believed to be the actual site of Arthur's last battle and the area is certainly full of very ancient remains; pieces of armour, rings, horse equipment have all been dug up, and an overlooking field was certainly the site of a genuine battle between the Celts and the Saxons that took place around 825 AD. Many historians believe more than one battle took place hereabouts.

In any case, Slaughter Bridge is haunted (perhaps appropriately!) by the sounds of slaughter, by heavy marching footsteps and all too often by an overwhelming air and sense of fear, and it is the fear of battle.

Stockbridge, South Yorkshire

Ever since it was opened in 1988 the Stockbridge bypass seems to have been haunted. There was accident after accident, death after death, pile-up after pile-up in the vicinity. The police insisted that most of the accidents were the result of driver error but there were town councillors and others who should know who believed the design of the seven-mile roadway was partly to blame and many of the drivers involved claimed they had swerved or braked suddenly to avoid a mysterious figure they had seen gliding across the road and their testimony was supported by several eyewitnesses.

All this before the bridge, a haunted bridge it seems, was put in place. While the bridge was still under construction it stood isolated by the side of the old road. One evening two men were driving towards the new bridge when they both clearly saw figures on the bridge. They looked like children playing among the struts of the bridge. Alarmed at the danger the youngsters could be in, the men stopped and went to warn them about how dangerous a game they were playing.

When they had parked their car and arrived at the bridge there was no sign of anyone among the struts or indeed anywhere on the half-completed bridge. Puzzled, they looked around and saw undisturbed dust and mud on the ground, but no footprints where they had clearly seen young people. As they returned to their car they noticed an odd figure on the parapet at the side of the bridge, a figure when they turned their headlights towards it, they saw looked like a monk wearing a habit – and then the figure suddenly disappeared.

The police, when they reported the experience, were

sceptical but a few days later two of their own officers had an even stranger experience at the same place. Two police constables were in a police car at night, when they pulled up at the side of the road, facing the bridge. They could see a white pallet box on the bridge but what puzzled them was a black figure, an indistinct form, that seemed to pass in front of the white box, pass behind it and then round to the front again. They watched as it carried out this performance several times and the constables decided to investigate. Keeping their eyes on the dark figure they got out of the car and had almost reached the box, when the figure completely disappeared.

The whole ghostly episode was recreated for one of Michael Aspel's *Strange But True* television programmes together with subsequent puzzling incidents which included a human form that appeared to be close to the police car and disappeared inexplicably; and some sounds that were equally unexplained. The screening of this programme brought other witnesses to the apparitional youngsters who some observers believed were dressed in seventeenth-century clothes.

There is evidence that a phantom monk has been seen in the area where the bridge now stands, for many years. Mrs Katrina Hewitt recalled hearing her grandmother talk about the ghost monk often seen there; she had been told that it all began when a monk was killed by soldiers on the sur-rounding moor, and it seems that he is still wandering in the vicinity and certainly there are reports of such a figure every so often hereabouts. Reliable sightings were recorded in 1990 by a lorry driver, in 1992 by a courting couple; in 1994 by a local lad; in 1995 by a local business woman; and in 1997 by a supermarket manager and his wife. After the intervention of a medium, things seemed to be better for a while but very recently, in October 2011, a local mother and her two children saw the ghostly figures and the same month a passing motorist reported having to swerve dangerously to avoid a monk slowly crossing the road, a monk who had disappeared completely by the time the motorist stopped and got out of his car to investigate. He searched thoroughly but could find no trace of the ghost monk.

Other Haunted Bridges

The hump-backed bridge on the Audley End Road near Saffron Walden in Essex is haunted by a phantom coach that emerges from the Lion Gate of Audley End House and after slowing down for the hump-backed bridge it then turns right into Chestnut Avenue but after that no one knows what happens to it. There are reports of it being seen on the main Newport Road.

The so-called Groaning Bridge at Brede Place in Sussex is a very ancient bridge that has always had a most unusual atmosphere. The site of the legendary death of a giant figure who is supposed to have devoured small children, it is a haunted place. Various occupants of Brede Place over the years, including Claire Sheridan, Roger Frewin and sceptical members of the British Army, who were at the house during the Second World War and also some Canadian military officers, all claimed to see ghosts there; Sir Edwin Lutyens described Brede as 'the most interesting and haunted house in Sussex'. Perhaps he was right.

A bridge in the garden at Slaybrook Hall in Kent has the ghost of 'an elderly lady in flowing robes', a figure known as the Grey Lady and reportedly seen on innumerable occasions, even by passing drivers who have wondered who the lady could be, standing out there in the middle of winter and in the heat of summer. She is thought to be Lilly Elsie, a music hall star of the early 1900s who lived at Slaybrook and was in the habit of dancing on the lawn and standing on the little bridge in the garden. The house occupants and visitors have also seen the figure I learned when I was there.

Trewornan Bridge near Wadebridge in Cornwall is, a knowledgeable and unbiased resident of Wadebridge once informed me, the oldest and the most haunted bridge in Cornwall. On many occasions, usually on nights of the full moon, a phantom coach and horses has been seen racing across the bridge but no one seems to know from where or to where it travels; the bridge itself seeming to confine the haunting; nor does there seem to be any story that may account for the arresting phenomenon. Today the bridge, in the interests of safety, is equipped with traffic lights which are presumably ignored by the coach careering at breakneck speed over the age-old bridge in this timeless countryside. One wonders whether this phantom coach has any association with the ghostly coach and horses that have long been said to gallop at midnight into the courtyard of the Molesworth Arms at nearby Wadebridge on occasions.

White Mill Bridge, Knowlton in Wiltshire is reputedly haunted by the bell-ringers who stole one of the church bells in a heavy snowstorm. Fearing detection after being followed by the traces they left in the snow, they threw the bell into the River Stour when they reached the bridge and their ghostly forms have been seen on the bridge and the dull ringing of a heavy bell from beneath the water here has been reported for many years.

The bridge at Oughtibridge ('Demon's Bridge'), Sheffield, South Yorkshire, is haunted by an enormous black form in the shape of a huge man, and a strange luminous form that sometimes crosses the bridge before disappearing. At one time security men were among the witnesses and a Church of England exorcism was seriously considered.

Part 5

HAUNTED GARDENS

Gardens with ghosts are legion and can be found all over the world. Gardens are where every human emotion is played out: love and hate, work and rest, happiness and unhappiness – small wonder then that some gardens – perhaps most gardens – are haunted.

Baddesley Clinton,
Warwickshire

A medieval moated manor house, beautiful Baddesley
Clinton Hall near Solihull has been described as one of the
most charmingly picturesque fifteenth-century domestic
buildings in all England. It has vivid memories for me as I
spent time there alone and among delightful company when
I took part in a televised report on the house's ghostly
inhabitants.

Here, where Guy Fawkes (1570–1606) may well have
lived – he certainly stored barrels of gunpowder here, and
Thomas Percy, one of the Gunpowder Plot plotters held the
lease at one time – there is an indefinable sense of the past
and a preponderance of ghosts. As I sat in the Great Hall,
facing the television cameras, I recalled the room known to
so many men and women over the past five hundred years
and where so many strange happenings have been experienced, and the years seemed to fall away and for a moment
all was as it had been long, long ago.

In Tudor times the battlemented mansion was the
residence of the Broome family. One violent member of that
ancient family, Nicholas Broome, is on record as having
committed at least two murders. An earlier member of the
family, John Broome, was killed in London during a dispute
with a man named Herthill, a death that was avenged by

Nicholas Broome three years later when he waylaid Herthill and attacked him so fiercely that Herthill died. Nicholas Broome did penance for the crime but in 1485 he returned home unexpectedly one day to find his wife in compromising circumstances with his domestic chaplain! Browne slew the man on the spot and he was in trouble again. This time he embellished the local parish church and paid for a steeple at another church by way of expiation. His ghost and that of the man he murdered here are still said to appear to this day and perhaps it is hardly surprising that a man so maniacally attached to his family and his property should remain here in some form. His shade has regularly been reported lurking in some of the many dark corners of this secluded mansion or hastening down one of the ancient garden paths.

The delightful Walled Garden is a favourite haunt of ghosts here or ghostly voices, and there are many accounts of muffled voices in argument; of apparent disagreement between several men; of shadowy and silent forms; of foot-steps – some stealthy and slow and others quick and fleeting, sometimes light and swift and at other times heavy, distinct and leisured. There have also been unexplained movement of objects inside the house and a really oppressive atmosphere: one lady felt she had to leave the Library immediately, or she would be attacked; another encountered an 'invisible but distinctly tangible' presence on a garden path so vivid and frightening that it sent her speeding back to the comparative safety of the house.

It is interesting to recall that the Library, in medieval times, was a first floor chamber adjoining the Great Hall (once part of the courtyard) and there is evidence to suggest that it was here that Nicholas Broome murdered the Baddesley priest. Certainly, an 'indelible' bloodstain in front of the fireplace was long regarded as proof of the place where the deed took place. Subsequently the chamber became a bedroom and, due to repeated appearances of a ghostly form there, it became known as 'The Ghost Room'.

Diary entries have been traced that mention a visitor being awakened in the middle of the night and seeing the ghost of a fair-haired lady, dressed in black, walking through the Ghost Room and vanishing through a closed door. This figure has always been seen on bright moonlit nights. Sometimes she is first seen standing beside a writing desk and sometimes she first appears standing close beside the bed. Each time, after a moment, the figure completely disappears.

The house has long associations with the Ferrers family and when Major Thomas Ferrers died in an accident abroad his ghost was seen for many years in the gardens. Some seventy years after his death his ghost was seen by a visitor and recognized afterwards from a portrait inside the house.

Unexplained footsteps, muttering voices, raps and taps and the sound of cloth being torn have all been reported time without number, especially in the very old parts of the garden. One visitor, after a night disturbed by various unexplained noises, including the sound of deep and heavy breathing, close at hand, decided to leave Baddesley Clinton to its ghosts as soon as she decently could but thought she would first take a last quiet walk in the gardens and was astonished to find herself, early in the morning as it was and in a seemingly deserted garden, surrounded by invisible men and women muttering and arguing; as she turned to hurry back indoors she found she was accompanied by a rather frightening gasping sound as if someone close at hand was completely exhausted. The sound suddenly ceased when she stepped inside the house.

The administrator at Baddesley Clinton in the early 1970s told me of many firsthand experiences of ghosts in the gardens and Mr Howard Heaton related how, fifty years

previously, when he knew the property well, he had encountered the ghost of a soldier from the time of Waterloo in the
garden. He believed some of the paths to be very haunted,
and he particularly mentioned the moatside path. There is
no doubt in my mind that this utterly delightful place is sat-
urated with ghosts, harmless ones for the most part, and you
are likely to meet one, doing no harm to anyone, almost
anywhere in the gardens that may be even older than the
present house.

Beaulieu, Hampshire

Beautiful and haunted Beaulieu Abbey, the Palace House
and perhaps especially the various gardens are situated pic-
turesquely beside the reedy Beaulieu River. I have been
there many times and each visit has enriched me and
provided me with more evidence for ghosts and hauntings –
of the quiet, gentle kind that have been experienced by so
many people; those who live here, guests who stay awhile,
visitors and even casual callers such as businessmen and
tradesmen.

I remember H. V. Morton, the distinguished and most
popular travel writer of the twentieth century, saying to me
on one occasion, 'There is no place known to me in which
you would be more likely to see a ghost in daylight than the
ruins of Beaulieu Abbey ... it is a quiet place, full of
ghosts.' And so it is.

Beaulieu Abbey was founded by Cistercian monks in
1204 and the story goes that King John summarily ordered
some monks to be detained for execution when they tried to
get exemption from taxation. That night he dreamed that he

was flogged for his cruelty and he awoke to find lash marks on his back. He promptly released the monks and gave them land at Beaulieu on which to build themselves an abbey. The Cistercians lived and worked at Beaulieu for the next three hundred years, until the Dissolution of the Monasteries in 1538. Soon ghostly monks began to be seen in the vicinity of the abbey ruins and such reports have continued ever since, together with nocturnal chanting of monks long gone from Beaulieu.

In the gardens here there are repeated reports of ghostly monk-like figures, strange and unexplained lights, the scent of incense not used here for many a long day, and the strange but peaceful sound of celestial singing and the chanting of invisible monks.

Disembodied footfalls have been heard approaching ancient doorways; the sound of low voices has emanated from deserted old pathways; the faint sound of ringing bells, of singing voices, the clink of keys, a choir singing; these and other echoes of the past are no rarity at Beaulieu.

The Revd Robert Powles died during the Second World War after spending more than sixty years as curate and vicar of Beaulieu and to him the ghost monks of Beaulieu were for years as genuine and as natural as any mortal; he completely accepted their presence as part of his daily life and when he spoke of them, which he rarely did, it was with reverence and complete conviction.

Once, two American army officers saw a group of monks in the Abbey grounds and the next time they saw the vicar, who acted as their chaplain, they asked him which order the monks belonged to. They were told that the Beaulieu monks had been Cistercians but there had been no monks at Beaulieu since 1538. The officers were so intrigued that they went to the trouble of ascertaining that no real monks had been visiting Beaulieu on that day and that there appeared to be no explanation for the clear and distinct figures they had seen.

A retired nurse once saw a monk reading beside a magnolia tree one Sunday morning; after a moment he had completely disappeared.

Many people are convinced that there are ghosts at Beaulieu and that many of the building and grounds are haunted. Sir Arthur Conan Doyle was among them. He visited Beaulieu on invitation and went away completely convinced that the place was full of ghosts. In 1965 I went to see author Diana Norman, wife of the authority on films and filming Barry Norman, to talk about her book *The Stately Ghosts Of England*, the result of visits to many English houses considered to be haunted in the company of my old clairvoyant friend Tom Corbett. Diana told me, unequivocally, 'We never encountered such a mass of evidence from one stately home as we encountered at Beaulieu.' Lord Montagu told them, as he has told me, 'You'll find ghosts are part of the scene here.' When I talked with him he told me he had never seen any of the ghosts to his knowledge but he fully accepted, on the available evidence, that the place was haunted. He has experienced the strong smell of incense that many people have reported from time to time.

Colonel Robert Gore-Browne, who lived in a house on the Beaulieu estate, told me he saw a ghost monk one evening at dusk as he was walking his dog along the lane outside his house. Some way ahead and walking towards him, he saw a figure wearing a long brown garment that brushed the ground. As he prepared to have a word with whoever it might be, the path went down a small dip and then up again, but when he reached the brow of the little hill there was nobody in sight. He looked carefully on either side of the path but there was no trace of the figure he had seen. 'It may well have been a ghost,' the colonel said. 'It may not – but some funny things do go on around here – that's for certain.'

When they first went to Beaulieu, the Gore-Brownes took with them a Swiss parlourmaid who always maintained she once saw a man with a bright red face and white whiskers who disappeared in mysterious circumstances. Her description resembled a former inhabitant of the house.

I remember talking to Michael Sedgwick when he was the Curator of the excellent Montagu Motor Museum and he told me he had twice heard chanting that was quite inexplicable. He described the chanting as 'very beautiful' but it came in uneven waves; at one moment it would be quite loud and then suddenly it would fade away, almost completely, and then return again, clear and distinct. A catering manageress heard very similar chanting late one night just before Christmas. She said, 'It sounded almost like a service but really beautiful singing; something I shall always remember.'

Paul Sangster from Bognor Regis, accompanied by two friends, spent a summer night at Beaulieu and sent me a full report. The night, I learned, was clear with a rising moon. The party positioned themselves on the east side of the cloister ruins and for over three hours all was quiet. The watchers then took turns for one of the party to rest for an hour every three hours. At exactly 2.15 a.m. the two investigators on watch saw seven small points of light moving from north to south across the centre of the cloister. A photograph clearly shows two groups of three lights followed by a single light. Was this some psychic repeat of past monks on their way to early morning Mass? Soon after, dawn broke at 4.30 a.m. and the two watchers on duty saw a shadowy but distinct figure in the area of a gateway directly facing them. The figure turned towards the north, to his left, and then back towards the watchers before turning the same way again and taking a few steps before disappearing. On immediately walking over to the spot where the figure had disappeared, the investigators discovered the temperature was ten degrees colder than on the other side of the cloister. The whole sighting, they told me, had lasted 'a good five minutes' but photographs taken at the time without flash on two cameras showed no such figure as they had clearly seen.

Do ghosts walk in the gardens at Beaulieu? It seems to me that there is good evidence to suggest that on occasions they do. As Lord Montagu once said to me, 'The ghosts here have never been evil; in fact I don't think they have ever been anything but extremely friendly but ghosts have certainly been seen and heard here by countless people.'

Bellechin, Perthshire, Scotland

The nineteenth-century mansion here, mostly demolished in 1963 because of dry rot, was a well-known haunted house in the 1890s. Renowned for its ghosts and ghostly activity inside and outside the house, the property was rented by the London Society for Psychical Research and subjected to intensive investigation. The resulting reports, especially *The Alleged Haunting of B— House* (1899), a journal kept by the central character in the affair, told of ghost dogs and nuns, a hunchback and other odd figures, not to mention disembodied hands, footsteps, voices, loud dragging sounds and other noises – all apparently vouched for by a responsible investigator. But all was not what it seemed and much of the alleged haunting is now discredited, although there are still occasional reports of ghost figures including a nun and a Grey Lady, seen by visitors on the drive near what is left of the enigmatic manor and also nearby.

Bordean House, Langrish, Hampshire

This attractive property in a small village within the administrative area of Petersfield, was built in 1611 by Roger Langrish, and belonged from 1878 to the Nicholson family until taken over during the Second World War by the Navy as a rest centre for sailors and members of the WRNS. Afterwards it became the home of an order of nuns, the Oblates of the Assumption; later still it became a Sue Rider Home. During all these occupations there were stories of ghosts, usually seen on the front drive or garden.

The three or maybe four main ghosts are those of a Cavalier with a plumed hat; a Lady in White who walks out of the house and down the front drive; and the survivor and possibly the victim of a duel between two brothers, resulting in the death of one of them. An indelible bloodstain on the floor of the chapel reputedly marked the spot. Author Joan Forman found the place 'taut and a little other-worldly' even in broad daylight. She talked with a night attendant there who left purely because of the 'unpleasant atmosphere'.

A member of the Nicholson family who owned the property for many years was Dr Christabel Nicholson who was formerly physician in charge at Charing Cross Hospital; for years she was Hon. Secretary of the Ghost Club (see my

The Ghost Club – A History 2010) and she remained a staunch and faithful member from the revival in 1954 until her death decades later. I treasure my long friendship with her and it was from Christabel that I first heard of the ghosts at Bordean House.

Dr Nicholson always maintained that the most active and most frequently seen ghost at Bordean was the so-called Lady in White who was invariably seen walking away from the house, down the drive and then disappearing. She was never seen approaching the house, as far as she and I have been able to establish. Christabel told me she had seen the figure several times and once a naval officer was walking towards the house at the time and she saw the two figures pass in the drive. Christabel met her friend when he arrived at the house but, in answer to her enquiry, he said he had passed no one on the drive – which was undoubtedly true. If he had passed a ghost he was not saying!

Another time, Christabel Nicholson saw the figure leaving the house and she managed to tell her brother who was in the garden at the back. He immediately went by a roundabout route to the main gate at the end of the drive at the front and was in time to see the figure of the Lady in White approaching. He said afterwards that he had never been so frightened in his life but the figure, making no sound, passed him without seeming to be aware of his presence and when he looked round after she had passed to see where she had gone, he discovered that she had completely disappeared. He said the face was that of a woman of about thirty years of age and he thought she looked sad and as if she had been crying.

The ghost Cavalier has usually been glimpsed inside Bordean House but occasionally in the front garden where the Lady in White walks. Over a period of the last ninety years this ghost has been reported frequenting various ground floor rooms but most often in one of the passages leading to the hall. He invariably seems to be in a great hurry and suddenly flashes by witnesses who always remark upon his fine plumed hat with the feathers swaying at his fast pace and the long cloak billowing out behind him. Once or twice a sudden gust of cold air has heralded his approach and sometimes witnesses mention the faint click or rattle, as of a sword – but perhaps these sounds are associated with the third ghostly appearance here, the pair of duellists.

The story goes that the duel was over a woman – the Lady in White perhaps – and one protagonist or even both receive fatal injuries. An 'everlasting bloodstain' was for many years pointed out on the floor of the chapel as evidence of the story, such as it is. Dr Nicholson always thought the sad-faced woman and the duellists were linked although they have always been reportedly seen separately. Very occasionally the sound of sword fighting has been reported in the front garden not far from the main driveway; possibly the scene of a preliminary skirmish between the brothers.

Buriton Manor, Hampshire

The Manor House here is unique in several ways, not only because the house in general and the garden in particular are haunted by the ghost of a suicide but also because here historian Edward Gibbon (1737–94) wrote much of his monumental *Decline and Fall of the Roman Empire*, that great panoramic history of the Romans from the reign of Trajan to the fall of Constantinople in 1452, and the fact that when the house was owned by Lieutenant-Colonel

Algernon Bonham Carter in 1957 he succeeded in getting his municipal rates on the house reduced because the house was haunted!

I talked with Mr and Mrs Miller-Stirling, who moved into the house after the death of Algernon Bonham Carter and they had no doubt whatever that the house was 'extremely haunted' during his time and that the front garden was always the most haunted part of the property, and it remained haunted.

There has long been a tradition that a female servant, possibly a chambermaid, committed suicide in the huge tithe barn facing the house across the front lawn many years ago and that it is her ghost that has been seen and heard so often emerging from the house, crossing the lawn and disappearing into the barn as she must have done just before she hanged herself. Incidentally, where the normal-looking but sad and dejected figure hurriedly vanishes into the now solid wall of the barn, there was once an entrance into the enormous tithe barn. Sometimes, hurried footsteps have been heard crossing the gravel in front of the barn where nothing is visible that might account for them. Such footsteps are always heard approaching the barn, but never returning.

In 1962 the Miller-Stirling's five-year-old son repeatedly complained that 'someone or something' kept trying to remove his pillow at night. Clairvoyant Tom Corbett told me, after visiting Buriton, that he saw the ghost of a friendly and kind woman there who could have been a nanny or children's nurse and he thought that perhaps it was her the boy was conscious of, as she tried to make him comfortable at night, and that she was adjusting the pillow rather than removing it. Tom found that the ghost's walk began inside the manor at the boy's bedroom, down a passage and into another small room, perhaps the servant's bedroom and he wondered whether the presence of the Miller-Stirling boy reminded her of one of her charges in her time at the manor.

Other children at Buriton Manor, relatives and strangers, have reported seeing a smiling woman watching them at play on the front lawn; a figure that seemed to be there one moment and gone the next. Usually these children had no knowledge of any ghost at Buriton. The Miller-Stirlings informed me that such descriptions as they had been able to acquire suggested to them a nursemaid from the time of Edward Gibbon and his father who died in 1770.

The same area, between the house and the barn, is also haunted by the figure of a monk or friar. On one occasion the son of the occupants of the house at the time was walking his pony past the barn when he was surprised to see a man standing beside a bale of straw. The figure was dressed in a long brown cloak and appeared normal in every way. Yet, as he watched, the figure did not move and the boy began to feel uneasy and became conscious of a sense of menace emanating from the silent and solitary figure. The experience was of sufficient significance to the boy for him to mark the event in his diary. A couple of days later the boy's mother saw the diary entry and mentioned the matter to the local rector who had a word with the boy who readily described in some detail the figure he had seen. From what the boy said the rector suggested the figure could have been a friar rather than a monk.

Interesting enough when the story of the boy's experience became general knowledge locally, other people came forward to reveal what they had seen. A churchwarden and her daughter had encountered a man in a brown cloak with a white cord around his waist; when he was almost upon them he suddenly disappeared. Another woman, walking with her dog, saw the figure of a monk some way ahead of her but a moment later he had disappeared; she then recalled that the path they were on was known as the Monks' Walk.

Heligan, Cornwall

The Lost Gardens of Heligan, north of Mevagissey in south Cornwall, have a magic all their own. People have lived at Heligan since prehistoric times and I have no hesitation in saying that from time to time something intangible from ancient times returns to this atmospheric place, and I am far from being the only person to encounter this indefinable sense of long past days at Heligan. There is often a deathly stillness in the Lost Valley where unexplained forms of primitive life have been glimpsed. And in the Old Wood there is often a complete absence of bird song although on other occasions wonderful bird singing of an overwhelming variety and quality fills the air. Sometimes the remarkable Lost Gardens return to life – but not always.

Tom Smit, who is largely responsible for the wonder that is the Lost Gardens of Heligan (and the author of an excellent book on the subject) told me in September 1977 that 'there have been many strange experiences at Heligan'.

The regeneration of these gardens – in less than five years the 200-year-old masterpiece of a garden was brought back to life – after three-quarters of a century of neglect, is a fascinating and uplifting story. With little help other than a few faded photographs and tithe maps, the original paths have been located and from the dim and distant past we may now encounter an original ghost in the Italian Garden, or in the Ravine or in the Crystal Grotto or in just about any of the many summerhouses on the Rides and the Lawns that have been hidden for so long.

A ghostly Grey Lady was seen many times nearly a hundred years ago when some of the original gardens were extant. In fact, part of a Ride between the house and the old woodlands is referred to on old maps as the Grey Lady's Walk. This phantom used to be seen 'quite regularly' walking away from the house. Now with the gardens much as they were it is perhaps not surprising that reports of glimpses of this ghost on her old walks have increased,

An Australian plumber working in Heligan House encountered 'something' in the then overgrown Melon Garden that so terrified him that he hurriedly gathered his things together and left, never to return.

Many parts of these atmospheric and attractive gardens seem to be haunted but perhaps especially the area around the Rockery, the region of the Wishing Well, the notorious Flower Garden, the Crystal Grotto and the Tump. All have reportedly been the centre of paranormal activity times without number. And in case you think that visitors, workmen and officials are affected by talk of ghosts and ghostly activity, dogs have repeatedly shown signs of terror in several places in these gardens. Elliott O'Donnell used to regard dogs as 'good psychic barometers'. Not that ghosts and suchlike are the only exciting aspects of the Lost Gardens; in 2011 the yellow legged Clearwing moth was seen and photographed here in Cornwall for the first time in thirty-eight years.

Since I mentioned the hauntings associated with the Lost Gardens in several of my books, *Ghosts of Cornwall* (1998) and *Haunted Gardens* (2009) in particular, I have received a number of letters from people who have experienced 'odd and unexplained' happenings in various parts of this haunted garden and especially, it would seem, in the vicinity of the Lost Valley where a strange and 'deathly stillness' has frequently been remarked upon, together with the absence of bird song; and then there are the disembodied voices, the mystifying odours and the inexplicable human and inhuman figures and forms that all go to suggest that anyone at any time might experience something not of this world at the Lost Gardens of Heligan.

Nanteos Mansion, Rhydyfelin, Wales

Located in the heart of a beautiful and secluded valley, a couple of miles east of Aberystwyth, and set in some thirty acres of pasture and woodland, Nanteos Mansion with its impressive lake sits in some of the least spoilt upland areas in the whole of Wales.

Dating from 1739, this fine property – perhaps the finest Georgian house in Wales – is now a high-class hotel within easy reach of golf, fresh-water and sea fishing, clay pigeon shoots, riding and the theatre and cinema. Once reputedly the haunt of such notables as Lord Nelson, Lord Byron, Richard Wagner and the poet Swinburne, the house and garden are said to be haunted by a Grey Lady, a Jewel Lady, ghost music and a phantom huntsman, the latter usually appearing near some shrubbery where he broke his neck in a fall, although some witnesses say they have seen and heard him riding up the drive towards the house at dead of night.

Janet Joel, the author of the authorized, informative and fascinating *History of Nanteos* (2013) is, not unnaturally, a treasurehouse of information on Nanteos and its reputed ghosts. She tells me the huntsman ghost seems to be well-authenticated and her information suggests the ghostly appearances resulting from a broken neck may be an entirely different ghost.

It may well be of interest to remember that a murder once took place at Nanteos. The head groom was murdered in 1782 by the head gardener and it is not beyond the realm of possibility that the unfortunate victim, the groom, may have been a horseman and over the years has been labelled a huntsman.

An official survey pertaining to the house contains an extract relating to the murder and states that what became known as the 'Garden Rake Murder' was committed by Mr R. Walter, a gardener and possibly head gardener on William Griffiths, the groom. While head gardeners saw themselves as very important figures on an estate, a head groom considered himself equally important and when, during an exchange of differences, Griffiths called Walter 'man', Walter found it extremely offensive, and he attacked Griffiths with a garden rake, the nearest weapon to hand, with such ferocity that Griffiths was fatally injured.

The Sessions Record dated 12th October 1782 shows that Walter was found guilty of manslaughter and sentenced to imprisonment for one year. Janet Joel's suggestion that the 'huntsman' ghost is in fact the murdered Griffith is certainly a possibility.

The so-called Jewel Lady is the best known ghost at this mansion and is believed to be Elizabeth Owen who lived at Nanteos during the middle years of the eighteenth century. She was in the habit of hiding her jewels, of which she was inordinately fond, and now her ghost haunts the property and garden searching for them. Her husband William was very much attached to her and showered her with valuable jewellery and he shared her anxiety as to what would happen to the collection when she died.

Knowing she was on the point of death she is said to have risen from her bed and hidden her jewels. Later that night she died. Over the years her ghost, shrouded in a long and flowing gown, still wanders about the place, still seeking the jewels she so loved. It is by no means impossible that she hid them in the garden just outside her bedroom; certainly there are reports of the ghost that is known as the Jewel Lady being seen in the garden. But ghost hunters and treasure seekers should know that Elizabeth Owen indicated that she would haunt anyone who dares to look for her treasure!

Another ghost here is Gruffydd Evans who was an accepted virtuoso of the harp and he entertained in the Music Room at Christmastime for no less than sixty-nine years! A relative of the Powell family he lived to be ninety-two and is buried in nearby Llanbadarn Fawr churchyard. There are many reports of the sound of his beautiful harp playing being heard on quiet and peaceful nights deep in Nanteos wood.

Yet another ghost at Nanteos was seen by Mary, a young nursery maid who worked at Nanteos for six months in the 1800s. She was sleeping in the Pink Dressing Room so that she could be close to her mistress who was sick in the next room. One night Mary awoke to find someone leaning over her. Startled, Mary screamed and the figure stood upright, turned and walked straight through the closed bedroom door. Mary never slept in that room again.

Evidence is mixed as to whether this unidentified ghost has revisited the Pink Dressing Room although a hundred years later two American ladies were staying at Nanteos, one occupying the Pink Dressing Room and the other the Damask Room. One night, after dinner, they went upstairs together and into their separate rooms but within moments the lady occupying the Pink Dressing Room came rushing out of the room, carrying her belongings, and invaded her friend's room saying earnestly: 'I'm not gonna stay in that room another minute!' Unfortunately she never revealed the reason for her sudden aversion to the Pink Dressing Room but catching a glimpse of the mysterious ghostly form others had seen in the room could well be the answer.

During the dear dead days when lavish parties were often held at Nanteos and the house was full of guests, an army officer was preparing to go upstairs to dress for dinner when he encountered on the stairs an impressive and striking-looking woman in evening dress who was carrying a rather strange-looking candlestick. Thinking she must be one of the guests, the officer bade her 'good evening' but he received no reply and the lady carried on down the stairs as if she had not seen him.

He thought this rather strange but went to his room and changed. Throughout the course of the party he made a point of looking for the lady he had seen but not finding her, he mentioned the matter to his host who immediately took him on one side and insisted he did not speak of the matter to anyone, adding that whenever the lady with the candlestick was seen, a death in the family followed. That night a Powell died at Nanteos. A week later a strange-looking candlestick was found on a dusty and disused shelf in the corner of the Silver Vault Room. Perhaps the curse played itself out for after the candlestick was found the mysterious lady was never seen again.

There is also the eerie ghost sighting near the front door of Nanteos. A witness saw what he thought was smoke but the smoke formed itself into a female figure wearing a long flowing dress. This so terrified the onlooker that he is said to have run all the way to Aberystwyth without once looking back!

Inside the house, ghostly activity includes the sound of disembodied voices. In the stable yard the sound of horses has repeatedly been heard, once on two consecutive nights around four o'clock in the morning, but when the witness peered into the yard, all sounds ceased. There have been no horses in the stables for many years now. On another occasion a horse and carriage was distinctly heard in the courtyard, followed by heavy footsteps entering the back door and walking towards the cellars. There followed a dragging noise and the sound of heavy chains rattling. No explanation was ever discovered for these sounds or for the phantom coach and horses heard and sometimes seen to speed up the drive to haunted Nanteos.

Sandford Orcas, near Sherborne, Dorset

This mellow Tudor manor house of yellow Ham stone harboured, if we are to believe former occupant Colonel Frances Claridge and his wife and family, who leased the house from the Medlycott family in 1965, many ghosts. Within a few years the house earned the reputation of being one of Britain's most haunted houses with something like twenty-five active ghosts inside the house and in the garden.

Witnesses included respected parapsychologist Benson Herbert from the Paraphysical Laboratory at Downton, who spent several nights at the house with a team of psychic investigators and concluded that 'a prima facie case has been made out for the house being haunted'. The colonel himself and his wife and family who admittedly provided most of the 'evidence' for ghosts at Sandford Orcas but previous residents and some visitors also saw them. The Claridge's daughter Anne claimed that there were twenty-two ghosts in the house and 'umpteen in the garden' and she said she had seen seventeen of them. Apart from 'beautiful music' and movement of objects there was a 'lady in green, a nobleman and a seven-foot villain'.

Inside the house, reputed ghosts included an elderly lady in a red dress, a man in a white shepherd's smock, cowled monks, a sex maniac, a naval cadet and many, many more. Outside in the garden the ghosts included a phantom dog, an Elizabethan woman, a man in modern dress, a gipsy lady and a white horse. There was also in the garden the ghost of a farmer – the house was used as a farm for some twenty years – and still Colonel Claridge seemed to produce a new one almost every day until the credulous came to believe that if the house was one of the most haunted in Britain the garden must be the most haunted anywhere.

But then Sir Christopher Medlycott, whose family owned the property, told me they had lived at the manor for forty-four years and had never heard or seen anything out of the ordinary and indeed had never heard anything about ghosts there until the Claridges moved in.

Whether there are or ever have been ghosts at Sandford Orcas Manor House I really do not know; the evidence is conflicting, but I thought the garden was and perhaps still is haunted. Certainly I know people who have had apparently inexplicable experiences in the garden in recent years and who have glimpsed ghostly forms in that fascinating garden. And there is the photograph taken in the garden of members of the family with what appears to be a man in a white smock in the background.

Scotney Castle,
Lamberhurst, Kent

Scotney Castle and its haunted gardens must be among the most beautiful in all Britain and the colourful tower of Scotney Old Castle and the moat must be one of the iconic images of rural England, The Bloomsbury author Rose Macaulay (1881–1958) said 'The beauty is quite breathtaking.' And so it is. I have lost count of the times I have visited Scotney but I never cease to enjoy the exquisite beauty of it all and its mysteries. But now there is a certain sadness to my visits.

I lived at Bentley in Hampshire for many years and my wife and I knew Christopher Hussey, the great architectural historian and explorer of ancient houses, and his wife; they lived nearby, and we had many mutual friends. Once, when I took a party of Ghost Club members to Scotney, I was much looking forward to seeing Christopher again for they had acquired Scotney; but I just missed him for he had recently died and when I visited in 2009, hoping to see Elizabeth Hussey again, I learned that she had died just a few months previously.

Many recent ghosts have been reported. Close to the keep the figure of a beautiful young girl has been seen from time to time in daylight, walking where no human being could walk. The story goes that she was crossed in love and when she became a nuisance she was murdered and her body hidden among the rocks and boulders where once she used to meet her lover and where now her ghost walks.

In the actual rock garden, constructed above a quarry, among the shrubs and trees the ghost of a man is not infrequently seen, dressed in clothes of the eighteenth century. Another daytime ghost here is a man who seems to be gazing wistfully in the direction of the 'new' house, long occupied by the Husseys and built in 1840 (Margaret Thatcher once had a flat there) and at other times he is seen facing the romantic and lonely old castle nestling in the quiet waters of the moat. No one seems to know who this ghost is or was, or why he haunts; perhaps like many of us he is enraptured by the many delights of Scotney Castle and its gardens.

Memories abound at Scotney; Christopher Hussey described the old castle as having 'the insubstantial fabric of a dream' while the breathtaking beauty of it all he always found 'quite overwhelming' and he confessed to me that he was convinced 'there are mysteries at Scotney still to be revealed'.

Sutton Place, near Guildford, Surrey

I knew this splendid Tudor mansion when it was owned and occupied by the American millionaire Paul Getty and he and I talked about the ghosts there as we walked together in his haunted garden.

The house itself has its ghost or ghosts for it dates from the 1520s when Sir Richard Weston, a favourite of Henry VIII, built this very early example of a mansion house as a peaceful home without any thought of defence. The Weston's only son, who had been a childhood playmate of the King, was accused of being a lover of Anne Boleyn and was beheaded on Tower Green. Elizabeth I was here two years after her ascension to the throne. When I was there the treasures of the house included pictures of Henry VIII, after Holbein; of Queen Elizabeth I, after Zuccaro; as well as paintings by Romney, Tintoretto, Landseer, Reynolds and Durer; priceless Brussels tapestries; seventeenth-century embroidery and painted glass of extraordinary beauty and rarity; a magnificent and enormous oak table once owned by William Randolph Hearst; a gold candelabra and other items of untold elegance and scarcity. The ghosts at Sutton Place walk on hallowed ground in venerable surroundings.

The commonest ghost at Sutton Place in those days and perhaps today (when another American millionaire is in residence) was the Lady in White, a mysterious figure seen with some frequency in the garden and grounds of which there were some 775 acres. Dorothea St Hill Bourne, the Surrey historian, was one reliable witness who told me she had seen the figure quite distinctly as did J. Paul Getty who was walking with her along the Yew Path.

Apparently they both became aware of the unidentified figure, which made no sound, at the same time and watched it together as it seemed to be taking a leisurely stroll in the quiet surroundings, its head somewhat bowed as though it was looking at the ground, but otherwise the seemingly solid and real figure was upright and elegant and took no notice of them; indeed it seemed totally unaware of their presence. Perhaps it was in another dimension, certainly it was in a different period of time. Within a few short moments the figure seemed to shiver or shimmer in the sunlight and the next second it was no longer there. Both Dorothea and Paul hastened to the spot where they had seen the Lady in White but there was no sign of her, or anything to suggest she had been there and certainly there was nowhere she could have gone.

Paul Getty seemed quite unconcerned, Dorothea told me. Presumably he was used to seeing the figure and he said his bodyguards and servants had also often seen the form – and made responsible investigations – but they had never found any explanation. It had been noticed that when anyone approached the figure, or after a few moments, it seemed to shiver, just as they had seen it do, and then it disappeared. It was not always seen in the same place, but in various parts of the garden and sometimes inside Sutton Place itself.

I liked the shy and quiet Paul Getty and found him more than willing to talk about the ghosts and ghostly activity in general that he had encountered at Sutton Place. On my first visit I remember we walked through the huge rooms of the mansion, which the Duke of Windsor described as 'spooky', and Getty's grandsons called 'dark and gloomy and scary' and he told me about the unidentified ghost in the Long Gallery, mentioned by a visitor as long ago as 1777 and by another as recently as 1980; and I recall as he talked of this ghost we suddenly looked at each other as loud crashing sounds abruptly accompanied us as we walked and preceded us as we entered the Great Hall. Paul Getty gave me one of his rare smiles and said, 'The ghosts are welcoming you, too!'

I should explain that the quite tremendous noise seemed to be almost by our side and then it transferred itself to just beyond the closed door through which we were about to pass, yet on entering the Great Hall there was nothing whatever to see that could have accounted for the startling sounds and the enormous room was certainly devoid of any human being.

Many visitors to Sutton Place have experienced similar quite inexplicable sights and sounds and in the haunted garden 'a fleeting form that sped with remarkable speed and agility behind a bush and then completely disappeared' has been repeatedly reported. White human-sized forms have been glimpsed out of the corner of the eye; the figure in the Long Gallery has been seen again and the Lady in White still walks in the gardens of Sutton Place.

Traquair House, Scotland

This ancient house with parts going back as far as the tenth century has substantial claims to being the oldest continuously inhabited house in Scotland, as the owner had no doubt when I was there.

Situated near Innerleithen, it is a house full of history with a definitely haunted garden. Alexander I was here in 1107 – the first of a long line of Scottish kings who have stayed here. Mary Queen of Scots visited with her husband Lord Darnley and infant son (the future James VI of Scotland) in 1566. Bonnie Prince Charlie visited as did Sir Walter Scott and Boswell and Johnson and King George V and Queen Mary, in fact some twenty-seven monarchs have visited Traquair.

The beautiful house and gardens ooze history and psychic activity and the owners at the time I visited were proud of the harmless ghosts that they were constantly made aware of, from reports from visitors, estate workers and themselves.

The ghost of a venerable old lady who walks in the grounds and gardens in daylight is thought to be Lady Louisa Stewart who lived to be a hundred years of age and was the sister of the last Earl of Traquair. She died in 1875 still loving the house and gardens as much as she had done the first time she set eyes on the place. A portrait of her hangs in the house and there have been occasions when a visitor or stranger has reported seeing an aged lady in the garden who mysteriously disappeared and then, seeing the portrait, has exclaimed, 'Why, that is the lady we saw!'

Bonnie Prince Charlie (Charles Edward Stewart 1720–88) is a favourite ghost in many of Scotland's great houses. His ghost has reportedly been seen here on many occasions. Traversing a long abandoned path leading to the house's famous Bear Gates is where he is most often seen. He was here in reality in 1745 and entered through the Bear Gates and the story goes that the 5th Earl closed and locked the gates after the Young Pretender left and vowed they would remain locked until a Stewart once again occupied the throne. They are still locked today. When I was there I asked about the frequency of ghosts in the garden at Traquair and was told the adjective 'often' would be appropriate.

Warleggan, Cornwall

The strange and almost hidden former rectory at Warleggan has a haunted garden, if ever I saw one. Even the brilliant sunshine on the day I first visited and sat in the silent garden could not dispel the gloom and apprehension and air of apathy that hung about the place. I was there again in 2010, in the company of Paranormal Investigation president Michael Williams and I found the garden, if anything, even more haunted.

The last incumbent to live in Warleggan Rectory was the eccentric Frederick William Densham, who served the parish from 1931 to 1953 and is thought to still haunt the house and garden. When I was last there the owner showed us round the house with its individual and sombre atmosphere and paintwork on the doors by Densham and rooms with Biblical names before we moved to the garden area, deserted but alive with past occupants. Here I felt, as so many before me have felt, the unmistakable presence of entities, especially children, from the past who enjoyed life in this now isolated place.

Frederick Densham became more and more peculiar as the years passed. He painted the interior rooms of the rectory red, yellow and blue and he painted the interior of his nearby church in the same glaring colours. He erected barbed-wire fencing all round the rectory and he protected the place with fierce dogs. He held church services at times most inconvenient for the few parishioners there were and generally seemed to go out of his way to live at odds with the local people.

There was an enquiry into his conduct in 1933 and the Church Council resigned in a body and never went to the church again and the rest of the local church-going people soon followed suit. Soon Parson Densham was preaching to an empty church and entries in the Service book read, for example, 'No fog, no wind, no rain, no congregation'. In what must have been profound unhappiness and frustration he cut out figures in wood and cardboard, painted faces on them and fixed them into places in the pews, and to such a congregation he preached and afforded absolution week after week.

In his rectory he painted large pink crosses on the doors, preserved for himself an ancient and secret hiding place in the cellars – but eventually he fell down the stairs I walked down (watching my step!) and he died because he could not reach the bell-pull that would have summoned help.

Years before the Revd Frederick Densham knew

Warleggan or the unhappiness he would find there, a previous building on the site was occupied by one Ralph de Tremur, who is widely believed to have practised the black arts, necromancy and forbidden procedures in his rectory (perhaps leaving behind some essence of the unholy) and he is generally thought to have celebrated Black Mass inside the church; certainly he burnt the Host there – small wonder perhaps that parts of Warleggan are still haunted.

But it is the garden that has always interested me. When I visited some years ago the house was empty and the garden overgrown and I put in my notes that 'both are certainly haunted'. There are many reports of the appearance of the ghost of Frederick Densham frequenting the empty church and the drive towards the locked and empty rectory with its then barred windows, and sitting where he used to sit and preaching where he used to preach in his torn cassock and dusty hat. Today the former rectory now known as The Rookery is lived in again, the garden is well-looked-after and welcoming yet somehow parts of the garden, once the place of fun and jollity is now a place of ghosts and hollow memories. Those who are sceptical of ghosts and haunted places may well change their minds if they are fortunate enough to visit Warleggan, now private property.

Other Haunted Gardens

Balgonie Castle, Fife, Scotland, haunted by the ghosts of a seventeenth-century soldier in the area where an outhouse once stood; he has also been seen walking about the garden and near the gateway of the castle.

Ballindallock Castle, Moray, Scotland has the ghost of its former owner General James Grant, who died in 1806, mounted on his favourite charger and seemingly admiring the fine gardens which he was largely responsible for and of which he was very proud.

The Binns, West Lothian, Scotland, a fine seventeenth-century castellated mansion has haunted grounds where the ghost of General Tam Dalyell rides on a white horse and also there is here the ghost of a Pict. This seems to be an old man gathering firewood, a peaceful enough happening that has somehow become embroiled in a time-warp and reappears occasionally.

Penkaet Castle, East Lothian, Scotland has several ghosts including that of a beggar-man who was thrown off the property and promptly cursed the house and its occupants for ever. He was eventually executed at Edinburgh but his ghost still haunts the garden and grounds near the castle.

The garden of Keat's House at Hampstead, London, is sometimes visited, according to reports, by the ghost of the great poet. The phantom form has been seen by many visitors, including Mr Gerry Sherrick, sitting in the garden reading a small volume of poetry presumably. There is a picture inside the house depicting the poet in such a pose.

And there are more, many more, haunted gardens.

Part 6

HAUNTED GRAVEYARDS

Traditionally, graveyards have been regarded as haunted places since time immemorial but in fact there are comparatively few that are genuinely and actively haunted.

Ghosts are popularly supposed to haunt the place of death or burial, again giving rise to the supposition that graveyards are haunted places, whereas evidence is overwhelming that the majority of ghostly manifestations occur where the subject's life was spent, where he or she was most happy or unhappy. Ghosts being seen at their places of burial are in a tiny minority.

Abbots Langley, Hertfordshire

The graveyard of St Lawrence Church contains the remains of Mary Anne Treble, a former housekeeper at the vicarage here just after the First World War.

This ancient village has other claims to fame, apart from a notable ghost, for it was the birthplace of Nicholas Breakspear who became Pope Adrian IV in 1154, the only Englishman ever to become Pope. He enjoyed an exceptional ecclesiastical career before becoming an abbot in 1137 and a cardinal in 1146 and then Pope for five years until his death in 1159. But it is not the ghost of an early Pope who haunts this churchyard, the nearby vicarage and the path between the two but that of Anne Treble who, it is said, was badly treated by the wife of the rector at the time.

I have visited this haunted graveyard several times over the years and am satisfied that the ghost of a female servant or housekeeper, from the look of her, has been seen by responsible people, locals and strangers, in the churchyard itself, inside the church, walking between the church and vicarage and in her old bedroom at the vicarage.

This bedroom was occupied on one occasion when I was there by the young daughter of the vicar who told me she always slept soundly in the room and never had bad dreams – ah, the innocence of youth! However it was a different story when I talked with a former vicar in the rambling Victorian house. This was the room that Anne

Treble had occupied and where she was so ill-treated that she died in the room, suffering 'a horrible death' I was told, 'and the room will never be free of her'. Among other depravities she was supplied with the meagrest amount of food and fuel to keep warm and she was forever trying to get what little heat she could from the fire by trying to draw the fire nearer to her. In the end the fireplace came away from the wall providing another excuse for more cruelty from the lady of the house, with less fuel, and the fireplace was never repaired.

One former vicar told me the ghost was very active when he first moved into the vicarage and, deciding that structural alterations were called for, he employed a local builder and when he came to the haunted room with its fireplace standing out from the wall, the builder said, 'Not much use repairing that; it will be out again within a few months.' He went on to say that Anne Treble had died such a terrible death in the room that she could never leave the chamber and there would never be peace there. Nevertheless the fireplace was repaired – and within six months it was out again! The vicar consulted a surveyor who blamed bad workmanship and again the fireplace was repaired and again it was out within a few months. It was then decided to leave it unrepaired.

This was the room in which the daughter of an earlier vicar used to find herself awake night after night and she would see the ghostly figure of Anne Treble, or so she believed, with her back to the bed, seemingly gazing out of the window towards the church and churchyard. This happened so often that the girl became accustomed to seeing the figure that never moved and she would turn over and try to resume her sleep.

The graveyard containing Anne Treble's grave is haunted by her ghost which has been seen, walking as in a trance, about the graveyard, restless and unhappy as she must have been in life. The same figure has been seen inside the church once, interestingly enough, by a young assistant curate who had noticed an unknown young woman at Mass, a woman who completely disappeared when the priest went to administer the rite to her. His description tallied exactly with that of others who claimed to have seen the ghost of Anne Treble. Another parishioner said she had seen the figure entering the church and had in fact almost collided with her as she brushed past her, but she felt no contact and when she turned to apologize, the figure had disappeared.

Perhaps even more interesting is the fact that this ghost has been seen from two different places at the same time. I talked with the daughter of one vicar who said she saw the figure several times from her bedroom window, walking away from the house towards the church. Once she hurried down, determined to follow the phantom figure but when she was outside the figure had disappeared but the occupant of a cottage facing the vicarage, just over the road, came hurrying out saying she had just seen the ghost coming away from the vicarage, but when she got outside, the figure had vanished.

At one time, I learned, several members of the church congregation and the then vicar reported the repeated appearances of the ghost to their bishop and Bishop Michael Furse carried out some sort of exorcism or blessing inside the vicarage and in the graveyard and while he was alone inside the church, he heard footsteps which he was unable to account for. Another assistant curate also heard disembodied footsteps approach from the west end of the church, when he was there alone one evening, and he knelt to pray. As he did so, he felt invisible clothes brush over his face and he heard footsteps he could not account for since the church was completely deserted apart from himself. He also heard unexplained footsteps one bright summer day in the haunted graveyard.

Nearby, the seventeenth-century almshouse, 16 Ann Seymour House, adjoining the graveyard was and perhaps still is haunted. Mrs Florence Buckland and her teenage daughter and young sons all experienced ghostly happenings: including a phantom figure they could not describe, humming, thumping and banging sounds and the movement of objects.

Canewdon, Essex

The graveyard here in Canewdon, long known as 'the witch village', has, according to Eric Maple, the renowned investigator, writer and lecturer on witchcraft, a reputation second to none as a home of black witchcraft and there is perhaps, no place in the British Isles where the belief in witches survived so long and so late and where stories of the old dark days of magic were told only a generation ago. A very old tradition has it that there will always be nine witches living in Canewdon – and many of the present inhabitants will not disagree! Little wonder that this whole district has always been known as The Witch Country. Eric Maple once led a party of Ghost Club members on a memorable Journey into Witchcraft, when he related the ghost lore and witch legends in the haunted churchyard at Canewdon.

An old tomb here has long been a great attraction to children who test the old belief that occasionally, with ear close to the tomb, the Devil can be heard rattling his chains deep underground.

The church, built on a hill and with a seventy-five-foot fifteenth-century tower, once used as a lighthouse, was partly built in the fourteenth century, perhaps by Henry V to celebrate Agincourt, and has been the subject of many legends and stories doubtless much warped over the years. A churchwarden, no less, told me that if a person walks round the church alone at midnight he will hear witches and ghosts singing and talking to him and he added this has been substantiated within living memory. I do know for certain that there have also been failed attempts.

Variations of this legend have it that walking round the church seven times on Hallowe'en will bring forth a witch and thirteen circles will cause invisibility.

In 1987 a vanishing Lady in Blue caused something of a stir and there have been many reports of mysterious lights hovering over graves and ominous-sounding footsteps that have no rational explanation.

One of the celebrated ghosts here is reputed to be a headless woman dressed in rich apparel who rides down the hill from the church and disappears near the river only to reappear on the opposite river bank.

There is also an ancient story involving a crinolined female wearing a poke bonnet who appears to rise from a tomb in the churchyard and proceeds to wander, sometimes floating above ground level, towards the west gate – which has been known to move inexplicably – and to eventually disappear in the direction of the river. She too, according to some versions of the story, reappears on the opposite river bank – but minus the bonnet and, say some, minus her head! This ghost seems to prefer moonless nights which make observation much less easy. She is presumably a witch who was put to death. It would appear to the unbiased observer that some of these stories have become intermingled and distorted over the years.

Nor are these the only strange happenings reported here. A curious entry in the parish register is written in verse concerning the burial of a lay impropriator of the great tithes then being taxed which evidently caused strong feelings in the breasts of the clergy at the time, circa 1636:

Lord! How he swells, as if he had at least
A Commonwealth reposing in his breast.
Prodigious stomach! Ah, cruelle deale
He could devour whole churches at a meale.
'Tis very strange that Nature should deliver
So very good a stomach to so bad a liver!

Daniel's Knowle, near Beaminster, Dorset

This private and walled burial ground contains the grave of one James Daniel. In fact, it is named after this lawyer from Beaminster, an attractive town situated among some of Dorset's lovely hills and associated with some of Thomas Hardy's best-known novels and a church with a Tudor tower of fine Ham stone.

Beaminster's ghosts include a Monmouth rebel's footsteps at Rose Cottage; a Lady in Blue at Bridge House; an unrecognized spectre at St Mary's church who is perhaps a remnant of the disastrous fire in 1684; the ghost of a murdered boy; a phantom coach and a highwayman. But it is the haunted graveyard that we are interested in.

At the late age of seventy-four, it would seem, James

Daniel joined the Monmouth Rebellion and fought at the Battle of Sedgemoor where the frightful defeat saw him fleeing the battlefield with many of his comrades, some of whom were chased and killed or captured but James managed to escape that awful field of death and to reach his home in Beaminster where he hurriedly hid himself for, being a man of influence and standing, he knew a reward would be offered for his capture, and so it was and a substantial one at that.

Soon James decided he must flee the town for the Bloody Assizes were taking place and, picking his opportunity, he fled again from the King's forces. Of the opinion, rightly or wrongly, that he had been spotted and was being followed he hastily hid in a barn amongst some piles of straw. Sure enough the King's soldiers, satisfied he was not at his home, made extensive enquiries and soon made for the barn where he was hiding.

They searched ruthlessly, thrusting their bayonets into the straw piles but miraculously he survived without injury. Once when they came close he pushed a sitting hen out of the straw and when the creature noisily ran from the hay, the solders decided the hen had disturbed the straw and they gave up the search.

James Daniel managed to evade capture and lived to the ripe old age of one hundred years. On his death in 1711 he gave instruction that the barn where he was almost captured at Knowle be removed so the site could become a private cemetery for his remains and those of his descendants at the place he always believed his life had been miraculously saved.

Near this private graveyard many ghostly encounters have been reported over the years. Peter Beer, who farmed Knowle Farm went out very early one morning to check on one of his pregnant cows pastured near the burial ground.

He found the cow had already had her calf and as he played his torch over the cow and calf he saw also two spectral figures standing close by.

Later he told the local paper: 'I picked out a woman and a boy. She was wearing a long white gown of some sort and the boy had on a dark outfit.' He said the figures appeared to be solid and natural in every way; he watched them from quite near by, only about ten paces away. The woman turned and looked towards him as the cow and calf stood up and then moved away. He saw the two figures walk slowly towards the cemetery and distinctly heard the clink of the opening and closing of the graveyard gates. As the figures disappeared Mr Beer became upset by the ordeal and realization of what he had seen and he rushed back to the farmhouse and blurted out his story.

Later that morning Mr Beer returned to the place where the calf had been born and he then visited the graveyard where he had seen the figures making for. There he found an eroded gravestone describing it as the grave of a couple and a child.

The Beer family moved to Knowle Farm in 1997 and knew nothing of the Daniel family or of the ghost incident at St Mary's church where the ghost of John Daniel's mother was repeatedly reported to manifest both inside the church and in the churchyard. The boy, it seems, was murdered and his mother died of a broken heart.

Descendants of the Daniel family approached Beaminster Town Council at one stage for help in restoring the family cemetery and in doing so they may have placated the ghosts of John Daniel and that of his mother, Hannah. However there would appear to be ghostly happenings still occurring at this little graveyard, for ghostly forms have been glimpsed in recent times; the unexplained sound of footsteps has been heard – possibly two sets of footsteps – and mysterious lights have been reported.

Hopwas near Tamworth, Staffordshire

Near Tamworth, once the seat of Mercian kings, the village of Hopwas has two graveyards, one attached to the church of St Chads dates from 1880 while a much older one in Hints Road once served the church of St John's. Both are reputedly haunted, the older one by the ghost of a young boy and the other by the stationary figure of a man in black apparel, possibly from the Victorian era.

One strange aspect of the ghost in the older graveyard is that the ghost is usually seen only by children. The local Women's Institute were attempting to list all the legible headstones in both churchyards in 1982, detailing the position, condition and other details. While careful not to disturb the tombstones or the graveyard as a whole, while working on some of the overgrown headstones, to decipher the wordings, it was necessary for them to remove long-standing ivy and weeds and one of the gravestones thus revealed was that of a boy who died on 15th March 1878 aged six years.

During the time that the Women's Institute members were bringing to light these gravestones from the past, Mrs Pat Waugh, according to David Bell, was walking past St John's churchyard with her three-year-old son Neil when, as they passed the graveyard gate, he said pointing, 'Look, Mummy, a little boy in there.' Later it was established that he was looking in the direction of the boy's grave that the Women's Institute workers had uncovered. Mrs Waugh had looked in the direction her son pointed but saw nothing. She stopped for a moment and Neil said he could still see the little boy who was standing and looking at them, but his mother, peering here and there as she might, could see no one and nothing that resembled a little boy. After a moment they walked on and thought no more about it.

The following day Mrs Waugh was chatting to her friend Gladys Smith who lived close to St John's cemetery and she chanced to mention an odd happening involving her young daughter Becky. Just the previous evening while they were all sitting in the lounge of their home, where a window overlooks the graveyard, across a path, the little girl suddenly said, 'Look! There is a little boy at the window!' Her mother looked but saw nothing and said so but Becky insisted she had seen a little boy looking in through the window. The fact that both the friends' children had seen a boy, that was invisible to them, the two mothers found interesting; rather too much of a coincidence, they thought, and a little disconcerting.

When the Women's Institute heard about the experiences they too were somewhat agitated and not a little worried that working in the graveyard may have disturbed things and they noted that it was springtime when the boy had died and that it was springtime a hundred or so years later that his ghost was reportedly seen by two children on the same day but on different occasions.

I was interested when I read the account because I received a letter from a resident of Tamworth who said he had become interested in ghosts after hearing that the grave-yard of St John's, Hopwas, had long been reputed to be haunted; he had talked with a longtime resident who said the reputation went back many years and as a boy he could remember hurrying past the place, especially at dusk in springtime.

Without knowing any more my correspondent decided to visit the graveyard and took with him his six-year-old son. They walked round the graveyard, reading the various head-stones and enjoying the spring day when the boy suddenly said, 'Who's that boy over there. Dad?' pointing in a certain direction. My informant looked, went nearer, really sought everywhere but could not find or see anything to account for the figure of a young boy that his son had seen. He said the boy was standing beside a gravestone and when they went nearer, suddenly he was no longer there. The gravestone where the phantom boy appeared was that of a boy who had died more than a hundred years before – at the age of six, the same age as his own son.

The ghost reported from the graveyard of St Chads is another still and silent figure but this one seems to be a middle-aged man in a long black coat and hat. Witnesses are suddenly aware that a man is standing some distance away, looking at them. When they wave or speak they get no response and should they go nearer, the solitary form remains exactly as it was when first seen – and then suddenly and inexplicably, it is no longer there.

David Bell recounts a somewhat similar figure being seen in the town cemetery off the Cheadle Road at Leek in the north of the county. When I first heard of this haunting, a good many years ago now, I visited Leek with Ghost-clubber Stewart Kiernander and we succeeded in tracing two further witnesses.

Originally, I had records of a stationary figure, a man wearing a long black coat and a tall black hat, seen standing on a bank beside a clump of trees in the graveyard. Several witnesses over several years reported to me what appeared to be an identical figure in the same place, a figure that dis-appeared inexplicably.

Stewart Kiernander and I made a number of enquiries in the immediate vicinity, saying we were interested in graveyards and gravestones and any stories associated with them. Two of the local residents, quite independently, told us they had seen, once or twice, the figure of a tallish man wearing dark clothes who seemed to be standing among the graves, looking towards them. No matter how long they looked back the figure remained there, motionless and soundless, seeming to be staring straight at them – or through them. When eventually a witness went forward, to speak to the somewhat strange figure, they always found that he suddenly disappeared before they were really close. Up to then he had appeared to be absolutely normal, certainly not transparent or anything like that.

In the middle of Staffordshire, Stone in the Trent Valley also has a haunted graveyard, a last resting place that contains the grave of Admiral St Vincent, the hero of the naval battle with the Spanish off Cape St Vincent in which Nelson participated.

The apparition of a young man was first seen here in the autumn of 1781, a spectre identified as one Tom Meaykin, who had died suddenly at the age of twenty-one. David Bell reports that Meaykin was born in a moorland village, Rushton Spencer, in the north of the county, and that he found work as a horseboy. He was a good worker and popular with everyone but he made the mistake of attracting the attention of his employer's pretty young daughter who fell in love with him. Meaykin realized the difficulties caused by their vastly different circumstances but the girl made no secret of her feelings for the servant and when the matter came to the ears of her father he was furious and tried to reason with his daughter but she would have none of it; she was in love and wanted to get married. Suddenly the situation solved itself for young Tom Meaykin died suddenly and unexpectedly and was duly buried in the local churchyard.

However, the growing frequency of the allegedly ghostly appearances of the young man during the winter following his death and burial, in the graveyard where his body lay soon gave rise to suspicions against his former employer. Had the young man who had infatuated his daughter not died rather conveniently?

As talk grew, the authorities became suspicious and a year after it was buried, Tom Meaykin's body was exhumed and examined. As soon as the coffin was opened suspicions were re-enforced. The body which had been buried in the normal position, on its back, was found contorted and lying face down. The conclusion was obvious: Meaykin had been buried alive! He may have been unconscious but he was not dead when he was buried. Everyone was truly horrified as they contemplated the dreadful image of the popular young man regaining consciousness inside the coffin and realizing that he was buried. No wonder his ghost returned, they said. While it was widely believed that his employer knew more than he told of the death of poor Tom Meaykin, nothing could be proved and no punitive action was taken. However, the young man's body was reinterred in the churchyard of St Leonard's church in his native village of Rushton Spencer in July 1782 where a worn inscription on the headstone can still be deciphered. It seems to be a mixture of Greek, Latin and English but in essence it tells of the death 'by violence, caused by the wickedness of man'. And this time the body was buried contrary to tradition with the head to the east and the feet to the west in order to ensure his ghost walks no longer.

Llanfaglan, Wales

The tiny church here, set amid fields, has an ancient graveyard that is haunted. Over the years I have received many reports of ghostly sounds and ghostly happenings there, not to mention ghostly appearances.

Jane Pugh, a journalist, author and biographer, in her 1990 volume *Welsh Ghostly Encounters* tells of a woman from Caernarfon who, one spring day in 1976, set out with her dog for a walk.

After about two miles and within sight of Llanfaglan Church, she paused for a moment to look out towards Anglesey. It seemed that one could almost walk across the sands to Llannddwyn Island, shrine of St Dwynan, but she knew the harmless-looking sands were in fact dangerous shifting sands.

The beautiful silence of the crystal clear day was broken by the plaintive and evocative call of a seagull as she looked out towards the Irish Sea. She turned back and looked again at the church, thinking how elegant and restful it all was when she became aware of a number of voices, bursts of laughter and the sound of tramping feet, yet she could see nothing; all around her was deserted space and there was not a soul in sight.

Then the sounds seemed to increase in volume, they were louder and less indistinct. The marching feet were not in step and some of the voices sounded raucous and harsh, yet still she could see nothing to account for the sounds. But now her dog showed signs of hearing the sounds or seeing something she could not see. The dog whimpered and whined and cringed close to her feet; then suddenly she saw the origin of the sounds. A crowd of men were approaching, old men and young men, some in elegant and elaborate Georgian apparel with tricorn hats on their wigged heads and carrying decorated canes and pomanders while others wore rags, handkerchiefs tied round their heads keeping their hair tidy and they carried bundles with them. She noticed two of the men were dressed more in the manner of Victorians. The motley crowd drew ever nearer, laughing and talking between them.

Completely flummoxed yet fascinated, the woman forgot any fear she may have had on first seeing them and as they neared her, she moved to one side out of the way. She wondered where they were going. On they came, still talking and laughing merrily among themselves and taking not the slightest notice of her, and on towards the little church. Sorting themselves into some sort of good natured order they trooped through the lychgate and into the graveyard. She decided to see where they went and looking over the churchyard wall she witnessed the gruesome finale to the vision. Each man selected a grave and disappeared into it – the earth closing over him! Some of the graves had masonry or headstones and these seemed to move aside to make way for the occupant of the grave.

By now, more than a little worried by what she had seen and what her dog had obviously been aware of, the woman, not knowing what to think, abandoned her walk and hurried home. Could it all have been a daydream? But what of the dog's reactions and what possible reason could there be for such a sight? Had anyone else ever seen anything like it, she wondered.

Back home she did not know what to make of the experience. After a few days she began to mention the graveyard to friends and neighbours, asking them whether there were any stories or legends associated with it and she was surprised to find there were some stories which she had never heard before.

One old man, born and bred in Caernarfon, seemed to know something about mysterious events there. He referred to the Bar with its dangerous cross currents nearby and said bodies from the many wrecks in the treacherous Irish Sea used to be washed up on the beach near the little church and they were always buried in the quiet graveyard, although in many cases it was impossible to know where all the men had come from. Among the corpses were pirates, professional people, seamen and travellers, men of every background but brought together in death. Some of the victims were obviously brigands and buccaneers and they were rewarded with a skull and crossbones on their headstones but most of the drowned bodies were unrecognizable and unidentified in any way and they went into unmarked graves.

The old man added that his grandfather often talked about a ghostly multitude who used to be seen annually in late spring or early summer; victims of ships wrecked off the coast. Yet the tiny graveyard could hardly have accommodated all those who had been tragically drowned thereabouts. Be that as it may, the pirate graves are there for all to see and the tiny graveyard, full of sadness and unfulfilled dreams, is invariably full of snowdrops and primroses and forget-me-nots at appropriate times of the year.

And still from time to time visitors to this beautiful spot report inexplicable sounds or equally inexplicable sights.

Ludgvan, Cornwall

The graveyard here, just north of Penzance, is haunted by an exceptionally tall figure, swathed from head to foot in white, that has been reported by many people of all ages over the years; a figure that not a few find frightening and a figure that invariably disappears into the solid churchyard wall. Also there are the ghosts of a young man and woman, hand in hand.

I talked with one witness, a stranger to the area who knew nothing about any ghosts in the graveyard at Ludgvan or anywhere else, and he told me he became lost while walking in the locality one night in the middle of a storm.

As he tried to decide on his best course of action he thought he would make enquiries at the next house he came to, when suddenly he became aware that he was being followed by a tall, white figure, a form that disconcertingly kept the same distance behind him, stopping when he stopped and hurrying forward when he hurried forward.

After a while our traveller found himself alongside a churchyard wall, over which he could see the drenched gravestones gleaming in the wet moonlight. He looked behind him and saw the tall white figure was still there and still the same distance away as always. Suddenly, as he watched, the figure turned and disappeared in the direction of Ludgvan graveyard. He saw it no more and soon found his bearings.

The area hereabouts has long had a reputation for odd happenings, including ghosts or ghostly figures in open spaces, in groves and graveyards and Cornish piskeys have even been reported. Piskeys are believed by some to be the spirits of the ancient race that once inhabited the far west of England. If Cornwall once had little people it may also have had giants. In 1761 tin miners unearthed a coffin at Tregony near Truro that was eleven feet long and, while the remains inside had crumbled to dust on exposure to the air, a tooth measuring two-and-a-half inches, supposingly the only surviving remnant of the corpse, has been shown in evidence of giants.

There is an old story, handed down as gospel truth, that a man named Glasson lost his way between Gulval and Ludgvan and no matter which path he took he always ended up back where he had started. At length he decided the piskeys must be leading him astray and he turned his coat inside out, the only way he could think of to break the spell, and lo and behold he soon found himself safely at Ludgvan.

Another strange story from Ludgvan describes how the local stream ran with wine one certain day each year, so long as no one saw it. One old woman desperately wanted to witness the miracle for herself and on the appointed day she carefully peeped from behind her window. She saw the stream running with wine sure enough but her actions broke the spell for ever.

One witness described to me seeing a tall, hooded figure in the entrance to the graveyard at Ludgvan; a figure that was there one minute and gone the next. It was almost as though the figure was visible to the witness from a certain distance; reduce that distance too much and the figure was no longer visible. Unfortunately the witness did not think of testing this idea until it was too late and he had left haunted Ludgvan graveyard.

Making enquiries locally I discovered that an abundance of similar stories created something like panic among the local people some years ago and no one would go anywhere near the burial ground after dusk. The unrecognized figure in the graveyard has by some people been connected with the publicly hanged and local murderess Sarah Polgrain.

Sarah was married to an elderly man named Polgrain and they lived at Ludgvan. Soon the tall and attractive Sarah became friendly with and then the lover of a young sailor, known as Yorkshire Jack. Anxious to be freed from the old man whom she no longer loved, Sarah resorted to a desperate measure and poisoned her husband with arsenic and she nearly got away with it. The local doctor never for a moment suspected the delightful Sarah of doing anything dreadful and was satisfied that death had been due to natural causes and signed the death certificate accordingly.

Immediately after the funeral, as Sarah and her young lover began to live together openly, rumours of the possibility of foul play began to circulate and eventually the body of old Polgrain was exhumed and found to be full of arsenic.

Sarah was arrested, charged with murder, and at the subsequent trial she was quickly found guilty and sentenced to death by public hanging. On the day of the execution Sarah, as her last request, asked that Yorkshire Jack might accompany her on the way to the scaffold. Together they mounted the gallows, the rope was placed around Sarah's neck and the couple embraced and kissed for the last time. Those spectators nearest heard Sarah say in solemn tones: 'You will – you promise – you will?' to which Jack replied, somewhat nervously but firmly, 'I will, Sarah, I will ...'

It was not long after the execution that the ghost of Sarah was seen in Ludgvan, sometimes on the high road between Penzance and Hayle and sometimes in the graveyard; both places where she and Jack had walked together and had been happy. And it was Jack who saw the ghost most often and everyone noticed a change in Jack. Gone was the happy, carefree sailor and in its place was a morose, short-tempered, restless and unhappy man who developed the habit of constantly looking over his shoulder. To some of his friends he confided that Sarah had never left him. 'She gives me no peace,' he used to say. 'She is there, wherever I go.'

Even when he was at sea Jack was still haunted by his dead love. His shipmates would chaff him for continuously turning from them and rebuking something they could not see; and at night he lay in his hammock, sleepless, silent, brooding, his eyes forever darting here and there and his companions admitted that sometimes they too felt that a strange, unwelcome presence was there in their midst.

After weeks at sea Jack's ship returned home and Jack was soon again in his beloved Cornwall, the only place he now seemed to feel comfortable, and at last Jack confided to his close friends the reason for his constant unease and apprehension and awareness of a form invisible to others. On the scaffold Sarah had extracted from him a promise that somehow or other he would marry her. Thinking to comfort her in her last moments, he had agreed and he ended his confession by saying: 'Not being able to wed me in the flesh, she means to bind me to her for ever in death.'

Soon, back at sea, Jack resumed his unhappy existence, still haunted, or so he believed, by the ghost of his one great love Sarah, and as the anniversary of her death approached, the day he had promised to marry her, Jack retired just before midnight and as he lay unsleeping, the ship's crew, as midnight neared, all heard the sound of light footsteps, as of a young lady, passing their rooms and traversing the passage leading to where Jack lay, restless and unhappy, in his hammock.

Suddenly he arose and climbed on deck, the tap-tap-tap of the light footsteps following close behind him. Once on deck Jack did not hesitate: he made straight for the bulwark, clambered over and leapt deliberately into the dark sea, far below. And he was never seen again. As he disappeared beneath the waves his shipmates heard the distant chiming of church bells and some of them believed they were hearing Jack's wedding bells; at last he had kept his word and he and Sarah were together again.

Ever since, far out in Mount's Bay, phantom bells have been heard at midnight from time to time and in the graveyard at Ludgvan a ghost couple have reportedly been seen, hand in hand, before disappearing among the grave-stones.

Monyash, Derbyshire

An old Quaker graveyard here, at the back of a Quaker chapel, overgrown and neglected when I was there, has long been haunted by a ghost figure wearing knee breeches and 'full bottomed' coat and a steeple crowned hat.

One witness, a tall and hefty Dalesman, decided to follow the figure when he saw it standing beside the grave-yard wall before moving away, but hurry as he would, striding quickly with his long and powerful legs, he found he could not catch up with the figure or even keep the same distance from it without considerable effort on his part. Eventually, the figure reached the graveyard wall opposite – and there completely disappeared.

Subsequently, the sometimes misty figure was seen by several villagers and, while admitting that the chapel itself and especially the graveyard were eerie places, especially at night, the witnesses I spoke to were convincing. And the history of the place is interesting.

Apparently, after the reign of Charles I, Monyash became almost entirely a Quaker community but as the years passed the young people sought pastures new and the old ones gradually died off and soon the village shrank to only a few inhabited houses. Wesleyan Methodism became all the rage and the Quaker chapel had no adherents.

During the last few months I have heard from a corre-spondent in Bakewell who tells me he has collected five reports of a ghostly form or figure being seen in the old Quaker graveyard.

Portsmouth, Hampshire

The graveyard of St Thomas's church (near Portsmouth Cathedral) in the High Street was long reputed to be haunted by a weird and very frightening apparition: so weird in fact that people who encountered the strange and awful appearance frequently fled away screaming.

This ghost seems to have been especially prevalent in the nineteenth century when the local military guarded Government House, the governor's official residence. Even stalwart and reliable soldiers became frightened and deserted their posts, according to reports, when, in the darkness of the night they saw the white, shrouded figure, taller than a man, leap energetically from gravestone to gravestone in the churchyard opposite. The military authorities tried time and again to catch whoever or whatever it was, standing guard in secluded parts of the graveyard and laying traps to catch the mysterious whatever it was, but they were never successful.

Today, the well-tended graveyard is still occasionally the centre of ghost reports. This 'haunting' may have been explained away as a hoax; a man covered in a bedsheet and with springs attached to his feet; but what are we to make of many recent accounts of visitors to the graveyard, with no knowledge of any alleged ghost, reporting the mysterious arrival and disappearance of a silent figure in daylight?

Mr and Mrs A. Morley were visiting Portsmouth during the summer of 2010 when they looked in at the cathedral church and then wandered into the adjoining graveyard. They were accompanied by their thirteen-year-old daughter and after a few moments, idly reading some of the gravestones, their daughter who had wandered off, came hurrying back to them asking about a figure she had seen jumping from gravestone to gravestone a little distance away. She took her parents to the place and then they too saw, a short stance away, an indistinct figure, looking taller than a man and clothed in white, hopping from grave to grave. As Mr Morley went towards the figure, enquiring as he did so, what the man thought he was doing – suddenly the figure vanished. All three members of the Morley family looked everywhere about them but could find no trace of the figure, nor could they find any possible explanation for what they had seen or for its abrupt and instantaneous disappearance. They had no knowledge that such a figure had been seen previously.

St Osyth, Essex

A very odd and ancient ghost, St Osyth herself, is reputed to haunt the graveyard here and the grounds of her priory amid the remains of the twelfth-century abbey and the vicinity of the massive fifteenth-century gatehouse which is joined to Tudor and later properties and provides an entrance to the haunted gardens.

Osyth was in all probability the daughter of Frithwald, the first Christian King of East Anglia, who was betrothed, against her wishes, to Sighere, an East Saxon king. At the marriage feast news came that a great white stag had been sighted in the locality and Sighere, a keen huntsman, at once left the marriage festivities and set out in pursuit of the stag. Osyth took advantage of the opportunity and fled the proceedings, taking herself to a nunnery, a following she had always yearned for, and there she determined to stay and take the veil. When he heard of her resolve, Sighere generously gave her a village where she founded her own nunnery.

St Osyth Priory prospered until one day in the year 653 Danish pirates came plundering through Essex and they sacked the nunnery at that time at Crich (the new designation arising with the canonising of Osyth) and legend has it that the Danes slew Osyth when she refused to give up her religion, striking off her head.

At once, so goes the story, Osyth bent down, picked up her head, and walked to the church of St Peter and St Paul where she knocked on the door with one of her bloodstained hands before falling down dead. Where she fell, still holding her head, a stream of water gushed forth from the ground, the source of the stream that runs to this day in Nun's Wood. And here, at least one night each year, maybe more often, her ghost returns to haunt the vicinity of St Osyth's Well and I possess several reports of sightings during recent years.

There are, perhaps more puzzling, reliable reports of the shade of a monk in a brown habit walking in the grounds of the priory.

The Great Gate House was the scene of a curious incident a few years ago when a passing motorist stopped to give a lift to a waiting girl who carried a posy in her hands. Soon afterwards the driver discovered that the girl had vanished from his moving car but the scent of her posy of flowers remained.

Writing in 1972 Andrew Green related that in 1969 and in 1970 a figure resembling a monk carrying a lighted candle had been seen 'gliding' among the priory ruins at dawn going in the direction of the watermill where he 'just vanished'.

At one time the priory was used as a convalescent home and a group of the occupants all saw a procession of ghostly monks which certainly had no reality. Here too there are occasional sightings of a spectre – whether male or female is not clear – dressed in a pure white robe; here again the figure does not seem to have any objective reality.

The history of St Osyth is interesting, quite apart from the ghosts. After the suppression of the monasteries the property was given by Henry VIII to his minister Cromwall and after he upset his sovereign and lost his head the possession passed to the powerful D'Arcy family. When Elizabeth I visited in 1561 she was alarmed by a terrific thunderstorm, so terrible that it was thought 'the world was at an end'.

As I write, a correspondent tells me that she and a friend saw a nun-like figure in the area of the graveyard here in January 2012; a figure that suddenly vanished. She noticed two men the other side of where the figure appeared who seemed to be puzzled about something and she and her friend went over and they too had seen the figure – from the other side.

Sanquhar, Dumfries and Galloway, Scotland

Lily Seafield is among those who have related to me the ghost stories associated with the kirkyard at Sanquhar, especially concerning the ghost of Abraham Crichton, who died in 1745.

Always a hard-working man, Crichton became wealthy and the owner of much land, yet he was declared bankrupt in 1741. But suspicions were aroused that he was not in such financial difficulties as he would have people believe. He had made a lot of money in his time and, rumour had it, he had secreted much of it away for his own use.

At the time there was a disused church in the district which some local people had voted to demolish but misfortune seemed to affect those involved in anything like demolishing the church and it still stood. There were those who said God would not allow one of his houses to be destroyed.

Abraham Crichton would have none of this. He could see money in the church site and he set about the demolition of the place. No sooner had work under Crichton's leadership begun than a great storm blew up out of nowhere and work had to be stopped for the day. The same day while riding home Crichton met with disaster. A bolt of lightning frightened his horse, Crichton was thrown but his foot became caught in a stirrup and the bolting horse dragged him at speed for miles. When it finally came to a stop Crichton's body was bloody and lifeless. Had divine retribution overtaken Abraham Crichton? It almost seemed like it for the church was not demolished and soon after his body was buried in the graveyard at Sanquhar there were reports that he had returned in ghostly form.

After that there were many and repeated stories of the ghost appearing in the graveyard and even of it leaving the burial place and following people into the fields next to the churchyard before disappearing and leaving very frightened witnesses.

Visitors, knowing nothing of the reputation the graveyard quickly acquired, would suddenly find themselves confronted by the ghost of the now long-dead Abraham Crichton, a figure that always seemed to be trying to speak or communicate in some way with the humans who witnessed his appearances, stretching out his hands for comfort but no one dared take hold of them.

As the years passed, the kirkyard became known as a haunted place, especially during the hours of darkness and local people and visitors, acquainted with stories of the ghost, would make detours of some considerable inconvenience and distance to avoid going near the haunted graveyard.

There has been talk of some sort of exorcism and at one time a bold minister armed himself with a Bible and a sword before attempting to face the ghost. He left in confident mood, not revealing what had happened but saying the ghost would haunt no more. For a while things were quieter but then reports surfaced again of appearances of the ghost and the tombstone of Abraham Crichton was secured in its place with strong chains, in the hope that this would stop the ghost walking.

In recent years there have been renewed reports of a ghost in the graveyard but whether it is that of Crichton or someone else is unclear.

Other Haunted Graveyards

The graveyard adjoining St Nicholas Church, Aberdeen, has long been regarded as haunted, in particular by the apparition of a woman wearing a white dress and veil. Witnesses, including two in 1982, say the figure had long black hair and disappeared at a corner of the church.

The churchyard of St Nicholas at Pluckley in Kent is haunted by the ghost of the beautiful Lady Dering and also by a Lady in Red searching for the baby she lost; these are just two of the reputed dozen or so ghosts that provide Pluckley with its accolade 'the most haunted village in England'.

St Alban's Abbey, Hertfordshire, has a churchyard haunted by the sound of footsteps, often reported, and by the ghostly form of Robert Fairfax, organist at the Abbey in the sixteenth century. Dr Tysoe, when he was Dean, told me there were several well-authenticated sightings by visitors and also the sound of organ music very late at night emanating from the empty church; and the sound of disembodied and hurrying footsteps.

The graveyard of Warblington Church in Hampshire is haunted by the ghost of the Lady Margaret, Countess of Salisbury, who lived at the sixteenth-century castle destroyed by the Roundheads in the Civil War. She lost her head at the Tower of London for opposing Henry VIII. Her ghost is also seen at the Tower but I understand her ghost has been seen at Warblington graveyard quite recently.

There is a haunted churchyard at St Michael's, Bishops Stortford, Hertfordshire where a Ghost Club member saw a female figure 'in a long dress and wearing a mob cap' walking through the graveyard at about 7.30 one morning. The graveyard is adjacent to a haunted house.

The churchyard at St Levan near Penzance in Cornwall is often haunted by the ghost of another woman in white, especially on summer nights, but who she is and why she haunts I have not been able to establish. The ringing of ghost bells has also been reported here.

The old graveyard beside the main road adjoining the church of St Mary's Latton at Harlow in Essex is haunted according to a correspondent, Mrs Jean Scarry, who wrote to me in July 2010 concerning the unexplained figure of a creeping man who appeared and disappeared as she watched.

The graveyard at Rye in East Sussex is haunted by a tall figure wearing leather boots and a long black cloak – a figure that makes no sound and leaves no footprints; possibly the ghost of a man executed in error for murder.

And there are many more ...

Part 7

HAUNTED HIGHWAYS
AND BYWAYS

It may seem possible, even probable, that a ghost might be met in a haunted building or close to a place once inhabited and frequented by human beings but can there really be haunted highways and byways, completely devoid of human habitation?

Evidence from all over the England, Scotland and Wales suggest that indeed there are such places, in many parts of Britain, where anyone is likely to encounter someone or something not of this world.

Annan, Dumfriesshire, Scotland

A quite remarkable experience reportedly took place on the stretch of the A75 between Dumfries and Annan one night in April fifty years ago when two brothers aged twenty-two and fourteen had the most frightening experience of their young lives.

Having spent a short holiday touring Scotland, they filled up their father's car with petrol and were all set for home when they ran into, literally, a bizarre and never-to-be-forgotten event. It was almost midnight and the dry and moonlit road stretched clear and deserted ahead of them.

They had just been discussing the fact that they seemed to be the only car on the road when a large bird, which they took to be a hen, suddenly flew towards them but then disappeared when it seemed about to hit their windscreen. The older brother, Derek, who was driving, automatically swerved to avoid the bird or whatever it was and both brothers felt shaken – but worse was to follow.

They had hardly recovered when they both saw the figure of an elderly woman rushing wildly towards them, waving her arms – and then she too completely vanished. But she was followed by what appeared to be an unending stream of forms and figures that loomed up out of nowhere and terrified the two boys. They saw great cats, wild-looking dogs, goats, hens and other large fowl, an old man with long hair who seemed to be screaming: horrifying and frightening sights that appeared to menace them and the car although nothing made actual contact with them. Derek zig-zagged along the road, swerving and breaking and repeatedly changing course as they pressed on through the night and into and through, or so it seemed, a menagerie of animal phantoms.

As they proceeded into the night, thinking any moment one of the creatures would collide with the car, both noticed an appreciable drop in temperature inside the car although both the boys were drenched in perspiration at the alarming and distressing events.

At one time, Derek felt as though some force was trying to gain control of the steering wheel and his driving became more erratic and difficult. They felt as though they were suf-focating and tried to open a window to get some air but it was bitterly cold outside and they closed the window and suffered as the sound of screaming, high-pitched laughter and cackling noises added to their alarm and seemed to mock them. Derek said afterwards that he became completely convinced that 'something' was attempting to force them off the road and he had an awful feeling that a fatal accident would result.

In the end, Derek stopped the car and immediately some invisible force seemed to attack the car which was bounced violently up and down and rocked from side to side. Then Derek, who had the feeling that he was going to be sick, suc-ceeded in wrenching open the car door and leaping out. Immediately all was quiet and the surrounding countryside was still and seemed to be utterly deserted in the quiet night.

Derek decided to press on home but as soon as he was back in the car with the door shut and he had restarted the car the night was again filled with weird and fearsome figures and terrifying noises that seemed to come from every direction. Trying to keep a straight course through the mass of strange figures that continuously loomed up in front of him, Derek was more than a little relieved to see some way ahead the red tail-lights of a vehicle. As he drew nearer he saw it was lorry, possibly a large furniture van. Yet no sooner had he been pleased to encounter something normal that night than he realized he was travelling too fast, he was swiftly approaching the slow-moving lorry and he found to his horror he could not move the steering wheel to avoid the lorry! Furthermore his foot would not move from the accelerator pedal and a collision seemed inevitable. He screamed to his brother to prepare for a collision – and then they were upon the van: and it had completely vanished!

Thankfully, the stream of entities had ceased and the night seemed normal at last. Derek now found he had complete control of the car and driving carefully and much relieved they found themselves approaching Annan. Their night of terror was over.

Subsequently, I was able to corroborate much of their experience with the brothers but later when I needed to check one or two points I learned they had moved to Spain and I was unable to trace their exact whereabouts. I have to say that I was never completely happy with the report although research by Peter McCue of the SPR in 2011 seemed to establish that the fifteen mile stretch of the A75 (possibly the *old* A75 rather than the present-day one) has been the scene of a number of unexplained happenings.

Andrew Green has referred to a lorry driver seeing a middle-aged couple walking along the road, arm in arm. When he stopped his van with the intention of remonstrating with the couple, he found they had completely vanished. Green also refers briefly to 'a ghostly car that suddenly disappeared'.

In 1995 a couple named Garson and Monica Miller were driving along the A75 when they saw a figure ahead of them. It looked like a middle-aged man who had his arms stretched out towards them and he seemed to be holding something. He was so close that the couple thought they must have hit him but when they stopped and searched there was no sign anywhere of the figure they had both seen.

In 1997 Donna Maxwell was driving along the old A75 when a man seemed to jump out in front of her car. She slammed on her brakes but there was no collision and the man she saw had completely disappeared. Her two children were with her in the car at the time and also witnessed the incident. Donna Maxwell later discovered she was not the only person to see a man who disappeared on that stretch of the road.

There are other reports, of a mist forming into a figure, of an old woman in Victorian clothes, and other odd and unexplained happenings on what has been called 'Scotland's most haunted road'.

Aylesford, near Maidstone, Kent

A stretch of dual-carriage roadway here replaces a short and steep hill that emerges just north of a public house, an area once known far and wide as Blue Bell Hill.

Off Old Chatham Road, in an adjacent field stands a famous Neolithic chambered barrow known as Kit's Coty House, consisting of three upright stones in an H-shaped plan, covered by a large capstone dating from perhaps three thousand years before Christ. It may have been a false entrance or part of a burial chamber. A sketch exists from 1722 showing a fourth large stone known as The General's Tomb which was blown down in 1867. The sketch also shows a long mound no longer visible and aerial photography reveals side ditches twelve feet deep. The monument is now enclosed with railings. It is not unlikely that four thousand years ago the area was associated with some kind of monumental preservation of human remains and artefacts. Nearby, a jumble of twenty sarson stones probably once formed a burial chamber; once known as Little Kit's Coty House they are now often referred to as the Countless Stones. There have been legends of ghosts here since time immemorial. A British chieftain is reputed to have been killed here in combat with the Jutish leader Horsa in 455 AD and to have been buried here. Phantom re-enactments of the battle are said to have been seen during 'uncanny silence'.

The stretch of road once known as Blue Bell Hill has also attracted a wealth of ghostly associations. There are stories of the ghost of a small girl who was run over in 1974; many accounts of the phantom hitch-hiker ghost story (a hitch-hiker is picked up and then vanishes) and stories of phantom people and phantom vehicles.

An SPR publication in 2011 referred to Ian Sharpe driving here in 1992 when he seemed to hit a girl – who vanished. Around the same time Christopher Dawkins had a similar experience. These are only two of the mass of strange experiences reported from this region which some call the Hill of Death. One hospital switchboard operator tried to locate actual witnesses who had picked up a girl who disappeared but he was not successful. Over a period of several months Tom Harber received nearly a hundred calls about local hitch-hiker ghosts but not one personal experience of the phenomenon. However, Harber did personally interview a dozen people who claimed to have encountered a hitch-hiker ghost on Blue Bell Hill and after careful questioning and cross-examination, he was satisfied that the testimonies he had heard were all solid and dependable. It might be thought that one or two or three could be dismissed but twelve similar stories from twelve different people on twelve different occasions, interviewed separately, must surely be seriously considered.

Those who look for some sort of link with actual happenings point to a car crash in 1965 or thereabouts resulting in the deaths of three young women.

Bath, Somerset

This magnificent city with its Roman ruins, Regency architecture and timeless air, has more than its fair share of ghosts. Local ghost expert Margaret Royal once told me that she had collected reports of every type of ghost under the sun in Bath. Not a few of them haunt the highways and byways of this gateway to Somerset, forever breathing the glamour of Beau Nash and his world of fashion. Bath vies with Farnham and York for the title of Britain's most haunted town. And two of its most famous ghosts haunt the city's highways.

During one visit to Bath, when I addressed the Royal Photographic Society on the subject of the Photography of Ghosts, I found evidence for the phantom 'man in a black hat' just about everywhere I went. This elegant-looking ghost must date from the early 1770s, the time of the construction of the magnificent Assembly Rooms, and it is

thereabouts in the quiet streets that this well-documented ghost is most often to be seen. He has never been identified. Margaret Royal collected evidence of this ghost that extended over several centuries.

The wealth of evidence includes the detailed testimony of Mrs Cynthia Montefiore who was walking from Portland Place to George Street when she became aware of a man approaching her, towards the end of Saville Row. The first thing she noticed about him was that he wore a large black hat, somewhat resembling the old-fashioned Quaker head-gear. She watched as he crossed the road and came abreast of her as she reached the end of Saville Row. There was no one else in sight at the time and suddenly something told her the figure was not human; for one thing she noticed it made no sound, no footsteps, no sound of the movement of clothing; nothing. Suddenly the figure was upon her, passing close but showing no sign of seeing her and still she heard no sound of any kind. As soon as they passed she turned to have another look at him and found he had completely disappeared! There was certainly no time for him to have entered any doorway or to have disappeared from view in any normal way.

The number of witnesses for a similar figure in the neighbourhood of Saville Row, Bennett Street and Russell Street is considerable. I talked with Mrs Harrison who saw the figure early one evening. She too remarked on the black hat; he also wore a black cloak and what looked like gaiters. She thought the man she saw looked ill. A local chiropodist saw the man in the black hat also early one evening. She described the figure as small in stature, wearing a black hat and gaiters and looking unwell. A Mrs Gittings gave a similar description but also noticed the man's pale blue eyes. She saw him at very close quarters as he passed her and she also remarked on his small stature and the fact that he clearly looked ill. A young employee of a local firm described the figure he saw as holding his head on one side; a small man wearing a black hat and cloak and looking sickly and distinctly ill and also there was something 'sinister' about him. As soon as the figure passed he swung round but there was no sign of him. He was very shaken by the experience which took place about five o'clock in the evening. A lady doctor living in Saville Row noticed the figure as she came out of her house late one afternoon; he was standing in the street and something about him looked strange. He was a smallish man and wore a black hat and cloak. A tourist supplied information to Margaret Royal concerning a man she had seen who vanished; she had seen him in Saville Row, a small man in a black hat and overcoat. She said he was clearly there but when she looked again, he was not there. A retired sergeant-major saw a man answering the same description and he was interested because the man seemed to be watching him; at first he was standing in the doorway of a house but, as he watched, the figure seemed to melt and then there was no one there.

All the witnesses describe the figure as wearing a noticeable black hat. Subsequent enquiries suggested the hat had a wide brim. The overall impression was of a dark figure, for everyone said the man wore a dark cloak or overcoat.

Another local witness saw the same figure from her window; he was striding along the street and then suddenly he was no longer there. She had not heard anything about a ghost and was very puzzled until she was told about the man in the black hat. She agreed that the figure she saw was wearing a black hat but she could not say anything more about his appearance. She was quite unnerved by the experience and now found herself often glancing into the street but she only saw the figure that once.

Margaret Royal showed me four sketches made independently by four different eye-witnesses who were complete strangers to each other. All the sketches showed a prominent black, wide-brimmed hat, and a long and dark coat or cloak. Two of the sketches show the face of the figure, looking sad and unwell.

Finally Mrs Eileen Parrish from Gloucester wrote in to say she had seen the 'man in the black hat'. She said she was in Bath and trying to park her car when she saw the man coming down Saville Row. He stepped into the road, hesitated, turned back and began to walk towards the front of the Assembly Rooms. Mrs Parrish says she took her eyes off the figure for a moment, attending to parking the car, and when she looked again the figure had completely vanished, although he could not possibly have got to the end of the road and out of sight in the moment she had looked away. She described the figure as dressed much like we see depictions of Guy Fawkes and, as he turned, his black cloak swirled out around him. He seemed to be wearing black breeches and gaiters. She never for a moment thought she was seeing a ghost; the figure seemed completely normal although somewhat oddly dressed.

Other street hauntings in Bath include a headless man in Perrymead, just off Prior Park Road; he has been seen in daylight and at dusk. One witness set out to follow him but after a moment found he was following nothing – the man he had seen had vanished. A figure, resembling a nun, has been seen walking on the busy A4 late at night. One lorry driver saw her at 2.30 one morning.

Another road-haunting ghost at Bath is known as 'Sally' and this ghost is another phantom blamed for accidents that have occurred at the particular bend in the road where the ghost has repeatedly been reported. She is said to be 'Old Sally', a gipsy woman who lived nearby for many years and was fond of walking in the road causing travellers to stop; whereupon she would ask them for alms. A television engineer told me he was driving through Bath with his girlfriend when suddenly she warned him there was a woman in the road ahead. He saw nothing and when he stopped the woman or whatever it was had vanished.

It is not difficult to find people who have had a ghostly experience at Bath and I am quite happy to label it one of Britain's most haunted towns.

Beaminster, Dorset

A phantom coach has long been said to haunt the road through this delightful little town of Elizabethan houses, forever associated with Thomas Hardy's *Tess of the D'Urbervilles*. The phantom coach is a stalwart component of ghostly tales world wide: the coach is often pulled by headless horses and driven by headless coachmen. In short, it's the stuff of dreams and imagination but the fact remains that phantom coaches abound and form part of many traditional and well-authenticated ghost stories, such as the famous Borley Rectory case. In his survey of *Supernatural England* (1977) Eric Maple, a pioneer collector of folklore and ghostlore cites more than a dozen phantom coaches while the Reader's Digest 2009 volume devoted to *The Most Amazing Haunted and Mysterious Places in Britain* lists twice as many. Interesting, since such supernormal spectacles would involve the seemingly miraculous manifestation of dead people, dead animals and non-existent physical objects.

Often there are plausible stories associated with such appearances and the one at Beaminster is no exception.

Sandford Orcas, Dorset. A photograph, taken on the lawn, looking towards the gate where a farmer hanged himself. The figure in a white smock, standing in front of the gateway and behind the dog in the centre of the picture, is thought to be the ghost.
(Photo: Peter Underwood Collection)

The winding road through the haunted Pass of Glenshee, Scotland.
(Photo: Peter Underwood Collection)

Battle Abbey, East Sussex, as it was in 1905. (Photo: Peter Underwood Collection)

Slaybrook Hall, Saltwood, Kent has a haunted garden, part of it was
once a battlefield and a haunted bridge. (Photo: J. A. Mackenzie)

Some of the mysterious carvings inside Royston Cave, Hertfordshire, looking north.
(Photo: Peter Underwood Collection)

A grave, possibly that of King Arthur himself, just upstream from Slaughter Bridge, the scene of his last battle. (Photo: Michael Williams)

The haunted garden at Sandford Orcas, near Sherborne, Dorset. (Photo: Peter Underwood)

The graveyard at Rye, East Sussex, haunted by the ghost of a man wrongly executed for murder. (Photo: Peter Underwood)

The author at Tintern Abbey where ghost monks still walk. (Photo: Peter Underwood)

The author amid the haunted ruins of Margam Abbey in West Wales.
(Photo: Peter Underwood)

The crumbling and haunted ruins of Odiam Castle, Hampshire. (Photo: Peter Underwood)

The graveyard and Bronte Parsonage, Haworth, West Yorkshire where ghosts of the Bronte sisters walk. (Photo: Marie Campbell)

Historic and haunted Hever Castle in Kent. (Photo: Peter Underwood Collection)

Hartley Mauditt in Hampshire where the silent pool is skirted from time to time by a phantom coach-and-four and where the little church has echoed with ghostly music. (Photo: Peter Underwood Collection)

The haunted sands of Lulworth Cove, Dorset, where the ghost of Napoleon has been reported. (Photo: Peter Underwood)

A simulated ghost at haunted Berry Pomeroy, Devon. A postcard that used to be sold at the castle. (Photo: Cox: Peter Underwood Collection)

The haunted pool of vanished Old Bayhall Manor, Pembury, Kent. (Photo: Peter Underwood)

The haunted ruins of Conwy Castle, North Wales. (Photo: Peter Underwood)

The haunted garden at Brede Place near Rye in East Sussex where several ghosts walk.
(Photo: Peter Underwood Collection)

Carew Castle, Wales, repeatedly haunted by a ghost known only as the White Lady.
(Photo: Peter Underwood)

The author dwarfed by some of the ruins at haunted Berry Pomeroy Castle in Devon. (Photo: Peter Underwood)

The Cloisters, part of the haunted gardens at Beaulieu in Hampshire. (Photo: Lord Montagu of Beaulieu)

Scotney Old Castle and the haunted moat. (Photo: Peter Underwood)

Montrose Airfield, Scotland, where Sir Peter Masefield saw an accident re-enacted fifty years after the day it happened. (Photo: Van Werninck: Peter Underwood Collection)

The strange and beautiful waterfall at haunted St Nectan's Glen, Cornwall.
(Photo: Michael Williams)

The Italian ship 'Silvia Onorato' meets its end on the treacherous and haunted Goodwin Sands, off Kent.
(Photo: Peter Underwood Collection)

The story goes that in 1790 one Ann Symes, a twenty-year-old girl, eloped to Gretna Green with her sweetheart, Samuel Cox, from the local manor house. Rodney Legg informed me that the garden door through which they escaped is still extant and proudly pointed out; it is known as the Wedding Gate.

The couple were duly wed at Gretna Green and later, when opposition was futile, in Beaminster at the parish church with its fine Tudor tower and subsequently they produced a large family. One of their great-great-great-grandchildren, Peter Cox, showed me the gate and told me the story when he owned and occupied Farrs. For many years another descendant lived at Beaminster Manor House.

Apparently, the families of the affianced had conflicting political views, one side supporting the Whigs, the other the Tories, and this may well have been the cause of the original opposition to the union. At all events the couple succeeded in escaping, although the noise of the coach and horses at dead of night awakened most of the neighbourhood, yet there was no chase. Over the years, on still nights, the resounding clip-clop of horses' hooves and the noise of the coach has repeatedly been reported and more rarely, but still not infrequently, a fleeting glimpse has been caught of an old-fashioned coach and horses racing at full speed through Beaminster.

Camborne, Cornwall

While walking her dog along a country road not far from Camborne, Mrs M. A. King had a curious experience, and she was kind enough to write to me and tell me about it. She

was on a continuation of Tehidy Road, which runs
alongside the Red River and joins the main road somewhere
close to Tehidy Hospital.

It was a fine Easter Monday and Mrs King thought she
would take the dog along the quiet byway in that
delightful countryside not far from her home. On this
occasion, as she and the dog were climbing a long and
steep hill, she noticed a woman quite near, facing her, on
the little road, walking beside her bicycle, about to
remount it. As she and Mrs King were both on the same
side of the road, it was obvious that they would be passing
quite close so Mrs King looked down and put her dog on
its lead; when she stood up again the woman had
completely vanished, as had her bicycle.

The road was especially steep at this spot but wide and if
the cyclist had changed her mind about the direction she
was going to take, and had gone back the way she had
come, she would have had to cross the road, turn the bicycle
around and begin pushing it up the hill when she could not
have avoided being seen. The only alternative would have
been for her to cross the wide grass verge and go into the
adjoining field, although there was no gate at that side of the
field and the hedges were high. In either case Mrs King
could hardly have failed to see her.

Trying to recall the appearance of the mystery woman
Mrs King found rather difficult. She had appeared to be
about thirty-five years old, slightly built with a sallow com-
plexion, rather poorly dressed in a grey cardigan and she
thought, but could not be certain, wearing a hat.

Both Mrs King and I made a number of enquiries pertaining to the possibility that someone, a cyclist perhaps,
answering the description of the woman seen, had been
killed on the road or had suffered a sudden attack of some
kind and had died there but neither of us was able to find out

anything that could possibly be related to the figure Mrs King saw. She has traversed the same route many times since that Easter Monday – as she had done many times earlier – but there was never a reappearance of the woman with her bicycle.

Camborne is known as a once notorious place for wife-selling; for popular songs of considerable antiquity, such as 'Camborne Hill'; and for a curate Parson Richards, who was frequently prevailed upon to lay ghosts by thrashing them with a whip, as he did on one occasion in the porch of the church; and for the roasting of live toads to break 'ill-wishing'. On ancient Carn Brea hill there is a ruined and haunted chapel and there can be found the Giant's Coffin, the Giant's Heart, the Giant's Hand, the Giant's Wheel and the Giant's Cradle: all said to have been the property of a giant who was one of the last of his race and whose beacon and bonfire were lit since time immemorial and sometimes young couples would leap through the flames to bring themselves good luck.

Although the Camborne area is full of legends and magic and maybe ghosts too, in fact, Carn Brea was an Iron Age hill fort, capped by a medieval castle and excavations have indicated a wall of Neolithic origin and, within, irregular huts which are probably the oldest in Britain, having been carbon-dated to between 3109 and 2887 B.C. All this is especially interesting in view of the reputed mysterious happenings there that include muttering sounds and the occasional sight of a human or sub-human form passing swiftly amid the ancient relics.

Flint, Clwyd, North Wales

There is still a dip in the A548 coastal road between Flint and Connah's Quay. Once it really was a dip that used to be known as Edmund's Hollow. This road with its spectacular views that overlook the mouth of the River Dee; a romantic castle; and a distant view of Liverpool Bay, is a favourite one for tourists who may not know that it is a haunted road with a history of tragedy.

When I was in Wales on one occasion I made a point of loitering there and was fortunate enough to meet a couple out walking who were on a visit from Cornwall. We talked of this and that and then the subject of ghosts and paranormal activity came up and the couple looked at each other and said they were sure the spot where we were at that moment was haunted. Twice, they said, they had seen a 'sort of misty figure' in the dip and they had had to brake sharply to avoid a collision. Yet when they stopped they was nobody there, either time. And once, while walking, they had seen a girl coming towards them dressed in very old-fashioned clothes. She seemed to be about to approach and say something to them, but then, suddenly, she vanished. Both of them saw her and both felt she was just about to address them when she abruptly disappeared.

I told them one of the stories associated with that very spot. A beautiful young dairymaid was herding her cattle at this place, many years ago, when a freak wave took her off her feet and she drowned. Outside a cottage where Charles Kingsley used to stay the body was washed ashore. The often irascible Kingsley was touched and wrote in her memory the immortal line, 'Mary, call the cattle home across the sands of Dee'. Where the body was found

became known as Edmund's Hollow, possibly after a pre-
siding officer for the district, or maybe it was the body of
someone who was found there; it had to be called
something because of the many accidents and curious happenings reported from that spot.

The stories of strange and unsettling occurrences taking
place at Edmund's Hollow are legion and many Welsh
people avoid the place if they can. Some say a weird force
operates there. Jane Pugh, in her *Welsh Ghostly Encounters*
(1990) recounts the experience of a friend of hers, an experienced driver, who was on the road one fine and sunny
afternoon, going towards Flint when suddenly a thick mist
engulfed her. It may not have been unusual for mist to lay in
the hollow that marred the road before it was more or less
levelled out but a bad mist is not common these days.

Jane Pugh's friend felt the steering wheel wrenched from
her control and she was forced towards the wrong side of
the road. As she emerged from the mist she found she was
on the right-hand side of the road and a car was coming
straight towards her. Somehow they missed each other and
all was well but, without acting promptly, things might have
been different. She added, as she described the incident;
'The place must be haunted.'

Jane Pugh also collected another story at the same place.
A Deeside businesswoman told her her father was involved
in an odd incident at Edmund's Hollow. He was cycling
from Flint to Connah's Quay one bright and sunny day
when he suddenly found himself in the middle of a thick
mist which hid everything but just before the mist
descended he had noticed a strangely tall and somehow
threatening figure on foot crossing the road just ahead of
him. In the sudden mist he realized he must be very near the
figure and he swerved to avoid it as best he could and he felt
the figure pass close behind him – and at the same time he

heard the sound of low and horrible laughter. Then, as he reached the end of the Hollow, thinking he was through the thick mist and would be out in the sunshine again in a moment, he saw the strange figure again, this time it passed close in front of him – and again he heard the deep laugh. Unable to control his bicycle he found himself catapulted over the handlebars and into a hawthorn bush at the side of the road. Of the mysterious tall figure there was no sign but, more than a little shaken by the experience, he tried to avoid the place after that and always said he felt there must be some supernatural force at work there.

Many people feel the same and cyclists, motorists and motorcyclists have all reported the feeling of losing control of their machines while pedestrians have felt the urge to walk along the dangerous edge of the road, and it is most often at a time when a thick mist has descended in Edmund's Hollow.

Honiton, Devon

Marlpits Hill near the church of St Michael at Honiton, once famous for its lace-making industry introduced to the town by the Flemish in the reign of Elizabeth I, has a phantom soldier who has long haunted the road. Exhausted and stumbling along the dusty road in a ragged brown coat of ancient design, he is thought to be one of Monmouth's men who fled after fighting at Sedgemoor.

When two schoolmistresses with a party of schoolchildren encountered the figure, the children bunched together, frightened at the sight. They all said the man looked totally exhausted, hardly able to put one foot in front of the other, wandering from one side of the road to the other and gazing dejectedly at the road beneath his feet. He took no notice of the schoolchildren or their teachers as he passed slowly by and then abruptly disappeared. A moment later a car appeared and sped along the path the soldier had just traversed. It almost seemed as though the approaching modern vehicle had destroyed the environment necessary for the appearance of the long-dead soldier

The teachers were so interested that they carried out some research and one of the first things they discovered was that some years earlier a local man had reported a similar apparition. He described the figure in almost exactly the same way as did the teachers and the school children. The teachers also established that the man's sighting had been at exactly the same place and at the same time of day.

Further research revealed details of a sad episode in the Monmouth rebellion. One of Monmouth's men who had fought at Sedgemoor was a native of Honiton and lived in a cottage on Marlpits Hill. He was one of the very few able to escape the scene of battle and, by moving only by night and living off what he found on his way, he eventually managed to find his way back to Honiton. His wife saw him coming and she and their three children ran to welcome him but, as luck would have it, a party of troopers rode up at the same time and seeing the 'deserter' they attacked him and slashed him to pieces with their swords. His distraught wife and children saw the whole sorrowful episode.

The moments before the unfortunate man's end seem to have become imprinted on the atmosphere and return occasionally when conditions are favourable. One researcher has suggested that, in some way we do not yet understand, the victim's distress as he stumbled on may have communicated itself to that spot on the road where his ghost appears.

As this account was being prepared I received a communication from a friend in Dorset who said he had been talking to a Honiton couple who had just witnessed the appearance of the ghost of an exhausted man in ragged clothes. Was there anything in my records of a similar nature?

Moffram, Cheshire

The road running between Hyde and Glossop is a haunted one. Some years ago a spate of sixteen unexplained accidents in three years led to repeated stories of a phantom lorry on the road. A bus driver was riding pillion passenger with his cousin one clear December morning when a crash, which no one saw, took his life and fractured the skull of the driver.

The driver said at the inquest on his cousin that he was driving normally with a clear view when he saw a heavy motor vehicle suddenly backing out onto the road on his left-hand side. There was nothing he could do and the accident occurred. Both he and his cousin were knocked unconscious.

The coroner was able to say that enquiries and investigations revealed there was no opening for any vehicle to have used at the place of the accident. Policemen and local members of the jury who knew the place agreed and no evidence could be found to support the view that a lorry or heavy vehicle was responsible for or even involved in the accident.

The driver insisted he had seen a lorry just before the accident and the remains of his motorcycle did not prove or disprove that it had collided with a lorry. Returning a verdict of Accidental Death the coroner referred to the 'phantom lorry'. And the driver insisted, 'Something happened. I don't know what.'

It was later established that there had been no fewer than sixteen accidents at the same place within three years, accidents involving motorcars, lorries, motorcycles and pedestrians, without any satisfactory explanation being given for any of them. Everyone agreed that mysterious accidents had happened on a perfectly straight road, with a good surface, in good weather conditions.

One local man told of hearing footsteps outside his house on many occasions at night, for which he could find no explanation. On one occasion he had sent his dog out, a dog that would normally tackle anything, but the dog turned tail and howled, terrified. And the footsteps continued.

When the inquest and its story of a possible phantom lorry was published other witnesses came forward. The driver of a heavy lorry going to Derbyshire said he was travelling normally along the road when he found himself unable to control the vehicle and it suddenly swerved to the left and described a complete circle.

A car travelling in the opposite direction late one night was apparently on a clear road when suddenly he found himself in collision with a lorry which seemed to disappear. After the collision the car driver found himself alone on the road and when he asked a passing pedestrian what had happened to the lorry he had hit, the pedestrian said, 'What lorry? There was no lorry.'

A motorcyclist, travelling on a clear road at a reasonable speed, suddenly found his machine unaccountably out of control and swerving to the left and the rider was pitched over the top of his machine which careered ahead for some yards.

Witnesses of a phantom lorry in the area surface from

time to time and unexplained road accidents occur with alarming regularity thereabouts; sometimes the two coincide.

Upminster, Greater London

In 1977 Richard Sage was driving with three friends along St Mary's Lane between Upminster and Cranham when they all saw the figure of a monk appear out of nowhere and cross the road a little way ahead of the car. He then disappeared.

They all agreed the figure wore a hood or cowl and seemed to drift rather than walk across the road. None of them saw the figure before it appeared on the road ahead of them and they all saw it safely reach the other side of the road.

Dee Goss, sitting beside the driver, said it looked like a monk who was lost or disoriented and although she saw the figure quite distinctly while it was on the roadway ahead, the odd thing was she saw no legs and it did seem to glide or float just above the surface of the road.

A couple of years later, at approximately the same place, Richard saw the figure again, behaving just as it had on the previous occasion and this time he reported the matter to the police who came up with the suggestion that it might be a tramp.

This was totally rejected by Richard who said the figure he saw was almost certainly a monk – just possibly a nun, but he thought it was a monk; that had been his first impression and he had not changed it.

During the course of enquiries in the area I discovered

that a mysterious monk-like figure had been repeatedly seen crossing the road at this place, or thereabouts, on a number of occasions over the years. Certainly in 1976 and 1978 and probably in 1998 and in 2010. One witness said the figure carried a folder or large pamphlet or book under one arm and all the witnesses agreed that the phantom monk appeared unaccountably in the middle of the road, crossed the road without touching the road surface, and then vanished when he reached the other side of the road.

There appear to be no record of any road death in the immediate area and this might be one of those apparitions that is a form of psychic impression on the atmosphere, an echo of a past happening, that returns when the climatic and other conditions are exactly right.

Whitechapel, London

This area of London is forever associated with the unsolved murders attributed to Jack the Ripper and the sites of some of these atrocious murders are haunted, as is the Whitechapel Road where several ghostly figures have been reported.

At the time of the Ripper murders, the autumn of 1888, the figure of a man was seen in the Whitechapel Road, standing on a street corner and another shadowy figure was often glimpsed in a doorway close by. Neither was ever identified or traced and there have been many reports of shadowy forms, both male and female, being seen for a moment and then inexplicably disappearing but whether they are figments of the imagination, phantoms from the past or merely individuals who for their own reasons keep to the shadows in this sordid and mean thoroughfare, is a matter for speculation. They are mentioned several times in police reports and court hearings.

What is more interesting perhaps is the evidence of more substantial reports in recent years. These include the couple who emerged from Whitechapel Underground station and saw ahead of them on the Whitechapel Road a couple dressed in Victorian clothes. They appeared to be in animated conversation with each other and the witnesses thought there must be a fancy dress party somewhere.

They were going the same way so they followed only a short distance behind the oddly attired pair. As they walked the husband remarked that the couple in front of them must be talking very quietly for no sound reached them and then they realized that they could not hear any sound of footsteps although their own were loud and clear. Then, as they watched the couple step through the numerous little puddles on the path, both noticed that the puddles in the paths of the couple ahead of them remained undisturbed as the pair, still seemingly immersed in conversation, continued on their way.

How could this be? They hurried forward and had almost reached the two people in Victorian dress when suddenly and totally inexplicably, they completely disappeared! They told me it was the most mysterious thing they had ever experienced. Apparently real and solid people – although completely silent – had been in front of them for several minutes and appeared to be completely normal, then abruptly and without any possible explanation, they had disappeared from the face of the earth. I saw these witnesses a couple of years after they had first told me about the event and I asked them how they thought about the matter later. They told me it had changed their lives. They had always been practical and down-to-earth individuals who never accepted anything in the realm of the paranormal. Now they were not so sure and they listened to other people's strange experiences with a new perception and understanding.

A few years ago I talked with a police officer who told me he had seen figures he could not explain in the Whitechapel Road; figures there one minute and gone the next. Had it not happened to him, he would not have believed it possible; and he never experienced anything of the kind anywhere else.

Elliott O'Donnell once told me he visited the Whitechapel area in 1895 and he was told that some of the streets where the Ripper murders had been committed were haunted by 'appalling screams and groans' and by unexplained and silent figures of men and women. Incidentally, O'Donnell was convinced that the Ripper murders were not the work of one man. 'Had they been, somebody would have given him away,' he said. So perhaps the streets of Whitechapel are haunted not only by the Ripper – or Rippers – but also by the ghosts of the Ripper victims. One way or another, violent death does seem to leave its mark.

A member of The Society for Psychical Research, Susan Allen of Bristol, reported to the Society a strange experience she had on the Whitechapel Road in 1973. At the time she was training to be a nurse at the London Hospital in the Whitechapel Road and one Sunday evening she noticed a woman walking towards her, a woman who wore a 'crinoline dress, very full and elaborate like her hairstyle, with its ringlets and curls dressed high on her head'.

Thinking the woman must be on her way to a fancy dress party, although it was a little strange that she appeared to be on her own, Susan Allen noticed, as the woman came close to her and then they passed, that no one else in the street took any notice of the figure who really stood out in that area. She also noticed the serious, almost deadpan, expression on the face of the woman who made no eye contact as she passed but just seemed to look straight ahead. Also and this she thought really odd, close up she appeared to be a greyish colour all over. Sodium lighting can affect colours but the appearance of the figure who had just passed her was quite different from anyone else nearby, her colour being altogether paler and her hair, skin and clothing all the same dull grey colour. And then the witness became aware of the strangest thing of all about the figure: she made no movement as she walked, no movement of her body at all; it was almost as though she were on roller skates and she glided past, noiselessly.

Once the woman had passed, all the little things that were odd about her tumbled through Susan Allen's mind and she wanted to look round immediately but thought it would seem rude and instead she strode on her way. A moment later she did turn round but could see no trace of the individual and unusual figure she had just seen. Other normal-looking pedestrians abounded but of the Victorian lady there was no trace whatsoever. Susan Allen had never experienced anything like it before nor has she since. She has always regretted that she did not have the presence of mind to reach out and touch the figure as it passed; that would have solved once and for all whether the Victorian lady was or was not a ghost – as must seem likely. One of many ghosts in Whitechapel, one of the oldest parts of London.

Winterbourne Abbas, Dorset

The old part of the present A35 road between Winterbourne Abbas and Dorchester has long been haunted. There is a report from over 350 years ago that first tells us of a phantom army here.

Most of this part of the Dorset downs has been unchanged for millennia. More than 2,000 years ago the Celts sought to cultivate the area which is rich in remains of prehistoric settlements. Then in 43 AD the Romans came and their methods of road building created long stretches of good road replacing the ancient trackways and such a one is the present A35.

Spectral armies in full battle array have always been reported hereabouts and the first recorded account, according to published information, is 29th June 1662. On that day two clergymen, travelling to Dorchester from Winterbourne Abbas saw, on a hill adjacent to the road they were on, what appeared to be a magnificent troop of mounted horsemen. The two men came to a halt at the arresting sight and then set off to get ahead of the procession and announce the arrival of the impressive army.

At Dorchester the excited pair loudly proclaimed the imminent arrival of the majestic troop of soldiers and while the town people quickly spread the news and collected to welcome the marching men, nothing happened. Everyone waited and waited, all in vain. On subsequently making enquiries of the authorities they learned that no such horsemen were in Dorset that day.

Did the two religious gentlemen catch a glimpse of the past? They may well have done so for where they saw the troop was one of the places where Roman legions once walked and where there have been many reports of super-normal appearances and phenomena. There have even been instances of nearby towns being alerted; the sight of the mounted troops suggesting an invasion or attack.

Such phantom armies have been seen time and time again down the years. There was one sighting in 1968 when Lady

Jane Culliford related how she experienced the phenomenon, noting the appearance of a great number of men on foot and on horseback, that turned out to be apparitions. And in 1970 an elderly local woman reported seeing a Roman legion in all its glory.

Other roads in the area, similarly haunted, include the Old Priest's Track at Swanage; the A252 at Abbotsbury Hill; the unused stretch of old Roman road at Ridgeway Hill between Dorchester and Weymouth and the roads near the ancient hill fort near Wimborne Minster.

Other Haunted Highways and Byways

The old military road running past Gairnshiel Lodge near Ballater, Scotland (itself haunted by the ghost of a former owner) has long been haunted by the sound of marching men, horses' hooves and the creaking of laden carts. The road was built during the Jacobite Risings and, although reports of these ghostly noises continue intermittently, no visual sights accompany the sounds.

A phantom coach is reputed to appear, usually around midnight, on the pre-bypass part of the A35 near Charmouth, Dorset (the scene of Charles II's attempt to escape to France in 1651), always going up the hill at Newlands and round the dangerous corner at Whitchurch Canonicorum where it has often been blamed for road accidents but the uneven surface of the road is a more likely cause. Although the local council do work on the road and erect warning signs, the 'unexplained' accidents continue and at one time an exorcism was carried out, with limited success.

The old road between Colchester and the Suffolk border, not far from Manningtree, at the head of the Stour valley, runs past a haunted crossroads. Women motorists in particular have complained about a phantom presence and there have been reports of a terrifying apparition haunting the area; a human-shaped form that seems to be covered from head to foot in matted hair. The hirsute horror stands at the crossroads and frightens all who see it.

A ghostly 'woman in white' haunts the A38 south-west of Bristol near the reservoir at Barrow Gurney. Many and varied are the witnesses who report seeing the sudden appearance of a woman in white on the road in front of them, causing them to brake violently and then the woman disappears. Many skid marks show where other drivers have also stopped suddenly.

A brightly dressed ghost haunts the road between Nunnery and Critchill near Frome in Somerset. Motorists have reported seeing a young man wearing a bright sports jacket who looks quickly both left and right time after time and then suddenly he vanishes.

The road below Dunvegan on the Isle of Skye is haunted by the ghost of a young hiker wearing full Highland attire, seen most often on moonlit stormy nights and disappearing almost as soon as he is seen. An American correspondent from Arizona saw him, tall, with a rugged face and sandy hair and wearing the kilt of the MacDonalds. Something she and her husband will never forget.

A thoroughfare at Leigh-on-Sea in Essex is named after a ghost. Crying Boy Lane is named after a little boy who was killed there and whose ghost is still heard crying in the lane.

Part 8

HAUNTED OPEN SPACES

It is interesting to realize that we may encounter a ghost or phantom or supernatural being or spirit or whatever you may call it, almost anywhere and at any time, especially, it would seem, in open spaces.

Here, where we might think we are safe from such manifestations and abnormalities, in fact, evidence suggests there are ghostly happenings of every kind out there in the open spaces all around us.

Bossiney Mound, Cornwall

Cornwall is a land of beauty and mystery where, around almost every corner, there are puzzling enigmas and unanswered questions. Where today only this mound stands there was once a castle and an important one whose architect was Robert, Earl of Mortoun, a half-brother of William the Conqueror; but then the bigger Tintagel Castle was built nearby.

A typical example of the strange happenings reported here was that experienced by Michael Williams, a Cornishman then running, with his wife Sonia, the Bossiney House Hotel. Later he ran the publishing firm of Bossiney Books and today he is the leading light and president of the organization Paranormal Investigation, specializing in West Country cases of psychic activity.

On Midsummer Eve 1965 Michael decided to take his dog for a walk, starting at nearby Bossiney Mound, just off the road that connects Tintagel and Boscastle. As Michael has said in some of his publications, the Mound is neither particularly photogenic nor today a landmark likely to attract the average tourist or sightseer. Gorse, ash bushes, brambles, hemlock, crowfoot and bracken are just a few of the ingredients which clothe the hump.

Yet legend and historical research suggests that King Arthur's Round Table lies buried beneath this mound and that it comes to the surface, a shimmering silver spectacle, just once a year at midnight on Midsummer Eve. Living nearby at the time Michael, ever the investigative and open-minded researcher, resolved to visit the Mound and test the theory.

In his magnificent volume on the Arthurian legend, Paul Broadhurst reminds us that at Bossiney Haven, with its beach and towering cliffs, there are remains of a medieval village and a petrifying well, where the mineral-rich waters can 'fossilize' a piece of cloth and that Bossiney was once a place of great importance. Its two members of Parliament would be inaugurated on the summit of the ancient earthwork now known as Bossiney Mound, now on private property and planted with trees and flowers. There is a very old well here, known as Jill's Pool that still produces a trick-ling stream and a stone bowl adorns the garden, 'looking for all the world like a giant grail'. Some of the Mound was removed many years ago but the Normans (probably the local Bottreaux family) treasured the place and it became the symbolic power centre of the whole wide area with the meadow in front serving as the village green where slaves and just about everything else could be bought or sold.

So important was the place in the thirteenth century that Richard, Earl of Cornwall, granted it rights and privileges equal to places far larger. Old maps show the Mound as a place of antiquity and Sir Francis Drake was once a member of Parliament for Bossiney and he built Borough House opposite which was later owned by J. B. Priestley who was fascinated by the concept of time.

The old legend attached to Bossiney Mound is detailed by Sabine Baring-Gould, that indefatigable collector of folklore and legend and he says: 'According to Cornish tra-dition, King Arthur's Round Table lies deep in the earth buried under this circular earthen mound; only on Midsummer's night does it rise, and then the flash of light from it for a moment illumines the sky, after which the golden table sinks again. At the end of the world it will come to the surface again and be carried to heaven, and the saints will sit and eat at it and Christ will serve them.' Arthur, of course, was reputedly born at Tintagel.

'Bossiney Mound is a place of strange atmosphere,' says Paul Broadhurst and I, for one, can verify that. On the occasions that I have been privileged to visit there is in the air a feeling of quiet energy, an energetic influence that perhaps contributes to the psychic happenings reported here.

As Michael Williams approached the small chapel built into the side of the Mound on one occasion when he was accompanied by three friends, he and those with him all saw glowing lights shining eerily through the windows of the quiet, deserted, empty and locked chapel. That something very mysterious happened on that occasion Michael has no doubt; indeed the experience had a profound effect on him and thereafter he never laughed about the supernatural. Furthermore, the strange light was seen by other people present – from different vantage points. And there was no natural explanation. Reflection, passing cars, moonlight, all were considered and rejected.

When Michael took his faithful dog Tex to Bossiney Mound that Midsummer Eve in 1965, he too showed signs of being aware of the strange atmosphere and environment of the place. They saw no Round Table rising from the Mound but they and I do not doubt that on occasions strange things have happened here and that reports that have occurred with some regularity concerning inexplicable sounds and sights here have authenticity; there have been many reports over the years of unexplained and fleeting shapes and forms seen around the ancient and historic Bossiney Mound.

Brooklands, Surrey

The concrete track at Brooklands, near Weybridge, on which the great amateur racing drivers used to roar round and round, in flimsy cars, from before the First World War until 1940, has all but disappeared. I remember being taken to races there as a boy, by an uncle keen on racing of any kind, and the spectacle of people like Bira, the Siamese prince, Kaye Don, Henry Seagrave and John Cobb, has never left me and nor have the memories of the cars themselves: the big Vauxhalls, the Napiers and Napier-Railton Specials, the Maseratis, the Leyland-Thomas, the Higham Special, the Lancias, the Indianapolis Duesenberta (driven by Whitney Straight), the fast front-drive Derby-Miller (driven by Gwenda Stewart) and the Barnato-Hassan Specials and the Talbots. My uncle told me he had once seen a driver flung high into the air as his car shot off the top of the banking. All heady stuff for a boy of nine or ten but probably frowned upon these days.

Today, a slice of the old banking can still be glimpsed from the railway if you look out of the window at the right moment, but otherwise the famous track has almost vanished. The row of pits where we would anxiously watch the drivers overlooking their urgent repairs became a row of odd-job machine shops although an advertising sign for BP-Ethyl petrol remained oddly fresh for years. It was the aeroplane and the aircraft works used to house it that really killed Brooklands with its famous pear-shaped track known as the Outer Circuit (there was also the less exciting Mountain Circuit). The track was less than three miles around and perhaps a hundred feet wide.

The tightest of the two great banked corners was thirty feet high with a gradient of 45 degrees at the top. Even when the track was opened, gleaming white, just a hundred years ago and through its heyday in the 1930s, it was no place for the faint-hearted, competitor or spectator.

Of course there were fatalities and the first occurred within three months of the track opening when a driver trying to overtake on a banking overturned his car and was trapped; the car incidentally belonged to the man who would become Lord Brabazon. Another early victim was a figure quickly popular at Brooklands, Percy Lambert, who had a tyre burst during a record attempt in October 1913. He died of a fractured skull and it may well be his ghost that has been frequently seen here. In those days the drivers wore only a cap and goggles so a crash helmet might have saved him.

The ghost of Percy Lambert has reportedly been seen at Brooklands on many occasions, often by night-shift workers, in the vicinity of the vast assembly shed that used to be called The Vatican, a part of the track at the end of the famous Railway Straight. This is where Lambert's accident took place.

Lambert was the first person to cover one hundred miles in an hour and among other psychic disturbances the roar of a racing car engine and the squeal of tyres have been heard. On more than one occasion the overalled, capped figure has been challenged and even followed and be seen to disappear into a wall. Perhaps Percy Lambert who lived for Brooklands and died there cannot leave his beloved racetrack.

Canvey Island, Essex

An island in the Thames estuary with an area of seven square miles, it was reclaimed from the sea in the seventeenth century. It now has a large population and is heavily built-up.

For many years there have been reports of the ghostly figure of a man, whom many witnesses describe as a Dutchman. The general attire of the figure suggest to many observers that he is an inhabitant of Holland but there seems little concrete knowledge or even legend to account for such a figure. Apparently he wears buckled shoes, full knee breeches with rosettes at the sides and is usually seen walking in a north-west direction from the Benfleet area up Church Parade and on to Oysterfleet. He passes through the garden of a house where the occupant has reported seeing the figure which she describes as a tall man wearing a pointed hat.

The point is 'the Dutchman' has been reported in various parts of the island and invariably, it seems, the mysterious figure carries a large bundle on one shoulder.

People whose forebears lived on the island seem to have been aware of stories of the appearance of the strange figure for scores of years. Sometimes the sound of running footsteps has been heard along the old track by the sea-wall from Wintergarden to Waterside Farm, especially around dusk.

Among the witnesses for the unidentified male figure are the occupants of a bungalow; some children playing in a garden and an aide-de-camp who thereafter refused to have tea in the garden during the summertime

Other hauntings on Canvey Island include a house where

an occupant appeared to his friend after death and where inexplicable footsteps were reportedly heard and a strange coldness pervaded one part of the house. When the oldest part of the property was eventually demolished a secret chamber was discovered containing unexplained articles including some ancient pistols. No disturbances were reported thereafter.

At Knightswish Farm, according to Jessie Payne, one occupant, hearing a strange noise, opened the door and saw a nun walking in the garden. She shut the door and then opened it again and was in time to see the 'nun' apparently disappear into the ground!

On Canvey there are many stories of a chapel or religious building of some kind at Knightswish that might account for a nun being in the vicinity. There are also lots of legends of secret tunnels, one running between Knightswish Farm and Hadleigh Castle, but this would involve the difficulty of passing under Benfleet Creek; although it has been suggested that the nun disappeared where once there had been an entrance to the tunnel.

The old Lobster Smack Inn has a ghost story of a kind. Years ago a girl named Lucy worked at the inn and she was to marry a sailor but before the ceremony could take place he perished at sea. Lucy pined away and died and was buried in the village churchyard in the wedding dress she had so looked forward to wearing in life. For years her ghost was said to walk along the path to the church, a path that became known as 'The Bride's Walk', accompanied by the strong smell of violets. This former rough track is now Hole Haven Road and the smell of violets has long vanished from the busy roadway, as has the ghostly form of Lucy who died from a broken heart.

Cwmdonkin Park, Wales

Much frequented by the sometimes brilliant poet and spinner of words, Dylan Thomas (1914–53) during his troubled life, this popular location in Swansea now seems to be haunted by his ghost.

Once when I was there I met a couple who, when I mentioned Dylan Thomas – but not his ghost – suddenly out of the blue told me they had both seen his ghost, in this very park. When I expressed a mild interest they informed me that one sunny morning they were taking their usual walk and anticipating a rest in the sun on their favourite seat when, approaching from the back of the seat, they saw it was occupied by a squat and chunky man who seemed to be talking to himself.

They decided to sit a while anyway and when they turned to do so, facing the figure, they both immediately recognized the unmistakable, almost doltish, curly-haired Welsh poet, and when he spoke, still to himself and completely oblivious of the couple now seated beside him, there was no mistaking the measured and musical voice. They looked at each other and then back to the seemingly solid and natural figure seated close beside them – and he was no longer there! He had completely vanished.

I talked with the couple for a few more moments and there seemed no reason to doubt that they had indeed encountered or rather seen the Welsh genius in one of the places he loved and often visited in his youth.

Dylan Thomas was a member of my London club and on one occasion when I was in Wales and at Swansea I took myself to Cwmdonkin Park, that favourite spot of his and where he played when he was a boy and where he wrote several of his early poems, including one about a hunchback who ate sardine sandwiches every day with his newspaper and was pelted with stones by children. Constantine Fitzgibbon, no stranger to ghosts himself, told me he was there when a carved stone monument was unveiled in memory of Dylan Thomas in 1963 and a dozen or more boys stopped and watched – and Constantine said he felt sure one of them disappeared, and he thought it could well have been Dylan as a child, watching. In later years, Dylan looked back on his innocent childhood with longing and delight. Cwmdonkin Park was for him a kind of Eden.

In 1980 a correspondent from the area, Margaret Hopkins, was kind enough to relate her experience in Cwmdonkin Park. Margaret met Dylan Thomas once and briefly but she never forgot the magic of his presence. As a young girl she and two friends were talking together at the entrance to Singleton Park when Dylan Thomas happened to chance by. One of her friends, rather older than Margaret, used to live near the Thomas family and knew him in his early days. By the time Margaret met him he was married and living at Laugharne and he was visiting his parents and some of his old haunts in Swansea. He was at a loose end and always enjoyed the company of girls. They all drifted off to the older girl's bed-sit where they spent a couple of hours drinking coffee and talking, with Dylan (who seemed to be somewhat inebriated) doing most of the talking.

After many years living away from Swansea Margaret had decided to visit her home town again and she spent a couple of weeks there during the summer of 1973. Most days she would spend an hour or two in Cwmdonkin Park before returning to her temporary accommodation and one day in the late afternoon she was in the park reading the local paper on a seat overlooking a stream and thinking it was nearly tea-time. The place was completely deserted at the time apart from a gardener working some distance away.

Suddenly a shower of small stones, clods of earth and twigs and pieces of small branches came hurtling down the slope and she immediately thought 'boys' and, a little annoyed at being disturbed, she turned to explore the slope behind her. The whole expanse was completely deserted. All was very quiet and there was not a soul in sight, except for the gardener, still busy tidying up. She shouted towards him, 'Did you see that?' but apparently he could not hear her and she realized that anyway from his position he would not have been able to see any boys who might be involved.

Margaret resumed her seat and suddenly had the distinct impression that perhaps the mischievous Dylan Thomas was up to his tricks! She mused on the thought and then recalled that early poem about the hunchback in the park who had been pelted with stones and rubbish. Had he sat on that very seat? she wondered. A curious incident and certainly reminiscent of the diminutive Welsh poet.

Dartmoor, Devon

There is nowhere quite like Dartmoor. With its craggy out-crops and rough moorland, treacherous bogs, purple peaks and high skies, this great lonely wilderness is peopled by ghosts almost everywhere you look. It is a landscape that has inspired great minds, attracted eccentrics and given inspiration to countless thousands. It is a place of mystery and, therefore, of ghosts.

I once spent a night, from choice, in a car with my wife

and our dog not far from Dartmoor Prison. It is a night I am unlikely to forget. We, that is my wife and I, saw nothing but we were conscious of invisible beings all around us and our dog, a lovely, quiet Springer Spaniel, hardly slept a wink, continually prowling round and round the car, obviously aware of something invisible, unseen, unwelcome and probably not of this world.

The prison, a remote and desolate place with a forbidding and macabre atmosphere, has been called the 'cesspool of humanity' and 'the abode of lost and forgotten men' and something of the hopelessness that pervades Dartmoor has transferred itself to the most forbidding building in Princetown – and many other places.

Of the many haunted spots on Dartmoor, Cranmere Pool takes some beating. Notorious for its evil essence and phantom forms such as Bengie Geare, a former mayor of Okehampton who returns here as a phantom black pony, the Pool, now drained, was once a bog where evil spirits from far and wide were consigned for ever.

Fox Tor contains Childe's Tomb a spot where a Saxon noble died after being lost in a blizzard on Dartmoor. So cold was he that he cut open his dead horse and crawled inside; and just before he died he scribbled his will in the horse's blood on a nearby rock. No wonder his shivering ghost has been reported here on cold winter nights; sometimes seen and sometimes heard crying for help through chattering teeth.

Among the host of haunted places on Dartmoor we will look in detail at just one, Fogging Quarry, close to North Hessary, not far from Princetown.

It is a place of shadows and solemnity although a veneer of pleasantness and charm sometimes seduces passersby. One such was a girl called Becky and she visited the area during the course of a school walking excursion. She immediately fell in love with the place, telling all and sundry that she would return and one day she would be married there!

A couple of years later, while on a short hiking holiday to Dartmoor with her boyfriend Stuart, she insisted on taking him to her adored and idolized Fogging Quarry, after spending a night at the Plume and Feathers in Princetown.

Stuart had not previously visited the place but had heard all about it from Becky. Almost weary of hearing its alluring qualities and pleasing environment he readily agreed to a visit although the weather was inclement and very different from Becky's first trip. In fact it had snowed during the night and snow and sleet showers continued throughout the day but, having made their decision, they set off, in a mist that lasted for much of the day. But they were determined to enjoy themselves, looking forward to the sights they hoped to see.

Stuart tells me he recalls the two of them walking along singing and joking together as they reached the disused quarry and walking through it, happy to be together and to have found this place they had talked about so often.

Certainly they had no thoughts of depression or unease but suddenly, as if they had walked through a curtain into a field or aura of a totally different kind, they both began to feel unhappy, uncomfortable, ill at ease and somewhat apprehensive. 'These feelings came from nowhere,' Stuart said. 'And they grew stronger and stronger as we neared the bottom of the quarry.' Upon reaching the bottom they found it to be largely covered by water – and even the still pools of water seemed oppressive to the solitary pair and although they were convinced they were alone they both became more and more uneasy and noticed a growing feeling that they were being watched by 'something'. Stuart says he uses the word 'something' because there were no people visible and due to the fact that they had walked around the highest point of the quarry walls, where the moor was visible for miles, they were confident that there were no human beings anywhere in the vicinity.

After a few moments, perhaps five at the most, Becky said she wanted to go, immediately. Stuart knew she was not the type of person to be easily unnerved and feeling much the same himself, he agreed straight away and they began to prepare to leave at once.

As they were making their way out of the quarry, around the pools of water to the opposite side, the feeling of insecurity they had both been experiencing, increased almost alarmingly and they found themselves running to get out. Indeed, such was the unease felt by Becky that she was unhappy about even waiting for Stuart while he took a couple of photographs.

Looking back Stuart realized that during the entire time they had been inside the quarry when he had repeatedly remarked on his feelings and impressions of the place Becky had made no comment – apart from saying at the last moment that she wanted to leave. However, once clear of the quarry and its haunting air, once they had left the whole vicinity, she hurriedly explained in a distraught and almost unrecognizable voice, that she had never, ever, felt so terribly unhappy and aware of some invisible, evil something, or ever been so glad to leave a place in her whole life.

Stuart told me, in relating the story of that unforgettable visit, that Becky refuses ever to return to Fogging Quarry and years later she still disliked talking about the place, becoming agitated and worried all over again when questioned as to her feelings.

The mention of water and its surrounding atmospheric conditions on occasions is interesting as there have been many supporters of the suggestion by G. W. Lambert, an SPR President and Tom Lethbridge and others that water can act as a kind of magnetic field with hidden power, a geophysical theory that could explain some paranormal activity. Stuart was aware of this theory of a magnetic field affected by water and perhaps playing back images and feelings and he told me he felt he knew exactly what such impressions, sensations and feelings were as the experience of Becky and himself were literally as though they had walked into and out of these irrational feelings, 'almost as if they were not our own'. Such have been the experiences of some visitors to Fogging Quarry on haunted Dartmoor.

Gibbet Hill, Hindhead, Surrey

Here for years criminals were hanged on a gibbet and their tarred bodies left to swing in clanking irons until they rotted. A remnant of the actual gibbet that once stood here is preserved in Haslemere Museum. Not surprisingly perhaps the area has long had the reputation of being haunted. Indeed so widespread was the reputation that the ghosts of executed criminals walked here that in 1851 Sir William Eric of Bramshott Grange arranged for an impressive granite Celtic cross to be erected near the site to try to dispel the ghosts and ghostly happenings hereabouts. Today the Celtic cross is a reminder of a once – and perhaps still – haunted spot. Even the official local guide mentions the hauntings.

Nearby on Hindhead Common, now belonging to the National Trust, there are reminders of the events of 24th September 1786 when an unnamed sailor was murdered.

It transpired that the sailor was walking along the turnpike road from Guildford to Portsmouth that Sunday afternoon when he decided to rest awhile at Mousehill near Milford where he encountered three other sailors, one of whom he thought he recognized as a former shipmate. As it turned out all three, Michael Casey, James Marshall and Edward Lonegan, were all short of money but our sailor, glad of some company after a long walk alone, suggested they continue to Portsmouth together and he said he would pay for refreshment on the way.

So it was agreed and before long, at the Red Lion, Thursley, they obtained sustenance before they all set off past the wooden belfried church where all too soon our friendly and unsuspecting sailor would be buried and where there is a sad epitaph on an elaborate tombstone (paid for by public subscription) to this unknown sailor.

At the top of the steep hill, whilst getting his breath back and perhaps admiring the wild landscape falling away into the Devil's Punch Bowl, the generous sailor must have turned his back on his companions for he was suddenly struck a hefty blow to the back of his head and he fell to the ground. All three assailants then drew knives and, obviously working to a previously agreed plan, each made two deep cuts on the unfortunate man's throat. One, determined to make sure their betrayed companion was really dead, made another vicious cut which nearly severed the head from the body.

Swiftly emptying every pocket, they stripped the corpse and dragged it a few hundred yards into the steep Devil's Punch Bowl. Satisfied with their evil work, they climbed back out of the Punch Bowl, made their way towards the old Portsmouth Road and quickly continued on their way.

Unbeknown to them, however they had not been unobserved. Two workmen from Thursley saw them drag and dump something into the Devil's Punch Bowl and they were horrified when they found the body of the sailor. Feeling unable to pursue the three thugs on their own, they hurried back to Thursley and, having gathered eight or nine men to help them, they all set off in pursuit of the murderers.

The guilty three were found and arrested at a public house in Rake, near Petersfield, where they were trying to sell the murdered sailor's clothes. Taken back to the scene of the crime each man in turn was required to touch the dead body of their victim in accordance with the prevailing superstition that the corpse of a murdered person would bleed when touched by its murderers. Although the result of this 'touching the dead' is not recorded, it is said that one of the men broke down and wept; the others showed no remorse. All three were taken before a Justice of the Peace in Haslemere and committed to Guildford Gaol. Tried for murder at Kingston Assizes, they confessed their guilt and were condemned to death. On 17th April 1787 they were taken back to the scene of the murder and there suffered for their crime by hanging. Afterwards the bodies were soaked in tar and riveted into iron frames and hung from the gibbet where they swung, the grinding of the iron frames creating an eerie sound when the wind blew; all creating a vivid warning to everyone passing thereabouts. As someone once put it: 'Hanging there both night and day, till piece by piece they dropped away.'

There have been a number of reported instances when the awful tragedy is re-enacted here ...

I gratefully acknowledge assistance with information for this entry from Matthew Alexander, Curator of Guildford Museum, who talked to me about the Hindhead murder at a meeting of the old Ghost Club, of which I was then President.

Glenshee, Perthshire, Scotland

In Gaelic, Glenshee is Gleann Shith – the Glen of the Fairies and few who know the place would deny its magic, its almost impossible beauty, its folklore, its history and its ghosts. This wild, romantic Highland glen is, in every sense of the word, haunted and haunting.

The winding road through the mountains is desolate and wild but unbelievably memorable and impressive. Many long years ago when I found myself at Glenshee, I knew the folklore and the legends, the stories associated with the stone circles there: some supposing they were places of execution or sacrifice. I also knew the stories of ghosts and haunting that abound there. I saw the nearby Serpent's Stone with its story of witchcraft; and I met more than one canny Scot who regaled me with personal accounts of odd happenings concerning ghosts and the supernatural in this unique and fascinating place. Its lasting allure, attraction and the mystery I found there has never left me and for many years now my house has been named Glenshee.

The present kirk at the head of Glenshee has a story that matches the magic of the place. This delightful little chapel was completed in 1822 to replace the primitive Chapel of Ease that once stood there. There were plans to build the new church at Runavey, more central to the Glen, they said; an ideal place the appropriate committee decided and work commenced. However, the fairies – never far from their very own Glen I was told – did not approve of the new site and each day the builders found the work they had done the day before, undone. This continued day after day, night after night, until the body concerned decided it was useless to oppose the wishes of the Little People and the new church was built on the site of the old one. Within living memory in this haunted place ministers would pray for protection from 'witches and warlocks and things that go bump in the night'.

During her early days visiting her 'dear, dear Highlands' Queen Victoria would journey through Glenshee on her way to and from Balmoral and on one occasion, at the foot of Glenshee, the horses drawing the Royal carriage took fright and careered down the hill until William Shaw spurred his horse to a gallop, overtook the leader, seized the bridle and brought the carriage to a halt. Ever after William Shaw used to declare with pride that he had once saved the Queen's life and he could well have been right.

But it is not this or other incidents involving the 'old Queen' that have left an indelible mark here but rather a somewhat mysterious death a century earlier

In 1749 Sergeant Arthur Davies was in charge of a patrol of men sent twice-weekly from Aberdeen to meet another patrol at Glenshee. Memories of the '45 were still vivid and among the duties of the patrol they were required to ensure that none of the local people carried arms.

Sergeant Davies was a keen sportsman and it was not unknown for him to wander away from his men in pursuit of game, although he had been warned that to do so could be dangerous for an Englishman. On this occasion when the patrol reached Glenshee Davies himself was missing and he was never seen again.

His wife, then staying near Braemar, stated that he had on his person at the time some fifteen golden guineas in addition to some silver, a valuable watch and two gold rings and this information gave rise to suspicions that Davies had been murdered. But where was the body? And was there any connection between the missing English soldier and the ghostly naked man now seen occasionally in this wild and lonely glen? A ghost that vanished from sight, it seemed, when it was approached.

Nine months after the disappearance of Sergeant Davies, a responsible local man who had known Davies, by the name of Donald Ferquharson, received a visit from someone named Alexander MacPherson who revealed that he was 'much troubled' by the ghost of the missing Sergeant Davies. He said that one night the figure of a man dressed in a blue coat suddenly appeared at his bedside and declared he was the ghost of Sergeant Davies and then promptly disappeared. Later the ghost returned, this time naked, requesting his bones be decently buried; telling MacPherson to visit Ferquharson and they would be shown where the bones lay. The two men were led to a local spot known as the Hill of Christie where, sure enough, they found the half-hidden and half-decayed remains of a man wearing a blue coat and other clothes. They buried the remains on the spot. They found no valuables.

Soon suspicion fell on a man of dubious character named Duncan Terig who, although previously penniless, in recent months had had money to spend. Furthermore he had recently married and Ferquharson testified that one of the gold rings worn by Mrs Terig was very similar to one worn by Sergeant Davies.

Five years after the disappearance of Davies the authorities who had been busy investigating every aspect of the disappearance, arrested Terig together with a man named Alexander MacDonald. Both appeared at the Tolbooth in Edinburgh charged with murder. Things looked black for the two men. Accounts of their movements at the time Davis had disappeared did not tally and was at variance with other evidence. Terig was then shown to have attempted to silence one potential witness and counsels for both men came to believe their clients were guilty.

When the matter of the ghost was discussed however, the trial took a totally different and unexpected course. Isobel

MacHardie, a former employee of Alexander MacPherson, testified that she too had seen the ghost, exactly as MacPherson described. When she asked him about the phantom form, he had told her not to worry for it would not trouble them any more. The jury, without exception, found the two men 'Not Guilty'.

The only fly in the ointment is that the ghost of the murdered English soldier is still seen from time to time in the vicinity of the Hill of Christie; some echo on the atmosphere perhaps of past events. And the Glen of the Fairies is as beautiful as ever.

Greenwich Park, Greater London

Situated on the south bank of the Thames Greenwich has several well-authenticated hauntings including the Queen's House where a remarkable and never explained photograph of a ghost, or ghosts, was obtained by the Revd R. W. Hardy and his wife, on holiday from Canada, who were not at all interested in the paranormal. It appears to depict a draped figure, or possibly two figures, climbing the Tulip Staircase which is not open to the public. My *Haunted London* (1973 and 2010) contains a reproduction of the photograph and the full story.

Also in Greenwich is the haunted and historic Royal Naval College built on the site of the old royal palace where Henry VIII was born and where Elizabeth I spent much of her time and where she still walks; as does the unfortunate Admiral Byng and an unidentified shrouded figure.

Charlton House has the ghost of seventeenth-century Sir William Langhorne. The Ship Tavern (once the scene of the 'examination' of witches) has long been said to be haunted but details are sketchy. The approach to the Blackwell Tunnel on the Greenwich side is haunted by a ghost motorcyclist; Trafalgar Road has a phantom coach and horse. But at present we are interested in Haunted Open Spaces so let us look at Greenwich Park.

I have heard from Eric Maple and others that Greenwich Park is supposed to be haunted by 'a monster, part human and part animal' that walks sideways like a crab but it is a story I would have completely ignored had it not been told to me by a respected member of The Folklore Society, The Society for Psychical Research and The Ghost Club – but I have yet to see this 'monster' or anything to suggest its presence.

A less alarming haunting or ghostly encounter, if that is what is was, has been sent to me by Mr R. Scott of Nottingham, who enclosed with his letter a sketch map showing the precise location and route of the figures he saw. I cannot do better than quote parts of his letter verbatim: 'The encounter occurred at the top of Observation Hill in Greenwich Park. At that time, during the Blitz, the gates to the park were open permanently to allow access for emergency vehicles The time was 18.30 in the evening of 31st December 1941. I had been working late until 18.00 on that occasion due to urgent war-work and was cycling home from Deptford to Charlton via the Greenwich Park roads, hurrying to attend a New Years Eve dance; "ghosts" were far from my mind at the time. I had just reached the summit of the climb to Observatory Hill and was taking a breather on the grass triangle there which occurs at the fork in the roads, when from the mists appeared what I assumed to be a courting couple (there being an Anti-Aircraft Battery on Blackheath). As the couple approached I suddenly realized that there was no sound; although they were traversing an area of loose gravel thrown up by the traffic cornering at the junction; I waited for them to get closer, as another couple were following about ten yards behind the first couple. There was still no sound and as the first couple passed between me and a park-bench I was surprised to find that I could see the bench through the figures! I watched and waited whilst the second couple passed the bench with the same effect – they too were transparent! As they proceeded about ten yards and turned to the left, I picked up my cycle bodily, turned it round and pointing directed at them I switched on the light and found the figures had disappeared. The public lamps had been switched off, essential during the black-out. Nothing further happened so I continued my journey home without further incident. I should point out that although it was frosty with a slight ground mist, there was a good moon and visibility was about two hundred yards. I noticed no colour but the clothing, although indistinct appeared to be medieval or Victorian, certainly not 1940s fashions. The fact that I describe them as courting couples is because they appeared to be arm in arm or arms round waists, as they casually strolled across the road and along the path past the park-benches towards Flamsteed House where they disappeared.'

The sketch map that Mr Scott provided showed that the sighting of the couples began, as far as I can make out, on the track by the side of the present cafe, crossed an area of loose gravel, turned towards the Royal Observatory, then turned left down a pathway to a path from the North Park Gates where the figures disappeared. Oddly enough in the summer of 2011 I received word of an almost identical manifestation by a correspondent from Blackheath.

Mr John Williams tells me that he was in Greenwich Park one bright afternoon in July 2011 where he and his wife had just enjoyed an ice cream and they set off for the Royal Observatory. They had with them their little grand-daughter aged four and a half and they thought they would take a photograph of her straddling the time-line. As they walked towards the General Wolfe statue they noticed a young couple walking slowly ahead of them. They took their time, hoping the couple would not linger near the Observatory and make the planned photography difficult. They were about twenty yards behind the couple and had almost reached the Observatory when suddenly the couple ahead of them were no longer there. Mr and Mrs Williams looked at each other. How could that be? They were there one moment and had completely vanished the next. Looking back they realized that they had not heard any sound from the couple, either talk or footsteps or anything. They asked their little grand-daughter whether she had seen the two people in front of them a moment before and she said, 'No, there was nobody in front of us . . .'

Other Haunted Open Spaces

Wotton, just east of Dorking in Surrey is where Mr and Mrs Barton walked into the mystery of their lives when, after visiting the church of St John the Evangelist at Wotton they turned right at the church gates and, reaching a seat, thought they would sit for a while. They suddenly felt icy cold and saw three men standing near some trees dressed in strange out-of-date clothes. One of them looked like a clergyman. They continued their walk, down a hill, over a weed-covered old railway line and eventually found their way back to Dorking and home. A short while later they decided to repeat the walk but found everything changed and nothing was as they had seen it a week or so before. Do we have here a haunted open space that completely changes? The very odd experience was looked into by experts from the SPR and other investigators but no satisfactory explanation was ever found.

A stretch of the North Downs Way near Bishopsbourne is haunted by an Irish wolfhound. The animal was lost on the downs early in the twentieth century and is often seen sadly making its way along the North Downs walk. Dorothea de Culwin, a longtime member of the Ghost Club, saw it three times. Each time it looked up at her with sad eyes before disappearing. Once she almost touched it but when she put her hand to it there was nothing there. Her aunt was walking with her three children once and they all saw it; after looking at them in a forlorn and sad way it turned and then suddenly disappeared.

A ghost monk in a brown habit has been seen on many occasions over many years in Denbigh Road, Haslemere, Surrey, on an old pathway from Steadlands towards Chiddingfold.

The village of Chewton near Bristol in Somerset has a group of ghost motorcyclists! In 1994 a correspondent informed me that just beyond Chewton village a road leads to Queen-Charlton. On the left-hand side a gateway opens onto a cart track and eventually to some old concrete works. This area is haunted by a group of motorcyclists dressed in Army outfits and riding Royal Enfield or Norton single-cylinder motorcycles who appear without warning and as suddenly disappear. During the Second World War there were two Army camps within a mile or so of this area.

Part 9

HAUNTED RAILWAYS

To anyone who has seen on stage or screen the entertaining and outstanding and enduring play, *The Ghost Train*, the idea that there are such things can be fanciful or intriguing, depending on your point of view. The strange reality is that there is in fact an astonishing amount of good evidence for ghost trains and haunted railways.

The idea that some essential part of ourselves may continue after death would seem to me just about possible but that inanimate objects can survive their passing from this realm seems quite incredible unless we consider some such idea as automatic atmospheric photography; some event preserved on the atmosphere that can reappear on occasions. That, to me, is plausible.

Brighton, West Sussex

Moulsecoomb Railway Station now occupies buildings that house the University of Brighton and the station is for the most part unmanned by human beings but perhaps inhabited by ghosts, according to the files of the Sussex Paranormal Investigation Society that are dated 1986.

Two young women had enjoyed an evening in Brighton and although it was late, about two o'clock in the morning in fact, they were reluctant to end the evening and they wandered into the station waiting room for a rest and a chat as they had walked the couple of miles or so from the town centre.

After a few moments they noticed an elderly man on the platform opposite. He was approaching the footbridge over the rail track and as they idly watched he began to climb the steps of the footbridge which would bring him to their side of the track.

Although they had felt quite comfortable in the subdued light of the station, the two girls now began to feel apprehensive for the station platform had deep shadows and they realized that they were alone on the station late at night.

Their apprehension increased when they failed to see the man emerge on their side of the footbridge and there was no sign of him coming down the steps; they were puzzled as to where he could have gone.

When quite a few moments had passed and there was still

no sign of the man, they thought perhaps they should see whether he had fallen or anything, so putting their feelings of unease on one side they moved out of the waiting room, walked along the platform and began to mount the deserted footbridge steps. There was still no sign of him. They reached the top of the steps and were then surprised to find the footbridge over the railway appeared to be deserted. Puzzled and beginning feel more and more apprehensive, they returned to the waiting room.

They had no sooner seated themselves and begun to chat when they heard a noise. They looked at each other. At first the sounds suggested youngsters larking about on the platform opposite but then the sounds came nearer and they changed. Now the noise sounded like an animal, a pig perhaps, squealing loudly. It was a frightening sound and the young women were petrified and they huddled together as the sounds came nearer and increased in volume.

The weird and extraordinarily intensive noise came ever closer until they seemed to be almost upon them and the girls felt very frightened, paralysed in fact, terrified to move. One of them had removed her shoes for comfort and she now sought to put them back on. Whilst she was doing so her friend began to move towards the door of the waiting room, unsure whether to face whatever was out there or to secure the door as best she could against anything getting in. Having decided to open the door, she did so and was in the act of turning to reassure her friend that all was well when she felt something screech past her head. Fear lending wings to her flight she tore out of the waiting room, along the station platform and towards the steps leading down to Lewes Road.

Her friend, now having got her shoes back on, ran and joined her but at the top of the steps so great was the terror – at what they did not know – that they felt they simply could not go down the dark stairs. At that moment they felt a 'presence' close beside them. They saw nothing but 'something' seemed to be so close that it was breathing on their faces. And then they heard the grunting noises again. Fortunately this proved to be the end of their frightening episode on Moulsecoomb Station. The breathing ceased; the grunting ceased and the feeling of 'something malevolent' close beside them vanished. Within seconds the oppressive and alarming atmosphere disappeared and they knew the 'dreadful creature' or whatever it was had gone. In tears and still quaking with fear of what might have been, they made their way to their respective homes having endured a night they will never forget.

Oddly enough just a few weeks after I heard about this curious, almost surreal experience, I received a letter from a student at Brighton University, who told me his mother and father spent an odd hour or so on the same platform. They had arrived early for an appointment with their son and the father being something of a railway buff, wanted to have a look at Moulsecoomb Station.

There the couple had a look round and took a couple of photographs, walked over the footbridge and back again and were about to leave the station when they both heard the distinct sound of a steam train approaching. They looked at each other, each thinking the other had heard nothing, but they had both heard the unmistakable sounds and an invisible train seemed to be approaching!

As they stood on the platform, outside the waiting room, they noticed an elderly gentleman on the platform opposite across the rails. They had not seen him previously and sought to catch his eye and wave a greeting and see what he made of the sound of an approaching train that they could still hear, but he seemed to be completely absorbed in himself and stood looking up the trackway from where the invisible train was apparently approaching. They saw nothing but what they both heard was the sound of a steam train pulling into the station. A moment later the loud sounds they had heard so clearly ceased. There was not a sound to be heard, indeed the whole place seemed silent in an almost unearthly and unnatural way. As they prepared to leave the station and meet their son, they remembered the old man they had seen on the opposite platform, apparently waiting for a train. The platform opposite was now completely deserted and of the man they had seen, a man who appeared to be completely normal in every way except that they could not attract his attention, had completely disappeared.

The train buff took the trouble to go over the footbridge and onto the other platform, returning to say there was no sign of anyone else on the station at all. Had the elderly passenger at last caught the train he had been waiting for?

Bury, Lancashire

The main line between Stubbins Junction and Helmshore north of Bury is a haunted line. Bruce Barrymore Halpenny told me at a meeting of the old Ghost Club about the cabin on the line that became known as The Murder Cabin.

The story dates from the end of 1959 when Bill Whitehead joined the railway construction team and was allocated to work at Helmshore. Soon the work gang moved down the line and Whitehead had his first view of the cabin where he was to experience a firsthand encounter with a ghost.

It started out as a fine and bright morning and Bill Whitehead walked along the line checking it thoroughly.

Everything seemed fine and correct and he began his return journey, but then it started to rain and soon worsened in intensity so that when the cabin came in sight, Bill decided to shelter for a while.

He said afterwards that he had been inside the cabin perhaps ten minutes, it could not have been longer and it was probably less, when suddenly 'this apparition appeared!' Bill, a practical manual worker, who had never thought much about ghosts, was faced with something the likes of which he had never seen before. 'It was shaped like a person,' he said. 'It was white in colour, such colour as there was because I could see clean through it. It was really weird. Then it moved and passed me and I felt an icy draught ...'

A moment later Bill Whitehead looked outside and was relieved to see the rain had almost stopped. He hurriedly left the cabin and continued on his way along the line and eventually rejoined the rest of the workmen. He was full of his strange experience but decided not to say anything about it, in case they thought he was mad.

Halpenny assured me that Bill Whitehead was a very sane and sensible, sober, solid and shrewd man with his feet firmly on the ground and that November morning ghosts were far from his mind; he was more concerned with making a good impression on his first day and, later, with keeping dry. He had not been told the cabin was haunted or anything about it so it was not a case of already half-expecting something unusual to happen. But haunted the cabin was although Bill knew nothing about the stories relating to it until after his experience.

About ten years earlier, in 1950, two platelayers, working with a gang on repairs and maintenance on that part of the line, between Stubbings Junction and Helmshore, had fallen out, had an argument that had escalated into serious disagreement and discord with harsh words being said on both sides. Within a short time the two men hated the sight of each other.

Although things were so difficult between them the two men continued to work together in the same gang.

One morning the two former friends found themselves alone while the rest of the gang went on ahead. As they passed a workmen's cabin one of the couple took himself off and, entering the cabin, found himself an axe and then hid behind the door, standing on one of the seats to remain out of sight.

His companion, walking past, noticed the cabin door partly open and knowing it should be shut if not locked, he thought he ought to look inside in case vandals had been there and caused some damage. He carefully pushed the door fully open and seeing nothing wrong he ventured inside. As he passed through the open door the axe wielded by his 'enemy' came down on his head, killing him instantly and without a sound he crumpled to the floor, blood spilling everywhere.

A week or so after Bill Whitehead had seen the ghost he was back in the haunted cabin but this time with the rest of the gang. They had just settled down for a cup of tea when suddenly the apparition appeared. The ghost made its way to a corner of the cabin. The whole gang saw it but showed no surprise or agitation 'That's Charlie,' one of them said. 'He often comes in for a warm in the winter; we've all seen him before. He won't do you any harm.' And a moment later Charlie disappeared.

Halpenny told me the line where the murder hut stood has now been closed completely. Bill Whitehead and the rest of his working mates moved elsewhere and the haunted hut was demolished. Bill told Halpenny he was very scared the first time he saw the apparition but afterwards he was not unduly afraid for he came to believe that Charlie was the ghost of the murdered man (or possibly the murderer!) but in any case he didn't feel the spectre meant any harm to the living but was merely revisiting the scene of the violent tragedy.

Some months later Halpenny told me he had heard that the haunted line had been re-opened and he wondered whether the ghost would return to the line if not to the hut.

Darlington, Durham and Teeside

In the latter part of the nineteenth century at Darlington North Road Station something paranormal seems to have occurred. This was before the North Road bridge was built and the old Stockton and Darlington Railway crossed the Great North Road by means of a level-crossing.

James Durham, an experienced and mature nightwatchman, had a hut near the crossing and he would frequently patrol from the old goods department to the passenger station, taking him near the crossing.

One night, having carried out his first patrol, he went to the porters' room at the station to partake of refreshments. This room had originally been part of the station-master's house and was equipped with a fireplace and with gas. The room also gave access to a coal cellar.

As he walked into the room on this occasion, from the station platform, Durham turned on the gas, sat down and was opening the package containing his meal when he was somewhat startled to see a strange man suddenly emerge from the coal cellar accompanied by a large black dog.

Jumping to his feet, the nightwatchman was about to challenge the intruder when he saw that the man made not the slightest sign of having seen him but simply walked towards the fireplace and then turned with one arm raised, threateningly. The nightwatchman, determined not to be intimidated or assaulted, decided that attack was the best means of defence and he struck a blow straight at the menacing figure with a yardbroom nearby, only to find the broom went through the figure in front of him and struck the fireplace!

The man or ghost, whatever it was, stumbled backwards while the dog reached forward and dug its teeth into Durham's leg. The mysterious figure, regaining its upright position, then grabbed the dog and they both retreated into the coal cellar from whence they had appeared.

James Durham sought to compose himself and, looking first at his leg where he had felt the teeth of the dog, he discovered no sign of any bite, no mark at all, nothing to show he had been attacked and bitten and no marks on his trousers. Thinking about the figure he had seen which he increasingly decided must be a ghost, he realized the man had been smartly dressed in a cut-away and fashionable jacket with buttons that shone, a stand-up collar and a smart cap. As soon as he felt more composed Durham decided he would find where the man and his dog had gone and he proceeded to procure a lantern and make his way into the cellar which he found to be completely deserted and he established that there was no other entrance or exit to the cellar.

Durham's story caused a considerable stir in Darlington at the time, being published and considered and commented upon by all sorts of people. There was no shaking the nightwatchman's story. He had not been drinking, he had never experienced anything of the kind previously and he had always been a trusted and reliable employee. Interest was intensified when it transpired that a railway clerk named Winter, known for always being well turned-out, and who owned a black retriever dog, had gone into the cellar with his dog one night and shot the dog and then himself. This tragedy was not widely known and certainly Durham claimed he had never heard of anyone committing suicide anywhere at the railway station.

Understandably, the nightwatchman, notwithstanding his reliability and responsible record over many years came in for a good deal of questioning by many people, one of whom, Edward Pease by name, went to considerable trouble to get to the bottom of the matter. In the nicest possible way he enquired whether Durham could possibly have been asleep. Was he subject to hallucinations or nightmares? Was there any possibility that he had been drinking, earlier? Durham replied that he was teetotaller, his mind was free of trouble at the time, he had no record of ever having visions, hallucinations or waking dreams, he had never experienced anything of the kind previously and his longtime working with the rail company had always been exemplary.

The Revd Henry Kendel, minister of the Union Street Congregational Church testified to Durham's straightforwardness and said he was a strong and reliable man who could be trusted. On behalf of the SPR, Professor Henry Sidgwick looked into the matter and established that Durham was a regular nightwatchman who slept during the day and was used to being on duty all night; furthermore he had only been in the station-master's room for one minute when the ghost appeared and he had had no time to doze.

The room in question and the cellar were visited and explored by various people including keen-eyed journalists and everyone was satisfied that the affair seemed to be an honest event that was well authenticated and inexplicable.

James Durham died at seventy-five years of age and is buried in a grave in the North Cemetery. One investigator wrote: 'The ghost fighter has now reached the blessed state where the wicked cease from troubling and the weary are at rest.'

Dunphail, Scotland

South of Forres and once a stop on the old Highland Line, Dunphail has long had the reputation of harbouring a ghost train.

In 1921 John McDonald, a much respected local man, claimed to see the phantom train that he had heard about but never believed 'existed'. It was on New Year's Eve and that might suggest the sighting was perhaps marred by spirits of a different kind but the really reliable John was adamant and subsequent accounts and enquiry suggest he may well have been telling the truth.

Certainly he never forgot the experience and said it was a most alarming sight. His unnerved companion was the first to see it and was immediately speechless with apprehension and trepidation, for he knew the last train had long gone; he mutely pointed and John, following the direction he indicated, saw the ghost train coming thundering down the track. Puzzled and not a little bewildered, the two men watched as the train passed, lights on in all the carriages and steam bellowing from the funnel but they saw not a single passenger aboard and further-more they both clearly saw the cab of the engine – and it was empty! No sign of any driver or assistant.

Subsequently there have been infrequent and irregular sightings by other local people who may well know the story of the ghost train but also, more interestingly, by visitors and strangers to the district who have no knowledge of anything of the kind. A family of four saw the phantom train one summer afternoon in 2001 and a visiting American and his wife saw the same apparitional steam train in 2009. The man was something of a train buff and was fascinated to actually see a steam train although he could not understand what was happening when he heard no sound as it thundered past and he watched it as it seemed to disappear while it was still in sight. His enquiries revealed that it could have been no real train he and his wife had seen and, utterly astonished, for neither of them had ever experienced anything of the kind before, he listened wide-eyed and amazed as he heard about the ghost train that sometimes ran where steam trains had run long ago.

Today the site of the haunted rail track can be perilous for walkers and investigators for several people during the last few years have reported that they have suddenly been knocked flat on their faces by some tremendous and invisible force that came out of nowhere as they strolled innocently along the track of the phantom train.

There are theories that, almost like batteries, some hauntings appear to run down over the passage of years, and if there is anything in this idea perhaps the phantom train is no longer seen but its passage is reflected in the power and force it once had.

Glasgow

The Glasgow underground system runs in a circle beneath the city centre and has played host to any number of strange and eerie happenings reported by scores of employees, workers, travellers and officials.

In the old days the only way to get railway carriages to the Govan sheds and workshops was by lifting the carriages bodily off the tracks and up through the pits into the workshop using a heavy crane. One night after the system was all closed down, when it was the practice for empty trains to be stacked end to end on the rails in the tunnels on each side of the sheds with the end doors of each carriage open to permit easy access for cleaners, some workmen encountered more than they had bargained for.

On that occasion, according to Bill Hamilton and Gordon Carsly, a team of five workmen were in the tunnel for working purposes and had just passed through train after train until they reached the last one where they found a colleague talking to a middle-aged man wearing a light-coloured raincoat who had apparently been asleep on the last train when it went out of service at Capland Road station. The stranger, who seemed dazed and confused by what had happened, was led back through the empty carriages to the sheds where he would be able to gain access to the street above.

Leading the way, a workman looked back at regular intervals to make sure the passenger was following and each time he was until they eventually reached the sheds where the workman found the man had vanished. He immediately went back through the trains and still no sign of the man. Enlisting the help of his fellow workmen they searched everywhere but of the stranger they could find not a trace. He had completely disappeared.

Subsequently they found, when they talked about the incident, that the Govan car sheds had long been reputedly haunted by the figure of a man in a light-coloured raincoat. The figure had been seen by cleaners and by workmen in the tunnels between Kelvinbridge and Hillhead stations.

There had also been many reports of the sound of human voices, sometimes singing and of an exceptional coldness just before the figure was seen. He never spoke and disappeared when those who saw him drew too close.

The tunnel near Shields Road station had the reputation of being haunted by a Grey Lady who was thought to be connected with a fatal accident in 1922 when a lady and her little daughter had fallen from a platform into the path of an oncoming train. The little girl was rescued and she recovered but her mother, wearing a grey overcoat, had been killed. The ghost of the Grey Lady was seen with some regularity for several years following the accident and then rarely until a similar accident took place more than fifty years later and thereafter the Grey Lady phantom was again frequently reportedly seen by railway staff, cleaners and by members of the public.

The tunnels for St Enochs and Bridge Street stations are also haunted, primarily by lights for which no explanation has ever been found. A pump engineer was working in the area and was about halfway between the two stations when he saw a flickering light and heard a hammering sound. He went towards the lights and the sounds, wondering what was happening, and he found the light receded as he advanced so that he could not reach it. After he had followed it for about ten minutes, it suddenly disappeared. The hammering noise, on the other hand, remained constant some way ahead of him and he felt he had almost reached the point from which it was originating when it suddenly stopped. He never found any explanation for the light or for the noise but he did discover that other workers on that stretch of line had reported mysterious lights and a hammering sound which they could not explain. One worker, Willie Baxter, ascertained that the area where the hammering noise was heard was near the point where the tunnels passed

under the River Clyde and he wondered whether it was possible that the noise was the propeller of a ship passing
overhead. Later exploration showed this to be unlikely.

Glasgow Central Station is reputed to be haunted by the
ghost of a murdered man. In 1911 twenty-seven-year-old
Joseph Patrick Noon was executed for the murder of a busi-
nessman on the Glasgow to Euston train. Travellers on this
line have reported finding themselves in a compartment
with a well-dressed man carrying a small case who, after a
few moments, vanishes. He is thought to be the victim who
was murdered on the train for the £200 he carried in a small
valise.

Hammersmith, London

There used to be a level crossing on the single railway line
that passed Bedford Park in the 1890s. In 1897 the artist
Camille Pissarro moved into 62 Bath Road, Bedford Park,
with his wife and son Lucien. At that time the house had
open fields on one side and the already infrequently used
railway line on the other with its gated level crossing and a
signal box. Among Pissarro's paintings there is one of a
train puffing towards the crossing; a picture that was
included in the 'Pissarro in London' exhibition at the
National Gallery in 2003.

A Russian anarchist named Stepniak was in the habit of
visiting Pissarro and his family and on one occasion he was
using the Bath Road level crossing at a leisurely pace,
seemingly oblivious to the possibility of the occasional
train. He was unfortunate in that one of the few trains using
the line came steaming up behind him. Too late the driver

saw a man on the crossing, too late he applied the brakes and as the heavy engine attempted to slow down it hit Stepniak with fatal results.

Long after the line was closed and dismantled – today there is no trace of there ever having been a level crossing in Bath Road – psychic traces of the accident still seem to recur, the shrill warning whistle, the screeching of locked brakes and the cries of alarm and an awful thumping noise have all been reported from the immediate vicinity, especially on dark winter nights, the time when Stepniak met his death.

Hayling Island, Hampshire

The former goods yard at the old railway station at what used to be called the Hayling Billy Line has long been regarded as haunted. The ghost is thought to be that of a former railway employee, Henry Wilkins, a signalman who made a mistake and was regarded as responsible for a number of deaths.

The station was converted into a theatre in 1996 and there have been reports of a ghostly figure resembling the dead signalman being seen inside the theatre, suggesting that the surroundings, the settings and the scenes are irrelevant to ghosts and they appear in the atmosphere, as it were, of the place where they lived or worked or died, and subsequent alterations, additions and later buildings occupying the site, have no effect on the appearance of a ghost that once haunted the spot when the surroundings were different. If this is so, and evidence suggests that in some circumstances it is, it makes sense of the reports of ghosts that do not appear to have any association with the existing premises.

At Hayling the ghost of the former signalman was apparently seen and reported locally in 1963 and 1973. In addition I possess statements that refer to sightings in 1975 and 1986 on the old railway premises and in 1999 in the premises of the succeeding theatre.

Isfield, near Uckfield, East Sussex

Isfield Station, on the famous Lavender Line, is reputedly haunted by the ghost of the young bride of an infantry soldier from the First World War.

Stewart Kiernander, a friend of many years standing, had shares in the Lavender Line and he first told me about the haunting of a phantom young lady in white and a phantom train.

The apparition of the young lady dates from the days, during the First World War, when the line was part of the old London, Brighton and South Coast Railway. The story goes that a local girl was newly married to a soldier and the time came when she bade him farewell for the last time on Isfield Station as he departed for France, never to return. When she received the dreaded news she walked to the station and threw herself in front of a train.

For nearly a hundred years there have been reports of a spectral woman in white being seen in the vicinity of the station. In the 1920s there were many reports and later when the line was derelict she was still seen and later still, when the line was acquired by the Lavender Line Preservation Society in 1983, she was still reported from time to time. The wife of one of the directors of the Society was a witness in addition to various members of staff and the public, travellers on the line and others visiting and local people. The form has often been seen to emerge from the station buffet, which used to be the Ladies' Waiting Room, and then walk along Platform One towards the level-crossing gates.

There is also some evidence for another ghost at Isfield Station, that of a man wearing old-fashioned railway uniform. He used to appear in the vicinity of a railway shed that was destroyed in the 1980s but, according to some people, the area where the building stood exudes a forbidding aura.

During the First World War, in the days of the L.B.S.C.R., the line was busy with trains carrying servicemen. It was a time when milk churns came to the station by rail and passersby would be warned at the level crossing by the ringing of a hand-bell from the signal box. On many occasions over the years, passengers, visitors and railway enthusiasts have heard the sound of a hand-bell on Isfield Station when the place is totally deserted.

The station was also used in the First World War by German prisoners of war, brought to the area for forestry work in the neighbourhood and marched back to the station at the end of the day. The sound of marching soldiers has been reported at dusk on many occasions in the vicinity of the station.

By 1939 and the beginning of the Second World War long distance trains had ceased to operate through Isfield; the milk traffic was carried on the roads and the station fell into disuse. It was closed in May 1969 and for a time the station lay derelict, apart from its ghosts, for at this time there were reports, not only of the phantom form of the young bride who killed herself but also of a phantom train that chugged its way through the station, invisible and unseen but heard at times when trains once ran there.

Thought-forms and timeslips may account for the phantoms reliably reported from Isfield Station but what are we to make of reports of a phantom train tearing through the silent station, whistling and with smoke streaming from the tall chimney, a passenger train that has been seen with some regularity, especially late at night in the winter months?

Two witnesses living nearby are adamant that they have seen and heard the ghost train and additional evidence comes from a railway worker who has helped to bring the station back to life and a visitor and her young son. They were staying in the area and the boy was unwell and restive one night when they both heard the sound of an approaching train and when they looked out they saw a passenger train flying through the station. Next day they learned that not only had no train run the previous night but that repair work on the line would have made it impossible for any train to run where they had seen one.

Maldon, Essex

Platform Two at Maldon East station had a ghost for more than fifty years. A striking and unusual station building, its ghost had a long·wait (and a wait stretching far ahead perhaps because the line has long been closed and the track dismantled). The ghost reportedly seen here is the ghost of a lady dressed in white; a passenger waiting for a train that never came.

In 1958 Muriel Andrews, wife of the then station master,

announced publicly that she had seen the figure several times. She saw the form gliding along the path towards the Waiting Room and standing on Platform Two. She also said that both she and her husband accepted the ghost and could always tell when 'she' was about to appear as the atmosphere became icy cold. Sometimes the apparition seemed to be accompanied by a weird groaning sound.

Maldon, one of the oldest recorded towns in Essex, is situated at the head of the Blackwater estuary and was the scene of a battle with the Vikings in the year 991; it has a fifteenth-century Moot Hall and nearby is haunted twelfth-century Beeleigh Abbey which I visited several times when it was owned by Christina Foyle, of bookshop fame, who had personal experience of the ghost there.

After the railway line was closed the station property was converted into a public house called The Great Eastern which, according to reports in 1975, continued to be haunted by the station ghost: the mysterious Lady in White and by other ghostly activity. In later years the property passed into private ownership.

Betty Puttick, who had a lifelong interest in the paranormal, once told me that she had traced more than a dozen people who, independently, had seen the unknown Lady in White at the station, without any knowledge that such a figure had been seen by other people for years. In each case they had only realized there was anything strange about the normal-looking figure when it vanished inexplicably.

Three of my correspondents, all from the Maldon area, inform me that they have either glimpsed the figure themselves or knew someone reliable who had. In every case the figure appeared to be solid and natural, although clothed completely in white, as far as could be seen. It made no sound and glided rather than walked when it was seen to move. There was a distinctly cold feeling in the immediate vicinity of the figure. Always it suddenly and completely disappeared when approached too closely.

The station at Kelvedon, seven miles north of Maldon, with its romantic ruins of seventeenth-century Felix Hall, was another haunted Essex railway station. The Victorian building was haunted for years by disembodied footsteps in the booking hall before it was replaced by a new station. The phantom footsteps there seemed to pass into oblivion with the destruction of the old station.

Rolleston, Nottinghamshire

A railway line, formerly part of the old Midland Railway, still threads its way through rural Nottinghamshire towards Newark and one of the places on this crossing-laden track is Rolleston and it has earned itself the title of Most Haunted Station in Nottinghamshire.

Until 1959 a branch line from Mansfield via Shortwell fed into the main line at Rolleston Junction and, when the branch line closed, the junction was removed in fact but not from the name of the station. It is possible to still find small remnants of the old track bed and branch line, a line that harbours a ghost train.

Mr R. Hoath, one of Rolleston's level crossing keepers related his experience to John Smalley, a railway enthusiast, saying that one warm April night in 1990 as he sat in his quarters he was astonished to hear the sound of a train on the disused branch line and it seemed to be slowing down as it approached the rail junction.

Conversant with trains and the sounds associated with them, he recognized a steam locomotive pulling some heavy goods, probably coupled coal wagons. He clearly heard the buffers clanking as the wagons ran into each other as the train slowed down. Rushing out to see what was going on he was astonished to see nothing whatever that could have accounted for the sounds he had heard! Not only was there no train or anything else within sight but, as he stood looking up the line, he heard the sound of steam hissing as would be expected if a locomotive was drawing near and he felt he could smell the steam and smoke but nothing that could possibly have been responsible was visible. The line was clear. He estimated that the whole episode lasted no longer than a couple of moments altogether. Looking back he tried to find a rational explanation for what he had heard and smelt, but he was totally unsuccessful. In the end he had to admit that a ghost train visited Rolleston Junction that night and he believed he had witnessed a replay of an event that had happened time and again in the past.

John Smalley visited Rolleston on 11th April 1993 when one of Mr Hoath's colleagues related some of his experiences including seeing the phantom form of a man at the crossing. A button on the gatepost is connected to a bell in the crossing keeper's cabin. When the bell rang the keeper on duty would walk down the platform to open the gates.

Time after time – interestingly enough soon after there had been an accident in which a lorry driver had been killed on the crossing – the bell would sound and a keeper would make his way along the 'down' platform. At the gates he would see a man standing, waiting; a man wearing brown trousers and a dark shirt. As the keeper approached and was almost within touching distance, the man would vanish, and there would be no explanation, either for the appearance or the disappearance of an apparently normal man or the ringing of the alarm bell. This happened frequently for quite a long time and the keepers became convinced that it was the ghost of the dead lorry driver at the gates, but they could never be sure who it was until the figure vanished and then once again they realized that they must have seen a ghost. As time passed, the sound of the bell ringing and the appearance of the phantom man became less frequent and eventually the phenomenon ceased altogether.

Another incident involving the mysterious appearance of what may have been a phantom man was associated with the up platform at Rolleston station which, incidentally, backs onto the Southwell Racecourse. Various crossing keepers have repeatedly reported seeing a young man in an ill-fitting suit looking at a half-folded newspaper, as though studying form in the racing section. One crossing keeper was on his way along the platform to open the gates when he noticed a man standing halfway down the platform, reading his paper. At the end of the platform he glanced back and of the man he had just passed there was no sign! It seemed quite impossible for him to have gone anywhere and the keeper was very puzzled until he related his experience to another keeper when he heard that the phantom man with a newspaper had been seen on many occasions. Those who saw the figure thought he looked as though he might have been the result of some kind of time-slip, perhaps from the late 1940s. I possess an additional two reports of a similar figure being seen at Southwell Racecourse!

Other seemingly inexplicable happenings at Rolleston Station include the sound of children's voices. There are stories of three children being killed on the station many years ago, either playing near the edge of the platform and falling in front of a train or being pushed by other children, in fun. At any event there have been innumerable instances of the sound of children on the deserted station, at first laughing and happy and then suddenly screaming. Some witnesses have reported that the voices seem to follow them or when they moved the voices seemed to move also, and there seemed no way of getting rid of them and they found it really uncanny, weird and spooky. Then, after a while, and as suddenly as it had all begun, the sounds completely ceased.

Other puzzling incidents associated with this haunted railway station include the unexplained appearance of an indistinct figure in black, always seen on the platform in daylight, a figure that seems to exude a sense of unease, menace even. Other witnesses have described seeing the figure of a nun who is there one minute and gone the next. An extraordinary number of motorists using the crossing have found their cars stop incomprehensibly on the crossing, sometimes being impossible to restart and having to be towed away. A responsible and down-to-earth railway-man from Fiskerton will only say he had 'the most terrifying experience of his life' at Rolleston Station; he refuses to elaborate and cannot bear to talk about the matter. The station at Rolleston can be a very eerie place, in sunshine or in shadow, and a place where perhaps, a real ghost train still runs.

The station at Fiskerton is only a few hundred yards down the track from Rolleston and both have level crossings with old-fashioned gates. At Fiskerton a small signal box is occupied by signalmen. At different times and by different signalmen unexplained footsteps have been heard inside this signal box.

One signalman says he was on duty and nearly at the end of his shift, one bright and sunny day, when having mopped the floor, being careful to work backwards to the door, he nipped outside for a moment. When he returned, seconds later, there were a series of footprints on the wet floor. He is convinced that there was absolutely no possibility whatsoever of anyone going into the signal box without him seeing them and in any event the footsteps walked across the wet floor – but did not return! Other signalmen have suddenly become aware of footsteps sounding inside the signal box that have no explanation. The sounds have been reported at different times of the day and night and do not relate to the approach or passing of trains and seem quite inexplicable. One man said the signal box at Fiskerton can be a strange place sometimes, at other times the atmosphere is fine; but sometimes it is really odd and there is the over-whelming impression of being watched by someone or something that is invisible.

Swanage, Dorset

Among the haunted stations I have visited I vote Swanage to be among the most attractive and perhaps the most haunted. And one of Dorset's little-known roadside memorials is to be found on the minor road from Bere Regis to Wareham, now mainly frequented by users of the caravan camp halfway along the road.

A short distance along the road there is a cross of stones, difficult to see if it were not for the upright cross bearing the date of 1928, a little memorial that recalls a holiday journey that went tragically wrong and the story involves the little end of the line Swanage station, as recorded by Theresa Murphy.

In August of the year marked on the cross, Iris Willis, an excited fourteen-year-old girl from south east London, pre-pared for a much anticipated holiday in delightful Dorset with David Evans, his mother and a cousin, Muriel. Iris was disappointed that her father Richard was unable to take a holiday at the same time but he had promised to make a day-visit to Dorset the following week and it was arranged that Iris would meet his train at Swanage.

The first days of the holiday were ideal but Iris was looking forward to seeing her father. On the appointed day, David Evans settled himself behind the driving wheel and prepared to take Iris the twenty miles to Swanage station. She sat at the front beside the driver and they drove out of Bere Regis and made for Swanage, taking in Sugar Hill where a lorry driver was having trouble with his vehicle as he climbed the hill although what the trouble was has never been established. What was established is that the heavy haulage lorry was on the wrong side of the road when David Evans came over the crest of the hill. A head-on collision resulted with the car's petrol tank exploding and the vehicle bursting into flames. Most of the passengers were thrown clear on impact but Iris, covered with burning petrol somehow found her way to the side of the road where the others, sick with helplessness, could only watch as she burned to death.

Once the police arrived and collected all the evidence from the survivors, arrangements were made for someone to meet Iris's father and convey to him the awful news. A week later Mr Willis was still overcome with emotion, as was David Evans who never really recovered from the shock of it all and even a policeman who attended the scene collapsed while giving evidence. The verdict was Accidental Death. It was a road accident; something that happens almost every day but the memory of what happened that fateful day in Dorset has survived in the memory of everyone involved and through all the years, even through the dark days of the Second World War, there has hardly been a day when there are not fresh flowers beside the little cross.

And what of the meeting between Iris and her father at Swanage railway station? A meeting that never took place. Could the thoughts of a dying girl and the utter and complete sadness of her father be the triggers for the ghostly appearances that have been reported from the station and its vicinity?

Whatever the source or origin of this psychic phenomenon there are many reports of the appearance on the platform of a phantom man in a city-style suit of the 1920s walking briskly along the one station platform or glimpsed at the end of the station or outside the main door to the station. Each sighting tells of an anxious, eager man hurrying to meet someone dear to him or waiting impatiently for somebody who never arrives. Other witnesses of what appear to be echoes of what might have been tell of seeing a young teenage girl wearing outdated summer clothes and looking extraordinarily happy, running along the station platform as though towards someone very special to her or, more rarely, standing looking down the platform, quietly expectant – before mysteriously disappearing. What never happens is that the two ghostly forms, the man and the girl, are ever seen together.

When I was last at Swanage, in the summer of 2008, the station staff I talked to were well aware of the sad story and of the platform ghosts that occasionally haunt the station and its precincts and they were able to tell me the names of several local people who had personal experience of the ghosts here, enabling me to obtain further confidential information.

Even after over eighty years the sadness of this tragedy still lingers at Swanage station and at the spot where the accident happened, and the memory of the depressing melancholy of it all pervade and saturates the atmosphere and perhaps provides the conditions required for such ghosts to appear.

Other Haunted Railways

Chiddesden not far from Basingstoke in Hampshire, where the station on the old Alton line lies, has long been the subject of interest to students of the paranormal on account of the sound of steam trains passing by when there is no train in the vicinity and no explanation for the sounds. In 2010 when I was there four independent people told me they had heard the sound of a train puffing past when the line was clear in both directions. The station was featured in the classic Will Hay film, *Oh! Mr Porter.*

The scene of the Tay Bridge (Dundee, Scotland) disaster in 1879 when a portion of bridge across the River Tay collapsed in a raging gale and some seventy-nine people lost their lives, although all the bodies were not recovered so we have no accurate figure, is said to be haunted. On and around the anniversary of the disaster, a ghost train has repeatedly been seen crossing the bridge from south to north.

Some years ago the Keighley and Worth Valley Railway Company were refurbishing the private railway running near Keighley in West Yorkshire and carrying out repairs to the Ingro Tunnel where, on several occasions, black smoke, as from a steam locomotive, has been seen emerging from the tunnel at times when there is no natural explanation for the smoke. Once, two investigators found the smoke to be coming out of the tunnel at a time when the wind was blowing in the opposite direction.

Among the ghosts on London's Underground there have long been reports of sightings of a ghostly 'thin man wearing a top hat and a dark suit' who suddenly appears and disappears. His most frequent haunt appears to be the vicinity of Covent Garden Underground station where staff and travellers have reported seeing the figure. Green Park is another haunted London tube station where the ghost is that of an older, well-dressed man, with a flower in his button-hole; he wears a wide-brimmed hat and has white hair. I have collected many reports of this unidentified dandy who cannot seem to leave Green Park station.

The railway embankment alongside Wong Lane, Tickhill near Doncaster is haunted on occasions by an old-fashioned railway train. Reports I have are dated 1964 and 2011.

Powerstock Station near Bridport in Dorset is a small branch line and here there have been reports of the sound of a train thundering over sleepers long vanished, A phantom little tank engine was once reported here.

Mayfield Station in Greater Manchester, now a parcel depot, but long a shunting yard, is haunted by footfalls on a deserted platform. Many witnesses include workers, porters, officials, and members of the public in addition to psychic investigators.

Ghost trains apparently still run on the Cowes to Newport line on the Isle of Wight and residents of Gordon Road, where the line used to run at the bottom of their gardens, repeatedly said they heard the sound of trains – and some say they have seen the trains.

The famous Bluebell Line in Easst Sussex is associated with a local murder and this is the reason given for several different phantom forms seen here; forms that appear and disappear mysteriously,

Part 10

HAUNTED RUINS

Atmospheric ruins should be haunted. Haunted ruins sounds right. Gaunt and hollow ruins of some formerly majestic building, set against a darkening sky with clouds passing over the moon – all it needs is a ghost or two to complete the scene.

And there are very many ruins that do possess ghosts. These places where once walked people who were happy or sad, devoted or fatuous – any of them may return and be seen or sensed by those able or lucky enough to attune their psychic powers as necessary. Occasionally the haunting entities at these poignant places seem to be able to manifest anyway and then those of us who are not psychically endowed may still see ghosts. We all live in hope.

Berwick-upon-Tweed, Northumberland

Once 'a city so populous and of such trade that it might be called another Alexandria,' one thirteenth-century chronicler stated. Today there are few remains to remind us of the once magnificent Norman Berwick Castle. Described as the cockpit of all the fighting between England and Scotland, and in the hands of first one and then the other country, until it was declared a neutral town in 1551, it had changed hands, it is said, more than a dozen times. A town with an unusually stormy history, Berwick is still essentially a border town as it has been since Hadrian's Wall was built. Even today for certain legal purposes Berwick is neither in England nor in Scotland.

The fragments of wall that survive are interesting in as much as they show the modifications in design which were thought necessary to combat the invention of artillery. The three noble bridges here are impressive, not least because the medieval stands side by side with the modern. The most recent, opened in 1928, has three spans and was designed to take the place of the seventeenth-century stone bridge of fifteen arches, while the third, the high railway viaduct was designed by Stephenson in the middle of the nineteenth century. All three bridges have had reported ghosts associated with them. The oldest is haunted by a monk-like figure; the most recent by the ghost of a workman who was killed during the construction, and the railway bridge by Stephenson himself. There used to be another bridge here; the first suspension bridge in England on a big scale, erected over the Tweed, near Berwick, in the 1800s, twenty feet wide and with a span of 440 feet. It was blown down in a storm.

The spectre usually associated with Berwick Castle is that of a Scottish piper who has occasionally been seen patrolling what is left of the ruined battlements and in the vicinity of the stone steps in the remaining castle wall, 'the white wall' as it is called, while the steps are known as 'the breakneck stairs' which suggests they were named following some tragedy. Our ghostly piper has also been known to appear below the castle remnants at the foot of the steep embankment by the river.

The present Berwick Railway Station is reputed to occupy the site of the former castle, or part of it; possibly the Great Hall but there do not seem to be any reliable reports of the haunting of that busy building. It must be likely that the reported ghost of Berwick Castle is a folk memory of some long forgotten incident and the 'pipe music' heard may well have a more prosaic and natural explanation – but then again, maybe not!

Caerphilly, Wales

Originally a Roman fort, today Caerphilly is perhaps the most impressive of all the castles in Wales, comprising some thirty acres; two lakes have been dammed to comprise the surrounding huge expanse of moat, and much of the present building dates from the thirteenth century. It is remarkably intact and haunted by at least three ghosts.

During a thousand-mile tour of Wales in 2008 I visited a great many wonderful castles but Caerphilly, which we visited early on, set a precedent that was never equalled.

The second largest castle in Europe, its haunted circular tower and impressive leaning tower, eighty feet high and ten feet out of the perpendicular – possibly the result of an explosion in the fourteenth century – its remarkable views and vistas and its overwhelming atmosphere all create a lasting memory, not to mention the ghosts.

There is a Green Lady, who is often seen flitting from one turret or tower to another and then back again. Once the phantom lady, who appears to be completely normal, was pursued by two local boys who had seen her before. Repeatedly they almost caught up with her before she somehow slipped away and appeared elsewhere. Many visitors allude to the lady who dangerously ran between the towers and disappeared in mysterious circumstances.

The massive flag tower is equally haunted by an active ghost and there were reports in 1984 from several of the security staff that they were increasingly aware of an atmosphere inside the tower and none of them liked going up there; they invariably felt that they were about to be confronted by something not of this world and often the scent of lady's perfume pervaded the air when no lady, visitor or otherwise, was present. Women visitors, as it happened, always give their companions some reason for not going up the tower. *The South Wales Echo* devoted a complete report to this very subject.

The present castle was the work of Gilbert de Clare, known as the Red Earl, the ninth Earl of Clare, Earl of Gloucester and Lord of Glamorgan, and it represents, with its inner and outer walls, the earliest and most complete example of the concentric castles of the type known as 'Edwardian'. The history of the castle includes an attack by the younger Llewelyn, enlargement by the Despensers (under whom it afforded a refuge for Edward II), capture by Owain Glyndwr and blockade by the Parliamentary forces during the Civil War. During the fifteenth century it was used as a prison.

The ghostly activity here additionally includes reports of the ghost of the wife of Gilbert de Clare who was banished to France where she died but she seems to have returned home after her death. Ghostly soldiers wander among the history-laden walls as they must have done in reality long years ago. There is also the ghost of a soldier in full armour, a screaming hag of a woman with red eyes who frightens those who see her as she is fond of running straight at people screaming harshly and flapping about the castle in a cloak before suddenly disappearing, and a goblin-like creature that darts out of dark recesses and disappears with lightning speed.

During the months that the castle was used during the filming of a series of Young Dracula films the cast and crew endured a number of puzzling incidents and experiences.

Caerphilly Castle was once known as a place of rendezvous for witches, warlocks, sorcerers and like-minded people who may have left behind something of the atmosphere and inhabitations that they engendered. At all events, Caerphilly Castle is still a most interesting place, historically, architecturally and psychically.

Castle Rising,
Kings Lynn, Norfolk

Castle Rising is now a popular tourist attraction but it harbours a screaming ghost that has been heard occasionally and is sometimes seen by officials, researchers, the visiting public and passersby.

There is a footpath leading from the old school house at Rising running east towards the mill and among the bracken and brambles of Castle Rising Wood – once known as Goos Wood – you may find, after diligent searching, an ancient barrow or tumulus which suggests the burial place of a person of some importance. Historians think it may be the last resting place of Hsris (or Horisi) a very ancient chieftain who may have founded the village of Rising.

Like Castle Rising itself, we simply do not know enough about it. Although we can start with the Romans, for coins and Romano-British pottery unearthed here show that the Romans knew the area, indeed it lay on their main route to their fortress at Brancaster, the so-called Peddlers Way.

The village is mentioned in the Domesday Book as Risina where its farming industry is emphasized. A Norman knight, the first Earl of Arundel, chose Rising as the site of his West Norfolk castle, and it was after the last of the Norman lords died without issue that its most famous occupant, Queen Isabella, came to Rising after the death of her paramour Mortimer. Her son Edward III and his queen visited on two occasions. Later the Black Prince held the castle, and then Richard III exchanged it with the Duke of Brittany for a castle at Brest. Until the reign of Henry VIII it was Crown property. Henry gave it to Thomas Howard, third Duke of Norfolk in 1544. In Elizabeth I's reign it was granted to Edward, Earl of Oxford and then to Henry Howard Earl of Northampton and then it was inherited by another Thomas Howard, this time the Earl of Arundel. In 1693 it was possessed by the family of the Dukes of Norfolk when it was sold to yet another Thomas Howard, this one was the Earl of Berkshire. Since that time it has remained in the Howard family.

There are the remains of a massive keep, very strong earthwork defences, an inner rampart and suggestions that this was surrounded by a wall. The Norman gatehouse is now ruinous, the keep is roofless but some ancient stone steps, the vestibule of the once great hall, a groined roof and a blocked-up doorway, originally the entrance to the hall, now a fireplace, remain. There are three Norman windows, some early relics of a guard-room, a narrow passage through the wall of the keep, a Norman chapel and quarters that may once have been occupied by the constable of the castle. In addition there is a dramatic staircase that has been described as 'pure Hollywood'.

The beautiful Queen Isabella, 'the she-wolf of France' was the widow of Edward II, the weak king who preferred the company of attractive young men, such as Piers Gaveston, to that of his queen and when she learned that Roger Mortimer, who became her lover, was conspiring against the king, she joined forces with him and the king was captured and confined in the castle at Corfe and then Berkeley where he was imprisoned in the castle dungeon and finally put to an agonizing death.

Incidentally, the shrieks heard ringing within the castle walls of Berkeley Castle, Gloucestershire, around 21st September, the anniversary of his death, would appear to be those of the king. When I heard that the renowned author Laurie Lee, whom I met at a literary function, was saying that people were still claiming to hear the dying shrieks, I asked him whether he could supply me with specific details. He said he was most interested in the whole subject of ghosts and ghostly activity but had no firsthand evidence but he added that his mother, whose forebears lived at Berkeley, often repeated the story to him and Sir Reginald Blaker of Sussex wrote to him quoting some very old and relevant lines which he had not heard before:

'Shrieks that through Berkeley's roof did ring,
Shrieks of an agonizing kind . . .'
The source of these lines is unknown.

When Edward III was crowned in 1327 he soon realized that he was king in name only and that the real authority rested with his mother and Mortimer and when he found that the couple were retaining two-thirds of England's tax revenues for their own purposes, he knew something had to be done. Soon he accumulated evidence that suggested that Mortimer was organizing a revolt against him. His mother and Mortimer were then living at the massive and impregnable (and haunted) Nottingham Castle and the king decided on a plan. An avenging party burst into the queen's chamber and seized Mortimer. He was taken to London and found guilty of having 'murdered and killed the king's father' and of usurping the authority of King Edward III. He was hanged at Tyburn and although no reference was made to Mortimer's liaison with Queen Isabella, after the execution she was imprisoned for the remaining twenty-eight years of her life at Castle Rising, where her ghost haunts the sombre ruins.

Marc Alexander told me he had seen convincing evidence that on occasions ghostly bursts of maniacal laughter fill the air, resonating hideously within the shattered remnants of the castle, suggesting she lost her reason before she died in 1397. Furthermore her demented ghost has sometimes been glimpsed hurrying along the ramparts and other ancient parts of Castle Rising. A 2009 *Reader's Digest* publication said: 'Her insane screams are still said to ring over the countryside.' I possess evidence that the shrieks were heard and the ghost seen in 2008 and again in 2010.

Colchester, Essex

The historic castle here, built by the Normans on foundations that could well have been a Roman temple, was once a noble edifice standing in the chief town of Britain, as important as London and probably as populous.

Sacked by Boudicca in 61 AD on her victorious march towards London, it was restored and fortified after the rebellion was quelled to become one of the most important centres of Roman life on this island. With the English rising Camulodunum fell but its walls were not entirely destroyed and in fact stretches of them remain to this day, inspiring monuments to the enduring nature of Roman work. The later Norman castle and numerous other structures used Roman bricks and tiles which can be seen in many buildings throughout the town.

The great vaulted basement is Roman and was once the substructure of some important Roman building, possibly a temple or basilica (where a Roman soldier has been glimpsed from time to time) and the excellent museum housed in the castle includes many important Roman objects such as a sculptured figure of a Roman centurion considered to be one of the best-preserved military memorials of the period to be found in Britain.

In 1648, during the Civil War, Colchester was besieged and subsequently some two hundred houses were burned and destroyed and many of its inhabitants left the town. It was a disaster from which it would take years to recover. In 1665 the town was scourged by the plague, and there is a room here where Witchfinder General Matthew Hopkins interrogated some of his unfortunate victims.

All these and other tragedies, bloodshed, violence and sadness have left their mark on Colchester for there is about the town and especially about the ruined remains of the castle, a mournful air of sadness and melancholy that has been remarked upon by many first time visitors.

And what of the ghosts? Unexplained 'shadows' and mysterious voices (some of which have been recorded) add to what can be an alarming atmosphere and it is all too easy to recall the terrified victims of fate and misfortune who once lived and died here. One named apparition is a Quaker who may have been called James Parnell. He is said to have died in prison here after being treated abominably and his ghost has been seen, heard and felt. There are several stories of groups of eager 'ghost hunters' spending a night in the dungeons but even more eager to leave the place when daylight releases them from where, they said, they never felt they were alone; always there seemed to be another, frightened and frightening, invisible presence among them. Other ghosts here include a young Royalist soldier and a Cavalier or trooper who parades the ground. And, almost anywhere about the castle ruins, it would appear, you are likely to bump into a Roman centurion who, oblivious of you, disappears almost as soon as you are aware of his presence.

Conwy Castle, North Wales

This historic castle, set in the interesting town of Conwy, or Conway or Aberconwy, on the north coast, is probably the most sturdy, romantic and impressive of all feudal castles, representing the high-water mark of thirteenth-century military engineering. Dating from 1283 with curtain walls fifteen feet thick and strengthened by eight great drum-towers, four of which still retain their finger-turrets, this haunted castle casts a lasting spell on all who visit it.

Entering at the north-east corner (there is no gatehouse as one was not considered necessary) the rampart walk commands arresting views of town and sea. The remains of the Great Hall, now roofless and floorless, can be seen on the south side of the Outer Ward, although in fact it was built long after the completion of the rest of the castle. For some unknown reason the Hall was only divided from the Chapel by a wooden screen. Only one of the original eight stone arches that supported the roof still stands. Be sure to inspect the Inner Ward or 'Palace', the Queen's Tower, with its lovely little oratory, and the King's Tower with its dungeon and the Queen's Garden where Eleanor of Castile planted the first sweetpeas in Britain; for these are places where the Conwy ghosts have repeatedly been reported – but you are likely to encounter a ghost just about anywhere here.

There is an unidentified cloaked figure (most frequently seen on the ramparts); a hooded monk in the Queen's Garden and also in the nearby churchyard and waterfront: a 'misty shape' often seen on the stone stairways and also in the King's Tower dungeon; the dark figure of a lost-looking soldier in the King's Tower and a girl in a floral dress in the Inner Ward and in the area of the oratory.

Once, as I explored this massive ruin, my companion and I both became aware of a very strong and somewhat frightening atmosphere in one quiet corner, it really felt as though a phantom form – and not a particularly pleasant one – would manifest at any moment. We continued our tour of the castle and half an hour later returned to the same spot but found the former definite air of expectancy had completely vanished. Many ghosts have been seen at Conwy Castle and I feel sure many more will be encountered in the future.

Corfe Castle, Dorset

A pretty village here houses a picturesque Norman castle ruin that has long had the reputation of being haunted. And well it might, with a history of ghastly deeds and great happiness and everything in between.

About 1571 Queen Elizabeth I gave Corfe Castle to Sir Christopher Hatton, her dancing Chancellor whose sprightly galliard of five steps and a leap in the air was much enjoyed by the queen. With the gift of the castle came responsibility for dealing with pirates and smugglers in the vicinity but there was the privilege of hunting red deer and rights to all the wreckage, which could be considerable, that was washed up on the beach nearby.

The gory history of Corfe Castle – parts of which we have looked at in the consideration of its Haunted Bridge – includes the murder of the boy-king Edward in 978 by his wicked stepmother who wanted the throne of England for her own son. Setting off on a hunt, the young Edward drank, at his stepmother's invitation, a stirrup cup. But the cup was no sooner at his lips than a knife was plunged into his back. The king spurred his horse on and away from danger but the wound was deep and he fell from his horse, one of his feet becoming entangled in the stirrup and he was dragged along until he died. The stepmother's son succeeded to the throne and became the king whose name everyone remembers, Ethelred the Unready.

Later another bad king, John by name, made the castle a royal residence and a typically unsavoury memory of his time there is his starving to death twenty-two French nobles whom he had imprisoned in the dungeons. Treachery often seems to have lurked at this castle and treachery brought about its own destruction. During the Civil War an officer of the garrison allowed Parliamentary troops to gain possession and the fine old building was undermined, blown up and reduced to a ruin. These spectacular castle ruins have long been haunted by unexplained lights and mysterious figures flitting about the broken walls. Smugglers may have been responsible for some of the sights and sounds here in the past but in recent years there have been many acceptable reports of inexplicable happenings.

The last time I was there, in 2008, I visited the sombre but impressive and wonderfully situated ruins with a friend and we both saw a figure we could not explain, a figure that disappeared in mystifying circumstances in a part of the ruins which we found it would have been impossible for an actual person to be; and we both felt the pull of this poignant place but we did not see the striking sight of the ghost of a headless woman who reportedly drifts across the road below the castle.

Hadleigh, Essex

The two circular towers forming the ruins of Hadleigh Castle that look towards the mouth of the Thames have about them an air of mystery and many are the stories of unexplained happenings in the vicinity of these ancient remains of a once proud thirteenth-century castle, painted by Constable in 1829. A royal property at an earlier date it was presented by Henry VIII to his fourth wife Anne of Cleves who appears to have accepted that it was Henry's idea of pensioning her off. A few years later the property was granted to Lord Rich of Leighs who was apparently content to allow the castle to decline into a ruin

The wealth of reported supernatural activity that abounded here in the middle of the nineteenth century was, almost certainly, encouraged, supported and aided by local smugglers who found such stories tended to keep the coast clear for their activities and offered excuses for what might actually be the sounds and sights of their furtive exertions.

Nevertheless there are ghostly tales associated with Hadleigh Castle ruins that have the ring of truth and might well be genuine paranormal activity. A woman in white has long been said to haunt the ruins and there is a long-standing tradition of such a figure being seen around midnight or in the early hours, with witnesses including a farm labourer, a local girl and a couple whose stories and descriptions are all remarkably similar, including the precise locality of the vision.

A footpath leading to the castle has been the scene of dis-embodied voices and there are reports of a ghostly young woman in grey; as well as a boy wearing knee breeches and a seemingly transparent white horse. All have been seen and heard in the vicinity of these interesting ruins and all are thought to be connected with the vanished castle at some period of its history. Who can tell?

'Hadleigh Castle stands today amid trees and bushes, the eyeless arrow slits gazing over the broad stippled tideways of the Thames, the misty marshes of Holehaven Creek and Fobbing with their many tales of smuggling and other, less easy to explain stories.' So said James Wentworth Day who was born nearby.

The castle was rebuilt by Edward III around 1365 and seems to have been actively haunted for many, many years. 'The place is full of ghosts,' one local man told me. 'And always has been.' Unexplained lights shining out of the yawning windows and strange figures seen among the historic ruins are just a couple of the ghostly happenings here.

Maiden Castle near Dorchester, Dorset

This great hill-top earthwork, some 115 acres in extent, and first occupied more than 2,000 years before Christ, must have been breath-taking in its heyday. Systematically excavated by Sir Mortimer Wheeler it has been established that there was a settlement here in the late Neolithic period and evidence of occupation by the Beaker people, and in the Early Stone Age, perhaps 350 BC, the site was extensively developed.

This, Britain's largest Celtic stronghold, was attacked by the Roman Second Augustan Legion and a fierce battle ended with the massacre of men and women. A kind of 'war cemetery' has been excavated outside the gates of the castle where the British hurriedly buried their dead. The name 'Maiden' could well have been connected with ancient stones and perhaps the Mother Goddess.

A ghostly re-appearance of the scene of battle here was sighted in 1983 by a woman walking the ramparts one still and quiet evening. She saw a group of Roman soldiers marching within the central enclosure being attacked and repelling the assault with ferocious tenacity. A moment later the place was deserted and peaceful but the witness was very frightened and hastened away from the place.

When Sir Mortimer Wheeler, then director of the London Museum, directed the excavations, he told me that Rachel Clay, a distinguished archaeologist, rather than travel daily from her home, camped at the summit of the site in her father's Great War tent and she often related how she heard the tramp-tramp of marching feet at the dead of night and once she saw a Roman standard being waved above a silent marching cluster of Roman soldiers, down below her; a vision or apparitional aberration that vanished as suddenly as it had appeared.

On a lighter note, during the dig rumour was rife that one of the Neolithic pits was inhabited by a crocodile. Rachel Clay investigated and indeed found a crocodile – 'a perfectly good stuffed crocodile' which, it turned out, had been discarded by a local museum. The archaeologist put a penny in the beast's mouth and buried it in one of the excavation tunnels. Many years later it was dug up by a baffled English Heritage archaeologist and Rachel Maxwell-Hyslop (as she then was) wrote to *The Times* explaining its presence.

Margam, South Wales

During many enjoyable visits to Wales and to its wonderful countryside and many haunted localities it has always seemed to me that one of the most haunted was ruined Margam Castle, south of Port Talbot.

In particular I continue to receive reports of a ghost monk wandering among the ruins, a Cistercian by all accounts. There is speculation that it may be the ghost of Twm Celwydd Teg, a monk from the days when there was a working abbey here. He was a man who had a habit of predicting the future. I wonder whether he saw himself centuries later still wandering among the picturesque ruins of Margam Abbey.

I have reports of his appearance on three separate occasions some years ago and twice a couple of years later; usually in the late afternoon or early evening. Most recently two visitors, with no knowledge of any ghosts at Margam, said how puzzled they were to see a monk disappear as they watched him.

There are not infrequent reports too of a Lady in White; a male figure in Victorian attire and the occasional fleeting form of a nun – quite out of place!

John Vivian Hughes, a Local Studies Librarian, told me of his long interest in the Margam Park area, his family having been associated with the Margam Estate for several generations, and I can personally endorse his considered opinion and that of his family and many other visitors to this atmospheric place, that the abbey precincts have a unique, overwhelming and fascinating feeling of psychic awareness.

Netley Abbey, Southampton, Hampshire

In 1967, soon after the demolition of the old Indian-style Victorian Military Hospital at Netley, the City Archivist sent me information about the building and its ghosts.

Queen Victoria herself laid the foundation stone on 19th May 1856, saying as she did so that she had sanctioned the naming of the building of the Royal Victoria Hospital and she was glad to think that her 'poor brave soldiers will be more comfortably lodged' than she was herself! Her words reflected the current public opinion that the design and facilities compared favourably with the queen's recently erected Osborne House. Later it was to become the subject of a national scandal and a War Office enquiry and be referred to as a 'horrid example' of nineteenth-century hospital construction. The first criticism came from Florence Nightingale and while it may be true that throughout its history Netley was a 'difficult, depressing and unsatisfactory hospital' as C. Woodham-Smith says in her biography of Florence Nightingale, nevertheless the building survived for over a century and catered for about a thousand patients for most of that time and in the Second World War managed to accommodate double that number.

The building was long reputed to be haunted by a nurse of the Crimean War period who committed suicide by throwing herself from an upstairs window after discovering that by mistake she had administered a fatal overdose of drugs to a patient.

Her ghost was always seen in one particular corridor. Officials and staff at the hospital, a clergyman, visitors and patients have all told of seeing the figure, although stories of the appearances were suppressed for many years because whenever the ghost was seen, a death seemed to take place in the hospital. A service of exorcism was held there in 1951.

The apparition was reported to be particularly active when the building was being demolished and one witness stated: 'The figure was dressed in an old-style nurses' uniform of greyish-blue with a white cap and was about twenty-five feet away from me when I saw it. She walked slowly away, making no sound and disappeared down a passage that led to the chapel.'

In 1936, a night orderly saw the grey lady pass a ward where a patient died the following morning. A night staff telephone operator, employed by the hospital for twenty-seven years, also claimed to have seen the ghost; he said that he heard the rustle of her dress as she passed and there was a perfumed scent in the air after she had disappeared.

On one occasion, three reporters from the *Southern Evening Echo* visited the former hospital when it was deserted and partially demolished hoping to catch a glimpse of the famous grey lady. They were accompanied by Bill Perry who was in charge of the demolition of the place. All four of them began a serious and systematic tour of the hospital including the ground floor corridors, what was left of the centre, and the south wing.

As they passed Ward 27 they all saw the figure and before order could be restored they were so scared that they all scrambled out of the building through a broken window!

One of the party, Brian Rivers, went back into the building wondering whether they had been the subject of a hoax but he and the others were convinced that the whole incident was genuine. The figure they all saw, apart from being completely silent, appeared to be completely unaware of the existence of the psychic explorers despite the torch-light, the shouting and the noise of the hasty retreat.

Mrs J. Allison of Peterborough was a theatre sister at the Royal Victoria Hospital in 1951 and during her night walks through the corridors she was in no doubt that the ghostly grey lady was there too. She could not swear that she had seen her but she and her companions were all quartered in the oldest part of the building and were very aware of the presence although they always tried to ignore it and get on with their work. She added that in all her travels in the Army, she had never been so fond of any hospital as she was of Netley and I am sure she and everyone else who worked there would be happy to know that today the pictur-esque and peaceful ruins and grounds form the Royal Victoria Country Park, a beautiful spot where many people enjoy a summer picnic.

Just along the road. the equally picturesque and peaceful ruins of Netley Abbey are also reputedly haunted. The last monastery to be established in Hampshire, it was founded in 1238 as a Cistercian establishment under King John and later Henry III. The first monks came from nearby haunted Beaulieu.

After the Dissolution of the Monasteries it became a private property and the home of the then Lord Treasurer, Sir William Paulet whom we have to thank for destroying much of the building. The present ruins are haunted by at least two ghosts. The one-time keeper of the abbey's treasure hid what he could of it at the time of the Dissolution and his white-habited figure is said to still haunt the vicinity. The treasure has never been found. There are also reports of the occasional appearance of a woman in white, carrying a parasol, walking across the abbey lawns. She is invariably taken for a real person until she suddenly disappears to the disbelief of many

witnesses but seeing is believing and the lady in white has
been seen many times.

Porchester
near Fareham, Hampshire

On Portsmouth Harbour, at the far end of the old village,
can be found the remains of what was once a magnificent
Norman castle built on Roman foundations. These Saxon
Shore Forts were built by the Romans during the latter part
of the third century AD in order to protect their province of
Britain from raids by Saxon and Danish pirates and a chain
of ten were built from the Wash to the south coast,
Porchester being the westernmost. They were commanded
by the Comeshitoris Saxonice who was known as the Count
of the Saxon Shore.

Nothing remains of Walton Castle near Felixstowe in
Suffolk, the last remains vanishing into the sea in 1933, or
of the fort at Dover and there is little to see at Brancaster on
the Wash or of Reculver in Kent, while of two more,
Ythancaestir (across the fields from Bradwell in Essex) and
Statfall on Romney Marsh, all that can be seen today are
remnants of grey wall. That leaves Burgh Castle in Suffolk,
Richborough in Kent, Pevensey in Sussex and Portchester.
Later, St Cedd built his church to St Peter and Murum
astride the Roman wall at Ythancaestir where it can still be
seen and at Reculver the twelfth-century towers exist of a
church founded in the seventh century.

These forts show the squat and massive walls, the
impressive wall-turrets and complicated angle-turrets

enclosing rectangular or oval spaces and are mighty reminders of the building power of the Romans. The builder in charge was the Roman usurper Carausius who was murdered around the year 294. Carausius was a Gallic officer formerly in charge at Gessoriacum (Boulogne) where he was accused of being in league with the Frankish and Saxon pirates and sentenced to death but he managed to get to Britain where he usurped the title of emperor in 286 but after eventually being recognized by the gigantic Roman emperor Maximinus, he was assassinated in 293. Emperor Maximinus was himself killed by his soldiers. Those were violent times: perhaps that is why they left behind so many ghosts.

Many of the ghosts – they have been reported at all the places mentioned – are somewhat transitory and insubstantial, but perhaps that is fitting for such entities; in any case, over the years there have been reports at these places of Roman origin of a somewhat nebulous phantom, a tall and white figure accompanied by a Roman soldier.

At Portchester there is a legend that in the sixteenth century an unfortunate lady was spurned and falsely imprisoned by her onetime lover and she is said, most frequently at times of the full moon, to appear, dragging her imprisoning chains, as she endlessly searches for the wayward lover for reconciliation or revenge. The same ghost (or is it a different one) is said to be a prisoner from long ago, fulfilling a vow to return after physical death.

There do appear to be reliable accounts of ghosts at Portchester Castle. A 'sensible' Porchester lady told Ian Fox of the experience she had one day on a visit to the castle. Standing watching some children playing at the front of the castle she was astonished to see a monk-like figure emerge from a small, iron-barred gateway to the left of the main entrance. The phantom form was extremely clear and the witness saw he wore a brown cowled robe with tassels of a corded sash swinging as he walked. After crossing the front of the castle he disappeared into the side of the bastion by the main Gatehouse. Years later another woman casually visiting Portchester saw what she described as a monk suddenly appearing and walking along the castle front before vanishing into the bastion wall.

There are records too of the wife of a former custodian encountering a similar monk-like figure immediately outside the Gatehouse. Other visitors have reported other ghosts. There is the man who saw, in 1980, someone bending over a grave beside the twelfth-century church inside the castle grounds; as he watched the figure suddenly dissolved before his eyes!

Less apparently tangible are experiences of many other visitors who have told of creepy, cold and forbidding feelings in the seemingly sun-drenched and warm ruins. Commander Bill Bellars, for example, encountered 'something' on the steps that descend to the dungeons. A friend ahead of him came to a rigid halt halfway down the steps and said she could not go any further as 'there was such an unpleasant atmosphere'. Bellars himself was much surprised at this sudden reaction by an outgoing, level-headed and usually cheerful person before he too 'felt something' and was glad to reclimb the steps and emerge out of the shadows into the sunlight. In Napoleonic times prisoners of war were held here in appalling conditions and it cannot be beyond the realms of reason that some people can sometimes pick up some of this awful unhappiness.

Tintern Parva, Monmouthshire

The magnificent thirteenth-century Tintern Abbey, in its romantic setting on the banks of the River Wye, is the best-preserved medieval ruin in Wales and its spectacular appearance and atmosphere have inspired many writers, poets and painters including Wordsworth and Turner.

Founded by Walter de Clare in 1131, the Cistercian abbey, one of the wealthiest foundations in Britain, is now roofless and the north arcade of the nave has gone but enough survives, including remnants of the cruciform church, the chapter house and the refectory, to illustrate the admirable proportions, the rich ornamentation and the beauty of the window tracery. These silent places, together with the former sacristy, the monks' parlour, the kitchens and other existing portions of this brooding and mysterious but splendid place, are undisputably haunted. Ghost monks have been frequently sighted here by all sorts of people.

In his monumental work, *Lord Halifax's Ghost Book* (1936), the author, a Ghost Club member, recounts the visit of a correspondent (referred to only as E.B.) and his psychic wife during the course of a tour of the area. (Together with many eminent Victorians, including Lord Tennyson, Mark Twain, Lewis Carroll, William Gladstone and Conan Doyle, Charles Lindley Wood, second Viscount Halifax, was a member of the Society for Psychical Research, founded in 1882 and much interested in spontaneous psychic activity.)

Arriving at Tintern, the couple, having found somewhere to stay, decided, after having a meal, to take another look at the majestic ruins. It was a beautiful moonlit evening and E.B.'s wife said she could sense an 'invisible agency' which apparently took control of her right hand and made it tap her

knee repeatedly. By a system of knocks for letters of the
alphabet, which they were familiar with during table-
rapping seances, she laboriously seemed to establish
contact with the spirit of a Saxon soldier who said he had
been killed near the abbey and his remains buried without
Christian rites, in the days of Henry II. E.B. interjected to
say that at that time the abbey did not exist but the response
suggested there had been an earlier one on the site. Then the
communicating entity suddenly requested a Mass be said
for his soul. Being members of the Church of England and
unfamiliar with Roman Catholic celebrations, the visitors
said they would see what they could do.

Next day they managed to arrange for a Catholic priest to
say Mass for the repose of the soul of the unknown soldier
and the following day the tourists spent sight-seeing in the
area, pleased to think they had helped the communicator.
That evening they again visited the abbey ruins and again
E.B.'s wife's hand began to move involuntarily and mess-
ages came through including a request for more Masses so
that his spirit could rest in peace for ever. When he was
informed of this request the Catholic priest agreed to
conduct further masses.

Some years later at an impromptu circle in their London
home a message of thanks was apparently received and two
members of the circle asserted that they could see the figure
of a bearded, middle-aged man, dressed in grey, ill-fitting
clothes. E.B. and his wife were much gratified and always
regarded Tintern Abbey ruins as haunted.

Once when I was there, one of the custodians told me that
not infrequently he and other members of the staff were
asked about a monk whom visitors had seen, sometimes
walking in the abbey ruins and sometimes kneeling beside
some stone steps just beyond an arched doorway at the
western end of the ruins. Visitors seeing the latter figure and

thinking he may have slipped or might be feeling unwell, have approached him to offer their help but suddenly the figure they have so clearly seen is no longer there. I have many reports of a phantom monk being seen among the ruins and invariably by people who have no idea that others have seen the same phantom or indeed that Tintern Abbey ruins are haunted. Tintern Abbey retains more than a little of its long and sometimes mysterious but always devout past.

Walsingham, Norfolk

These magnificent ruins, comprising chiefly of the gateway and the eastern end of the chancel, rise above well-kept lawns. This was once one of the richest monasteries in the world, due to the continual stream of pilgrims to the world-famous shrine of 'Our Lady of Walsingham'.

The former Holy Shrine, according to a fifteenth century manuscript, was founded in the eleventh century and modelled on a replica of the Virgin Mary's home in Nazareth, where the mother of Jesus received the divine message. Lady Richards, wife of a Norman lord, started it all when she had a vision here in 1061 in which the Virgin Mary appeared to her.

The original house of Nazareth fell into the hands of the Mohammedans and the story circulated that the Virgin deserted the Holy Land for Norfolk. At all events, her shrine here is believed to be the first in Britain to be dedicated to the Virgin Mary – who is so-called nowhere in the Bible.

Until the Reformation, Walsingham was almost as popular as Canterbury as a place of pilgrimage and its holy relics included a phial of the Virgin's milk, hence the pilgrim way across Norfolk leading to Walsingham from Ely was popularly known as the Milky Way. Another suggested reason for the name was that the pilgrims were as numerous as the stars.

Robert the Bruce of Scotland was one of many monarchs who visited the shrine; later Henry VII was there, after the defeat of the impostor Lambert Simnel, and gratefully presented the Virgin with the upstart's banner. Edward the Confessor, Richard the Lion Heart and Henry VIII also visited.

The illustrious commoner, Erasmus, visiting the shrine in 1511, wrote deliriously, 'Before the chancel is a shed, under which are two wells full to the brink: the water is wonderfully cold, and efficacious in curing pains in the head.' Even today miraculous healing powers are attributed to Our Lady's Well. Pilgrims were allowed to use both the wells, providing they understood that they had to throw money into the wells for otherwise their wishes would not be granted!

Among the treasures here are relics of the True Cross and of St Thomas of Canterbury together with stones from many holy places including the Grotto of Lourdes; St Peter's Rome; Westminster Abbey; St Augustine, Canterbury; the Colosseum, Rome; and a fragment from the Cave of the Nativity at Bethlehem.

Visions and unexplained appearances of nun-like forms are common here (as perhaps might be expected) as are reports of mysterious twinkling lights and soft bell-ringing, for which no rational explanations have ever been discovered.

Other Haunted Ruins

Bayham Abbey near Lamberhurst, Kent, is a beautiful collection of religious ruins dating from 1200. Spectacular and evocative they are haunted by spectral monks, phantom bells and ghostly voices. This place of absolute peace is visited by ghostly forms and ghostly happenings at all times of the day and night. The vicinity of a holy water stroup and the forlorn remains of a tomb seem to be especially haunted. Ghost monks have frequently been glimpsed at this lovely place; snatches of a whiff of incense have also been reported – not used here for five hundred years. The faint sounds of sacred music and voices chanting in unison have also been heard. Here one really feels one is walking along the edge of the unknown.

The ruins of Barnwell Castle near Oundle in Northamptonshire are haunted by the ghost of a woman prisoner, Marie Le Maine, who is said to have been walled-up alive there soon after the castle was built in the thirteenth century and whose skeleton may still be in the existing left bastion of the historic gatehouse. Patrolling policemen, a practical postman and passing pedestrians are among the many witnesses of the distraught Le Maine ghost.

Middleham Castle ruins, near Richmond in Yorkshire have long been the scene of odd happenings: the sound of old-time music, a ghost knight on a phantom horse, the sounds of clashing swords and an inexplicable blue light at the top of the South Wall, the clop of invisible horses' hoofs and a phantom foot soldier. All have been reported in recent years.

The great ruined abbey at Bury St Edmunds in Suffolk is reputedly haunted by the ghost of Edmund whose body was brought here three hundred years after he was martyred by the Danes. His ghost has been seen passing through the great Gate. I was there more than fifty years ago when I heard the ghost had been seen the previous month and in

2010 a resident informed me that it had just been seen by two visitors who thought the phantom form was someone taking part in a pageant, until it suddenly disappeared.

Careleon, Wales, was once the fortress of Rome's Second Augustan Legion comprising 5,000 men. The impressive remains of their fortress, the baths and the amphitheatre can all be visited – the latter is haunted by the sound of tramping soldiers. When I was last there I was told the sound of marching feet had become more frequent in recent years, or rather reports were more frequent.

The crumbling ruins of Odiham Castle in Hampshire are haunted by a phantom minstral and ghosts of prisoners once held there.

Ruined Carew Castle in Wales is haunted by a White Lady, last seen by a family of four on a summer day in 2011.

The remains of Berry Pomeroy castle in Devon are some of the most haunted ruins extant. The reported ghosts include an ancient de Pomeroy walking the ramparts; a woman in blue who smothered her baby; knights on horses plunging to death rather than be captured; Lady Margaret starved to death in the dungeons, and various other forms and shapes that are often frightening.

Tintagel, Cornwall, where King Arthur may have been born, is said to be haunted by his spirit to this day.

Part 11

HAUNTED SEASCAPES

Seascapes usually bring memories of lazy days on beaches looking out to sea among other happy holidaymakers but sometimes, and perhaps more often than we like to imagine, these scenes are peopled by ghosts.

The unknown and in many ways mysterious sea, it has been suggested, is a natural breeding ground for strange happenings and stranger beliefs.

If all life came from the sea, is it not possible and even likely that the shades of people who have been wonderfully happy or those who have been terribly sad might return to the edge of the sea and become a part of a haunted seascape?

Beachy Head, East Sussex

This is a promontory between Eastbourne and Seaford standing some 575 feet above the sea and forming the termination of the South Downs. The view from the head in clear weather extends to the Isle of Wight and the coast of France. It has long been a favourite spot for suicides. The Belle Tout lighthouse, 282 feet above sea level was erected in 1831; it was replaced in 1902 by a lighthouse 125 feet high at the base of the cliff.

This notorious place is associated with many ghosts and the seascape here is undeniably haunted.

Back in medieval times, Beachy Head was the scene of witchcraft rituals used to deter possible French invasion and much later Aleister Crowley, 'the wickedest man in the world', held demonic and witchcraft rites at The Devil's Chimney, one of several chalk pillars that split away from the cliff proper and became popular for its name and locality for sinister rituals. Crowley was photographed on The Devil's Chimney in 1894 and is thought to have acquired something of the ominous and poignant atmosphere of the place which he used in other rituals. His life ended along the coast at Hastings; his Sicilian villa which he used for orgies and daubed with explicit frescoes, until Mussolini expelled him in 1923, was sold in 2010 for over a million pounds, but Crowley was long dead.

The Devil's Chimney and other chalk pillars eventually eroded and disappeared into the sea in the early 1900s.

I knew a man whose wife drove to Beachy Head, carefully parked her car and then jumped off the cliff to her death. Belatedly, the husband heard from her mother, whom she had telephoned to say goodbye, and he rushed to Beachy Head and seeing the car thought he was in time to save her life. As he hurried towards the deserted car he heard a strange whistling sound that increased in volume the nearer he was to the cliff edge. Discovering that the car was empty he stopped, broken-hearted, at the top of the cliff when he noticed the strange whistling sound had changed to a soothing melodic sound that seemed to lull him into a sense of safety as he went nearer and nearer to the brink, until he felt that the quiet and gentle music allayed all fears and he felt the thing to do was to throw himself over. The sound of a police car, his wife's mother having alerted the police, broke the spell and he retreated from the brink of the cliff and back into normality.

He has always thought the ghost music here encourages would-be suicides and he is convinced that Beachy Head is haunted. Many people have reported feelings of sadness and hopelessness in the immediate area but my widowed friend tells me he keeps away from the place because he feels he could be affected by the mysterious sounds there and become another Beachy Head suicide.

Once the haunt of smugglers, who may have enticed vessels by setting up false lights and then plundering the stranded ships, there have been reported sightings of dark and muttering figures seen hereabouts, the ghosts of long-dead wreckers perhaps or a smuggler or two at their work. Such figures appear on dark and stormy nights which perhaps suggests they are indeed the ghosts of men who used the dangerous coastline for their own purposes on such nights.

Birling Gap was used by smugglers and two very old stone huts, high on the cliff overlooking the Gap, have their own ghosts. From time to time there are reports of two children, a boy and a girl, being seen here playing happily together but they seem to be reclusive and unsociable children who disappear mysteriously when they are approached or spoken to. They may be ghost children but their story, their origin and indeed their purpose in appearing, are quite unknown. Perhaps they are recordings of ghosts that reappear where they were once happy and confident before something happened to shatter their enjoyment in each other and their appearance has nothing to do with their wishes, being merely a photographic record of a past event. However, as is the case with this type of ghost, when those who see them go towards the forms, thereby altering the angle necessary to see the apparitions, they vanish. There have been instances when witnesses to such appearances retrace their steps to where they were when they first saw the figures, those figures then reappear.

Some of the suicides at Beachy Head have been known to reappear as ghosts. A woman who threw herself to her death here in 1856 has reappeared at more or less regular intervals ever since. Another apparition here, according to Janet Cameron writing in 2010, is that of a farmer's wife who stepped off the cliffs carrying a baby in her arms. Yet another is called the Lady in Grey who seems to be fond of dogs but when she gets near to one, a real one, and stoops down to stroke it, the animal invariably shows signs of sudden terror, racing back to its owner with its tail between its legs. The Lady in Grey has reportedly been sighted in 2008, 2010 and 2011. If you go looking for her, it might be kinder to leave your dog at home.

In 1988 an article appeared in the *Eastbourne Herald*

exploring the reasons why people commit suicide at Beachy Head and while there appeared to be many different reasons, one common assertion was that the evil aura of the place lures people to jump to their deaths. It was even suggested that an 'evil presence might play a part' but one of the interesting findings of the investigation was the number of people who claimed they heard voices and music luring people to their deaths. Certainly there are many reports of mysterious music and the sound of voices when to all intents and purposes the place is deserted.

There are also repeated stories of a phantom monk who has evil on his mind. The story goes, and was publicised as recently as June 1988, that during the Reformation the monk's place of abode was sacked by Henry VIII's men and although the monk in question managed to escape at the time, hiding in a nearby manor house, he was hunted down and captured, shackled and thrown over Beachy Head to his death. His fearsome ghost, a figure in black, haunts the place of his death around midnight and by way of revenge, seeks to entice visitors to jump over the awesome cliffs to their deaths. There are also conflicting stories suggesting the killer monk races along the cliff top and those who have followed find themselves stopping just in time at the brink of the cliff. There have been suggestions too that a light-house keeper once took his own life and his ghost haunted the lighthouse; this is the old Belle Tout lighthouse on the cliff top.

Whatever the explanation, Beachy Head continues to be synonymous with suicides, from the first recorded here in 1600 to the present day. Haunted Beachy Head has much to answer for.

Boscastle, Cornwall

I have been visiting Boscastle twice a year for a good many years. To me it is the very essence of Cornwall. Here is the rugged coast, the quiet inland, the gentle slopes, the wildness, the legends and the history, and the green, green coastal paths, the mysteries and the sometimes sinister air that I have never found together anywhere else, here or abroad. All this and ghosts too!

There are ghosts at the Old Mill, long referred to locally as 'that haunted place'. The mill was once worked by a one-eyed miller who died among rumours of having been murdered and of having hidden 'something valuable' some-where inside the building. The ghost figure of a one-eyed man has repeatedly been seen in the building over the years, sometimes disappearing into a wall in the basement; and there have been numerous experiences of unexplained foot-steps in some parts of the building.

Nearby, The Wellington Hotel, where I have spent many happy holidays and enjoyed some fantastic meals, has long been haunted. When Victor and Solange Tobutt were there, Victor saw a frock-coated figure on a landing of the main stairway; a pony-tailed young man wearing a ruffled shirt and leather gaiters, suggesting a coachman or stable lad. When Victor went into the bar and began to describe the figure he had seen, the head barman Tom Gregory interrupted him with an exact description himself. Tom had worked at The Welly for about twenty years and said he had seen the same ghost figure several times.

Here too there used to be sightings of a man who com-mitted suicide, and of a young girl, said to have been crossed in love, who has been seen on a landing at the top of the tower. A retired police officer was one witness who said she appeared to be completely solid and natural until she disappeared through a closed window. Another witness said she saw the girl materialize out of a wall before fading away again. Eighteen months after he had first seen the phantom girl, the former policeman saw her again, but by this time a flat had been built in the adjoining attic and where there had been a window there was now a door. The girl disappeared through the closed door.

Rooms 9 and 10 have reportedly been the scenes of unexplained happenings. Some of the staff told me there is a distinct feeling of a presence sometimes in Room 10 and on one occasion a little old lady was seen sitting on the bed of the vacant room. Debbie Jordan was checking the room one day when she saw the form of an old lady go through the door of Room 9, which she understood was vacant at the time. When she reported back to the receptionist, Jackie Yates, she confirmed that the room was indeed vacant and they checked the room together. It now appeared to be deserted but Debbie then realized that the old lady had gone through the door and had not opened it. Her description tallied with that of witnesses of a similar ghost in Room 10.

Once a visitor who was interested in paranormal happenings asked whether he could have a look at the allegedly haunted areas and he returned to say he had seen and communicated with the little old lady in Room 10 and she was grateful that Sandra had not spent long in the room at 2.30 p.m. and that she had not been disturbed. He assured the staff that the ghost was a friendly one. Sandra was astonished: she had indeed checked the room at 2.30 p.m. when she normally checked the housekeeping. Afterwards she always made sure she kept the time she spent in that room to a minimum.

Once when my wife and I were stopping at this hotel we

passed the doorway to the older part of the building and made our way up the final set of stairs to our room. There my wife mentioned, quite casually, that there must be some sort of celebration going on, judging from the decorations she had noticed as we passed the open doorway. I said I had not seen any decorations and popped down to look. I saw no decorations although the door of the room was indeed open. My wife immediately confirmed this – much to her surprise. That night my wife found herself suddenly wide awake in the middle of the night and aware of someone standing beside the bed close to her. It was not in the least frightening but she was certain that someone, a man, was standing there. She thought about waking me but decided not to disturb my rest and after a little while the 'impression' vanished and she went back to sleep.

At the top of Penally Hill, leading down into Boscastle, nestling among trees overlooking lonely Boscastle Harbour, stands Penally House, built by a wealthy wine and spirit merchant, William Slogatt, in 1836, with seventeen rooms. Local people suspected Slogatt of being involved in smuggling and using the house as a second storehouse, although nothing was proved. Subsequently the house passed through many hands and Carolyn Dymond, who was born there, revealed that it is a haunted house. She thought the ghost was a previous owner, one Colonel Hawker, and that the mysterious footsteps heard in various rooms, were his. Mrs Frances Baxter, who bought the house in 1954, saw someone pass the window of her room and waited to see whether it would pass the other window, but she waited in vain, no one passed the second window. She immediately went outside but no one was in sight and she made extensive enquiries and established that no living person had passed her window at the time. She thought it might be some kind of psychic echo from smuggling days. Penally

House has played a large part in the history of Boscastle
and there have always been stories of underground tunnels,
secret shafts and unexplained footsteps and other sounds
including horses' hoofbeats on the private road that Slogatt
cut out of the solid rock from the house to the harbour.
(Slogatt's three sons were transported to Australia for smuggling.)

The unusual harbour at Boscastle is certainly haunted.
Tucked inland, it consists of a massive breakwater and then
a second one, making the way tortuous and difficult. It is
not unknown for a boat to find itself in difficulties and the
cliffs and impressive rocks give an impression of reluctance,
resistance and independence.

David Waddon-Martyn from Tarbarwith went down to
Boscastle Harbour one late afternoon in November 1970
with the idea of doing some fishing. As he went down the
harbour towards some moored boats he noticed the figure of
a man standing alone just past the boats at the top of some
hewn stone steps. At first he thought it must be a holiday
visitor out for a walk, admiring the little village and inner
harbour but, as he approached and began to himself ascend
the steps he saw that the man was in fact not looking at any
part of Boscastle; it was he, David Waddon-Martyn, who
was being stared at!

As he drew nearer still, David became somewhat
nonplussed and he found the man's set gaze rather unsettling. The man's eyes were looking directly at him,
seeming to follow his every move and yet they seemed
'distant eyes' as though they were grounded in the past.
The man was dressed in heavy tweed clothing and
carried a stick. As David got really close, the man still
stared at him, then he took a pace back, turned round and
melted away. He disappeared so quickly that David
thought he must have gone over the rocks and into the

water and David quickly searched the whole area but there was no sign of the man.

Several times I have made enquiries in Boscastle and I met two residents, completely independent and living at opposite ends of the village, who both told me when I simply said I found a strange atmosphere in the harbour area, that they had seen phantom figures there. The first who lived on Penhilly Hill said he had twice seen the figure of a man in the harbour that a moment earlier had been deserted. A moment later there was no one there. When he spoke to a local fisherman he was told the harbour was completely deserted, there had not been a soul there for the best part of an hour, but he had often seen figures himself, usually a man but sometimes a middle-aged woman, who were there one minute and gone the next. He had got used to it; they never did anyone any harm.

The second person lived near the harbour and she said she 'often' saw a man pass close to her window but whenever she quickly went outside, to see what he was up to, there was never anyone there and, more times than she could remember, she had seen the figure of a stranger, a man with a walking stick, on the rocks overlooking the harbour, a man who disappeared suddenly. Once or twice when she saw the man she determined to keep watching as she approached the harbour and the man himself and she did, not taking her eyes off the unmoving figure but each time when she was quite near she had unthinkingly moved her gaze for a second, looking where she was going, and when she looked back the man had completely disappeared. It was well-known, I was told, that Boscastle Harbour had long been haunted by harmless ghosts.

Isle of Iona, Argyll and Bute

This holy, peaceful and magic island is the burial place of some sixty Scottish, Irish and Norwegian kings, and the ancient monastery founded, it is said, by St Columba who was here in the year 563, harbours many ghosts from Viking marauders and their longboats, to massacred monks and phantom bells, ghostly music and twinkling blue lights, not to mention the strange 'call' of this enchanted and irresistible island.

The ghostly forms of Viking longships have reportedly been seen here since time immemorial, gliding noiselessly into the little harbour and expelling the fierce and well-armed Norse invaders as they did many times in reality. The much-visited monastery has had to be completely rebuilt after being repeatedly sacked. Sometimes the Vikings would slip ashore elsewhere, perhaps at the White Sands, a spot beloved by artists and most certainly haunted. I have a batch of reports extending over many years detailing sightings of the phantom ships and of the massacred monks.

Tommy Frankland, an ex-RAF officer and management consultant, and John MacMillan of the Iona Community, were walking one evening in the middle of summer towards the bewitching White Sands, heading for the north of the island. Suddenly as they approached the White Sands, sparkling in the late sunshine, they saw a fleet of Viking longboats emerge from behind an islet and make for the north shore. They counted fourteen ships and, as they drew nearer, watched fascinated at the rhythmic swoop of the oars as the ships drew gracefully nearer and nearer. They could see the Viking emblems on the great square sails and the fierce-looking men seeming to be shouting and gesticulating as they neared the shore, although no sound accompanied the scene. Then they saw, calmly watching the approaching attackers, a group of monks standing on the sands, directly where the Vikings were heading for.

Aghast, they watched as the invaders flung themselves upon the monks who made no attempt to defend themselves and when all the little group of monks lay motionless on the sands the Vikings ran off over the hill towards the monastery. Tommy told me that he and John MacMillan realized they had been seeing some sort of replay of past events and as they made they way towards the huddled bodies and the Viking ships with their crews resting in the shallow water or pulled up on the shore, suddenly the whole environment seemed to change; a chill wind blew up and as the sun disappeared the place became alive again and they suddenly heard the cries of birds replace the total silence. The whole location returned to normal and they found no sign of the monks or the Viking ships or the invaders. Whatever they had seen had vanished as completely as though it had never happened.

Later that evening, John MacMillan sketched the coloured emblems they had seen and Tommy subsequently consulted the appropriate authority at the British Museum with the drawings and he was told they were authentic Viking designs and belonged to the tenth century. They found other people who had also seen Viking ships and fighting men and ghostly monks on the White Sands. It is a matter of historical fact that in the year 986 a party of marauding Danes descended on the island at the place now known as the White Sands and there slew the abbot and fifteen of his brethren before plundering the abbey buildings and setting them on fire. Sir Walter Scott knew all about the supernatural aspects of Iona and was well aware of these re-enactments, sometimes in bright daylight. Of another haunted place in Scotland he said, after spending a night there, he felt too far from the living and too near the dead!

I knew Lucy Bruce when she had a home on Iona and she told me she had seen ghostly monks in the island several times, Columban monks with brown robes and coarse ropes round their waists; they never spoke or made any sound and seemed to be oblivious to her presence. She and some of her friends and lots of the helpers at the community heard the chanting of invisible monks and sometimes saw twinkling blue lights out at sea. Haunting and haunted Iona has ghosts and ghostly activity in profusion.

Lindisfarne, Northumberlandshire

Widely known as the Holy Island, this isolated place can be reached by causeway only at low tide twice a day. It is a unique place and famous as an important centre of early English Christianity, the religious connection being the basis of most of the many mysteries relating to the island, just off the north-east coast between Bamburgh and Berwick-on-Tweed.

St Aidan founded a monastery here in 635 AD; St Cuthbert became its bishop until he died in 684 AD. Long threatened and eventually sacked by the Vikings in 875 AD – an event that was predicted, it is said, by fiery serpents and unprecedented storms. The monks fled, taking with them the preserved body of St Cuthbert, eventually to Durham. There are still legends here of bread falling from the skies and wine appearing in a bottomless cup but of the silent, harmless ghostly monks of Lindisfarne there is much more and better evidence.

The ghost of St Cuthbert is still said to haunt this romantic and lonely place, still producing 'St Cuthbert's Beads'. These discs, from the 'stem' of an animal known as acrinoid or sea lily, are considered by those who find them to be good omens that augur well for the future. They are sold in local shops but these do not have the power of ones that are found, it has been said.

The castle, built about 1550 and once the home of Sir Edwin Lutyens, comprising stones from the original vanished priory, was a royal garrison before being besieged and taken by Parliamentary forces in 1644 immediately before the Battle of Marston Moor, which may account for the ghost of a Cromwellian soldier that actively haunts the castle.

The late Revd A. W. Jackson talked to me at length about the ghost monks of Lindisfarne whom he identified as St Cuthbert and the Brotherhood of the North. He became interested in the case when one of his choir boys revealed that he often saw 'a tall man carrying parchment' who disappeared into a solid wall. The man wore a dark brown habit tied with a rope round his middle; he had long hair cut away at the back leaving part of the head bare in the shape of a half-moon. For a long time this half-moon tonsure puzzled the Revd Jackson until he learned that this was in fact a characteristic tonsure of Celtic Monasteries, superseded by the circular tonsure in the seventh century.

The choir boy, guided by his vicar, became something of a spontaneous medium and received thousands of apparent communications from St Cuthbert and the whole story was published, with a Foreword by the then Vice-Provost of Southwark Cathedral, the Revd John Pearce-Higgins in

1968. The ghost of St Cuthbert has been seen by many other people, at Lindisfarne, and similarly described; indeed ghost monks have been reported here for many years. Elliott O'Donnell (1872–1965) stated categorically in one of his many books that the island was haunted by the ghost of St Cuthbert, and Sir Walter Scott (1771–1832) refers to the haunting in one of his poems.

The ghost monks are most frequently seen in the area of the causeway linking the island with the mainland. They are thought to be some of the monks cut down while fleeing from the Viking invaders in a particularly dreadful raid in 793 AD when the Danes ran their dragon ships onto the curving shore of golden sand and pillaged, sacked and destroyed the monastery and just about everyone in it. The ghost monks are usually described as 'grey-clad' figures and in recent years reliable reports have dated from 1962 (by two visitors from Worthing), 1999 (by a visiting university professor) and in 2011 (by a member of the Ghost Club).

Perhaps it is relevant that Lindisfarne is an old and sacred place unsullied by civilization.

The Mumbles, near Swansea

Amid as fine coastal scenery as you could find anywhere. Mumbles Head is a special place. One Swansea man certainly thought so. He habitably travelled to Mumbles most mornings and most mornings were routine and uneventful although he always felt a lift when he entered the seaside town but this morning, although the road ahead was clear, something told him to slow down although he was well within the speed limit. As he did so, he had the strange feeling, something he had never experienced before, that there was someone sitting on the back seat of his car. He slowed right down and was very pleased that he had done so because the next moment he came upon the scene of an accident that had just happened.

A few months later he suddenly had the same feeling, again at The Mumbles, that someone was sitting in the back seat of his car, although it was certainly deserted. Again he had the sudden inclination to slow right down, which he did, and a moment later a child appeared from nowhere and ran in front of his car. He was easily able to stop and the child was unharmed but if he had been travelling any faster, it could have been a very different story.

At Mumbles, on the Newton Road, stand the well-preserved remains of Oystermouth Castle that dates from the thirteenth century. These are haunted by the ghost of a young woman in a torn white dress who seems to be crying and displaying weals that suggest a flogging, perhaps to death. She wanders sadly about the castle walls and has been reported by numerous concerned visitors. Ominously, a medieval whipping post may be seen today in the castle dungeons. Near the castle there is an eerie cemetery haunted by a fleeting figure in black.

Visiting Mumbles on a beautiful day, as I have done, is a blissful experience. The promenade, the views, the colourful ironwork pier, the castle hiding in the trees and the lighthouse topping the headland, all help to make a perfect day even more perfect. Once a fashionable Victorian seaside resort, it has never forgotten its roots as a small fishing village. And the ghosts and ghostly activity here are quiet but convincing at this gateway to the glorious Gower peninsula, an area of unspoilt natural beauty.

The Mumbles has always been considered different, a

place apart; and an old snatch of poetry neatly pin-points the place:

> Mumbles is a funny place
> A church without a steeple
> Houses made of old shops wrecked
> And most peculiar people.

Haunted Mumbles Pier opened in 1898 and stretches nearly a quarter of a mile out into blue-watered Mumbles Bay. Once upon a time, White Funnel paddle steamers from Bristol would dock at the pier, unloading tourists who would then continue on their way into Wales via the Swansea and Mumbles Railway, one of the world's first passenger railways, remains of which can still be seen.

One of the ghosts at Mumbles is that of a young woman wearing a dress and a scarf covering her face. She has been seen many times on the road leading towards the pier and on the pier itself and she disappears when anyone gets close to her. Another phantom figure here is the rather alarming figure of an old seafaring man, wearing a coarse navy jersey, coarse trousers and sea boots, who looms up suddenly in the grassy area overlooking the pier near Mumbles Head and then, just as suddenly, disappears. Yet another ghost at Mumbles is a blacksmith who used to work his forge in a building that is now a house in Titchbourne Street; this ghost appears to date from some two hundred years ago.

More recently, the much altered house was owned and occupied by a hospital chaplain and he and his family were all aware of the ghost who had been seen frequently by the previous occupants and by people in neighbouring houses. Interference with material objects was one of the chief manifestations, including the repeated opening of windows, even in wintertime, almost as though the ghost was still experiencing the red-hot heat of the forge that had once burned there.

Yet another Mumbles ghost is that of a Victorian cockle-seller, wearing the patterned clothes those women wore travelling around the country. They were often to be seen at Mumbles in its heyday, where they also sold pins and needles and the like.

There have been many reports from visitors who have said they have been intrigued to see a large woman in old-fashioned clothes carrying two baskets, one containing cockles and the other odds and ends. At first she would hold out a basket for the contents to be examined but when the visitor went forward to see what was in the basket, the figure was no longer there. A visitor was sitting on a seat facing the sea when suddenly such a woman passed her, exhibiting her wares. The visitor thought she would give the old woman something and she searched her bag for a coin or two. When she found something and leaned forward to pass on the money, the figure, who had stopped in front of her and had waited while she searched her purse, was no longer there. She had completely disappeared. She asked another person sitting on the seat where the woman selling things had gone and the woman looked puzzled and said she had seen no one. I must say that on one occasion at Mumbles I thought I briefly glimpsed such a woman with baskets selling goods but she disappeared before I could really establish her presence. A similar figure used to haunt the Victoria Gardens in Neath, the other side of Swansea, I am told.

Purbeck Hills, Dorset

These haunted hills in southern England have magnificent views of the sea on one hand and the deep and enchanting Frome valley on the other.

Their crown is gaunt Corfe Castle and they sweep down to what is now part of the wonderful Jurassic Coast which well repays exploration by land and sea. The shelly limestone marble that is mined from these hills can be found in many of the cathedrals of England. Here between Flowers Barrow and Grange Hill the steady tramp of a long-dead Roman army has been heard many times and those who do not hear it 'uncomfortably feel an inexplicable presence' and on those nights 'no rabbits and no dog can be induced to go near'. In 1970 an elderly lady saw and heard the Roman soldiers, as did a boy a few years later.

These gentle hills where once dinosaurs roamed overlook haunted Worbarrow Bay and haunted Lulworth Cove.

Lulworth Cove is a magical place. It is almost as though a giant has taken a bite out of the rocky coastline and the uniquely circular sea-filled bay has an exceptional atmosphere.

Once there were real smugglers here, and now their ghosts haunt the narrow beaches; the ghost of a girl who committed suicide walks; a ghost dog, black and silent, swiftly appears and disappears; the cries of the drowning sometimes rent the peaceful ambience of the place; and the unmistakable phantom form of Napoleon himself has been seen on the beach here. There has long been a tradition that he visited the Dorset coast looking for the perfect landing place and that he was seen walking up and down the beach here, studying his maps and looking out to sea. Now his ghost, recognized by his distinctive hat and squat figure, strolls along, deep in thought, and then he turns suddenly and quickly vanishes.

The famous chronicler of Dorset, Thomas Hardy, who was born, lived and died in the county, thought he had invented the idea that Napoleon had visited Ludworth Cove, when he used it in one of his short stories. But perhaps it was a psychic memory for he soon discovered from friends that there was a very long-standing tradition to this effect and furthermore the ghost of the brilliant but vain little man had repeatedly been seen at the romantic cove. One witness described to me her sighting of the singular ghost, saying he seemed to be very agitated and was continually darting looks here, there and everywhere; and he was slimmer than she had thought. The results of my researches showed these attributes to be typical of the man.

One student of English folklore, a university graduate in philosophy, told me that he had collected reports of Napoleon on the beach at Lulworth that suggested he had with him a companion, but Lulworth evidently did not impress him as a landing place and he was heard to mutter, 'impossibilité' several times before folding his maps and returning to his boat. There have been witnesses who claim they have seen the ghost of Napoleon here from 1930 at irregular intervals up to 2009, to my knowledge.

I visited Lulworth Castle after it had been restored following the disastrous fire in 1929 when it was the magnificent home of the Weld family. After the fire there was much speculation about the fate of twelve maidservants who all completely disappeared. Whether they had perished in the flames or left the area in a body without telling anyone or whether they had met a sinister or tragic end has never been established. They were quite simply never heard or seen again.

At the time, a story circulated that all twelve girls had been seen walking along the cliff path to Durdle Door and had probably been washed into the sea and perished without anyone seeing their end or hearing their screams for help. Such a tragedy could explain a number of reports, including that of a former naval commander, claiming that sometimes the frightened figures of a group of distraught girls had been seen and their screams had been heard in the vicinity of Durdle Door very late at night.

The naval commander, who never experienced anything of the kind before or since, was in his cabin on board ship anchored off Lulworth and it was getting late when he heard what he described as 'a wild crescendo of screams' and he hurried up the companionway but could find nothing to account for the sounds. Then he heard them again and they seemed to come from the black space away from the ship, loud one minute and faint the next. Then all sound ceased 'as abruptly as if the dark waters had quenched it'. Then, by the light of the moon as it shone between clouds, he thought he could see a number of girls on the coast. He watched for a moment; then they suddenly disappeared. When he reported the incident and talked to people about it he learned that others had heard similar screams and seen the forms of agitated girls in the vicinity of Durdle Door.

Sandwood Bay, Sutherland

In the extreme north-west of Scotland, a few miles south of the lighthouse at Cape Wrath, Sandwood Bay is a particularly remote and beautiful place, lonely, quiet and haunted. Here one can walk for a whole day among the rocky hills and great lumps of stone slowly disintegrating over the years, without meeting another living soul, although one may well meet a ghost.

Antony Hippisley Coxe described the place as 'a very haunted spot'; locals call it the 'Land of the Mermaids'; John Fraser of the SPR refers to it as 'the ultimate in ghost hunts'; and it assuredly deserves a place in any volume on haunted Britain.

The place is interesting for several reasons. Its very remoteness makes it an unlikely candidate for contrived deception although the same remoteness hinders ease of verification. At all events, the evidence for varied paranormal activity over a period of years at Sandwood Bay is impressive and several responsible investigations have proved 'interesting', if not entirely supportive scientifically.

Looking at the evidence in some sort of chronological order it is possible that some ghosts here go back more than three hundred years when a Polish ship was wrecked in the bay with the survivors settling themselves locally in a tiny place called Polin, the place of the Poles. Of those who drowned, one at least has been seen wandering about the area, a stranger in a strange land and dressed in a strange sailor's outfit.

Jumping forward to the early 1940s, a local shepherd, Sandy Gunn, who died in 1944, accompanied by George McKay and William MacLeod saw the figure of a bearded man walk behind some rocks in the bay and disappear. Gunn seems to have been a great story-teller with many legends at his fingertips but he was also highly intelligent and a much respected member of the community who was known to be a man of his word. However he told the author Robertson Macdonald that in January 1900 he was checking his sheep when he saw a mermaid, very beautiful but marooned on a rock. He and his dog turned and fled but forty years later he still stuck to his story saying, 'You may scoff as much as you choose and attribute my story to whatever you will but I know what I saw and it was a mermaid.' In passing perhaps it is worth recalling that two girls in the 1930s also claimed to see a mermaid in Sandwood Bay, slipping into the sea from a rock; and a woman, fishing from a boat in 1939, also claimed to see a mermaid here and a local man admitted that a mermaid had sometimes been reported thereabouts. Doubtless what was taken for a mermaid was in fact a seal or something of the sort, perhaps bedecked with seaweed.

But the ghostly sailor is another matter. Sandy Gunn and his two friends saw the figure in bright moonlight and interestingly both McKay and MacLeod thought they recognized him as a Polish neighbour. When the three man approached the figure they knew they were mistaken; there was something strange and even uncanny about the large and bewhiskered man that seemed to be unreal. As they watched, he turned, walked away and disappeared behind some rocks. Although there was nowhere he could have gone without them seeing him, when they reached the rocks he had completely disappeared.

In the 1940s, a crofter and his son were gathering driftwood in the bay when they suddenly found themselves confronted by a large and bearded man who was standing quite close to them. Their pony, normally a very quiet and docile animal, became restive and as they sought to calm the animal, the figure they had both seen so close beside them, disappeared as mysteriously as he had appeared. Afterwards both father and son remembered brass buttons on the man's tunic, his worn sea-boots, faded sailor's cap and the dark, weather-beaten clothing that he wore.

Also in the 1940s there are records of a farmer, searching for some of his livestock, seeing the figure of a tall man among some nearby rocks. Thinking it must be a local man, he called out a greeting and went towards the figure but as he drew nearer he saw it was someone he had never seen before. When he was within a few steps of the figure, it completely disappeared.

Early one afternoon in 1949, a fishing party from Kinlochbervie rounded one of the big sand dunes that dot the area of Sandwood Bay and they all clearly saw a figure wearing a sailor's cap and seafaring clothes striding along the crest of a sandy knoll not far away, They caught a glimpse of brass buttons glinting in the sun as the figure disappeared behind a hillock. One of the party, an attendant to the sportsmen, had with him his stalking-glass and he trained it on the figure, thinking he might be a poacher and he set off to track the man down only to return to say there was no sign of the man they had all seen, anywhere in the bay, nor were there any footprints or anything to suggest anyone had been where they had all seen the figure.

In 1953, on a bright summer day, a party of picnickers from Edinburgh were enjoying the peace and beauty of Sandwood Bay when they saw a tall, bearded sailor apparently gazing at them from the crest of a nearby hillock. They all saw the figure and looked back at him for some minutes before he appeared to take a step back – and completely disappeared. Puzzled they went to the spot but could find no trace of anyone having been there, not even footprints where they had seen him standing.

A walk of about two hours from the parking site and twice as long from the nearest inhabited dwelling brings you to idyllic Sandwood Bay and the little that is left of the once substantial cottage that stood there and was the scene of much reported psychic activity.

There are stories of an old shepherd seeking shelter in the cottage and having retired to a room upstairs, waking during the night to hear footsteps padding about downstairs inside the cottage. He got up and heard the sounds move from one room to another and back again, time after time. At length, having lit a candle, he quietly went downstairs again and searched every inch of the cottage. He found nothing whatever to account for the sounds he had heard and he returned to bed and spent the rest of the night undisturbed but for the rest of his life nothing could convince him that the cottage was not haunted. 'You spend a night there,' he used to say, 'and you will know its haunted.'

There is also a long-standing story about a wealthy Australian who visited Sandwood Bay by chance and fell under its spell to such an extent that he visited every year and each time he was more loath to leave. At length, just after one of his annual visits to the area, he died in Australia and it has been suggested that his spirit or some vital part of him returned to Sandwood Bay and is still to be encountered in the place he loved so much.

Later, a woman on a visit from Edinburgh took back with her as a reminder of the visit and the wonderful ambience of the cottage, a small portion of the then existing wooden staircase. Back at home she experienced a wealth of strange and inexplicable happenings: loud knocks, crockery breaking, the strong smell of alcohol, the repeated rattling of the purloined piece of staircase and the appearance of a phantom bearded sailor.

Some years later still, an old fisherman was caught in a heavy storm and decided to spend the night in the deserted cottage. He made himself and his dog as comfortable as possible in the fast disintegrating building. Around midnight he was awakened by his dog and he heard the footsteps of someone approaching the cottage. Then there was a knock on the remaining window and he saw, in the bright moonlight of the clear night that followed the rain, the unmistakable figure of a bearded man apparently seeking entry to the cottage. After a moment the figure drew back revealing that he was wearing a short black coat with brass buttons, like a sailor, and wearing a peaked cap. On opening the door, the fisherman could see no sign of a sailor or anyone else and when he and his dog went all round the cottage they found no trace or sign of anyone having been there.

In September 1970 two walkers from Surrey made their way from Durness to the Cape Wrath lighthouse and then towards Kinlochbervie but with the sun setting as they reached Sandwood Bay they decided to spend the night in the deserted cottage and resume their walk the following day. First thing next morning they fled the cottage and regaled the first person they met, the local postmaster, with details of the ghastly night they had spent in the haunted cottage. In the middle of the night they had been awakened by fearful noises from downstairs. There were crashing noises and sounds of things being broken. In fact it sounded to them as though the whole place was being smashed up and the cottage itself seemed to vibrate as it might in a violent storm but the night was fine and dry. After a while the rocking ceased and the crashing sounds died down to be replaced by the sounds of a horse stamping and pawing the ground and snorting, but these noises seemed to come from above them, where there was nothing but the empty air of Sandwood Bay. After the noises ceased, the disturbed couple sat huddled together dreading further disturbances and, although they heard nothing more, as soon as dawn broke they fled from the haunted cottage that does not like to be visited.

In April 1988, John Fraser, a respected and experienced psychical researcher, visited Sandwood Bay and spent a night in the cottage. He told me afterwards, 'As night falls it gives the impression of being one of the most lonely and desolate places you can imagine.' The cottage by this time was a two-roomed shell, the upper storey long gone, and he thoroughly checked the place out. It was getting dark so he tried to light a fire but somehow he couldn't manage to do so. He then set about positioning his equipment but he discovered the cameras containing the infra-red film had been damaged beyond repair and the new batteries he had brought refused to function in the tape-recorder and, with no torch, he was completely in the dark.

The atmosphere and circumstances appeared to be ideal for 'something' to happen but nothing of consequence in fact took place during the whole night and next morning he quickly packed up his things and made his way back to civilization, making several calls on local people to see whether he could find anything more about the various stories associated with the cottage.

He did learn that an old Glaswegian named James MacRory Smith fitted admirably the description of the ghostly sailor, down to the bushy beard and peaked sailor-type cap. However, as far as could be established, he never occupied the cottage at Sandwood Bay or a bothy not far away which was in better condition. He certainly used to frequent the area for some twenty years as a summer resident.

John Fraser found a neighbour of the witness Sandy Gunn and learned that he was regarded far and wide as an honest man who never told a lie and he certainly claimed to have seen a mermaid. He could find no confirmatory evidence concerning the Australian but did find that a book by Robertson McDonald, long out of print, entitled *Scottish Highland Folklore* contained much information about the sailor ghost and later writers and students of the subject could well have used this book as a source of information.

The visit by John Fraser was by no means entirely negative. He had been able to find out contemporary evidence from people no longer alive and, in spite of most of his equipment not being in working order, he did take a number of photographs and on one of them there appears to be the outline of a bearded man.

In August 1996 Trevor Kenward led a party of four to Sandwood Bay on an investigative visit. They found the cottage in an advanced stage of deterioration with no roof, no floor and walls that were falling down. They cleaned and tidied the place as well as they could; took a number of photographs (experiencing some difficulties with the functioning of the equipment), took measurements of the whole cottage, took a lot of video film – one frame showing what looks like a face and another some strange lights – and they recorded some 'strange' sounds. They had no result from the placing of 'trigger' objects (including brass buttons) although one appeared to have moved sideways about one inch. They encountered a fog of most unpleasant Scottish midges. They found the bay much more frequented than they had expected and were told that it is not unusual for a hundred people to be wandering about Sandwood Bay on a sunny August afternoon.

To sum up, it would seem that there have been several good sightings of the same alleged ghost over many years; the ghost is usually but not always nocturnal and appears to be solid and real in appearance. Attempts at conversation have come to nothing. His appearance is that of a bearded sailor from a bygone age; dressed in peaked cap, boots, dark clothing and with gleaming brass buttons on his jacket. Who he might have been is unknown. He has an almost proprietorial air about him, according to most witnesses, and he always disappears suddenly, unexpectedly and in inexplicable circumstances, leaving so traces behind him.

Anyone now seeking shelter in the remains of the cottage at Sandwood Bay would be likely to find what is left, if anything is left, falling about them. It has been suggested that the only reason for the appearance of ghostly forms here is not malevolent but merely a wish on someone's part to be where they most want to be. It is likely that with the total disappearance of the cottage the ghosts will disappear also.

Sennen Cove, Cornwall

The white sands of Sennen Cove, just north of Land's End, are haunted by a ghost long known as 'the Irish lady'. The sole survivor of an Irish ship which foundered in the bay during a storm, she managed to swim ashore and to haul herself to safety on a rock or so she thought but the sea was so rough and the storm so severe that it was impossible to rescue her. For days the storm raged and anxious people on the shore watched helplessly as she waved imploringly at them to save her. Eventually she died from exhaustion, hunger and thirst and the unrelenting waves took her back into the sea. Ever since, when stormy seas cause high waves at Sennen Cove, the ghostly form of 'the Irish lady' is often seen clinging desperately to a rock that is forever associated with her.

Sennen Cove is also probably unique in having the tradition of harbouring a guardian spirit. A hooper – so-called from the hooting or hooping sound it makes – was thought to have appeared out of the sea in a cloud and come to rest on the rocks called Cowloe from whence the hooper would be heard calling and it was found that whenever the strange noise was heard, a storm followed so the fisher folk of the area always made sure they were ready and never set to sea when the hooper was in the cove.

This area off Land's End has long been reputedly haunted by phantom bells. Stanley Baron was just one witness who told me of the eerie sound he heard in that beautiful part of the world. Stanley was staying with friends locally and one night, just after eleven o'clock, having completed an article for a national daily to which he regularly contributed, he retired to bed but not to sleep. He lay awake for what seemed like hours listening to the distant sea, a stone's throw from his window and then, at about one o'clock, he noticed that in addition to the usual regular sounds of the sea, there was also a rhythmic clanging of bells. At first he thought it was his imagination – bells at one o'clock in the morning! – but as the sounds continued he told himself there was no doubt about it. He could hear the faint but distinct sound of bell-ringing. It continued for a while and then ceased. Some three hours later he was awakened by the sound of long, low pealing of what sounded like muffled bells. Again he was adamant that he did actually hear the bells. Very gradually the chiming diminished and faded and again the calming sound of the sea lulled him back to sleep.

At breakfast, Stanley asked his hosts whether they had been awakened during the night by the sound of bells. They said they had slept soundly that night and had not been disturbed but they had heard the bells on other occasions; the Lost Bells, he was told. Then Stanley recalled the story of the Lost Bells of Lyonesse. According to Cornish tradition the land of Lyonesse was overcome by two mighty surges of the ocean, one in 1014 and the other in 1094.

The Lost Land of Lyonesse – pure legend or historical possibility? So asks my friend Michael Williams in one of his many books devoted to his and my beloved Cornwall, could Lyonesse have once joined Cornwall to the Isles of Scilly, forty miles away. The evidence is conflicting; geologists have searched in vain for irrefutable evidence but personal experiences tell of masses of trees sometimes being seen beneath the clear waters and white sand extending far out to sea; even of tree stumps, pieces of old stone columns, glass windows and various utensils that may have come from the Lost Land. Fishermen, years ago, used to say they saw the roofs of churches and houses beneath the calm waters on clear days.

Then there is the evidence of Edith Oliver, one-time mayor of Wilton near Salisbury, who wrote the preface to an edition of the enigmatic volume called *An Adventure*, written by two academic ladies about a visit to Versailles, France, where they apparently stepped back in time. Edith Oliver, who while she found the whole story 'extremely convincing' still wondered whether a solution to the mystery of Versailles might be found in the theories of relativity and of serialism which alter our conception of time and space. A plausible possibility certainly but one that remains elusive and unprovable. It was this same sceptical, practical and level-headed Edith Oliver who, making her first visit to Land's End on a bright and sunny day, stood at the very edge of the cliffs, looking out towards the vastness of the sea, saw to her considerable astonishment but with a clarity she never forgot, what appeared to be a town of some importance, seemingly miles out to sea, and she gazed at a jumble of towers, domes, spires and battlements. At first she thought she must be seeing the Scilly Isles, but surely she would not be able to see such detail nearly forty miles distant.

As she looked at the distant domes and towers she saw a coastguard approaching from Land's End and she turned and asked him the name of the town she could see, to which

he replied. 'There is no town out there; only the sea ...'
When she looked back there was no sign of the town she
had been looking at for some moments. Making enquiries,
Edith Oliver discovered that she was not the only person to
see from the precipitious coast at Land's End what appeared
to be the roofs of a city, and everyone she spoke to who had
seen anything 'out there' believed that what they saw was
part of lost Lyonesse.

A year or two after Edith Oliver's experience, Miss
MacPherson, accompanied by a friend, was driving towards
Land's End one wet and blustery evening when she saw
towers and spires and domes far out to sea. As she peered at
the strange sight her friend suddenly asked, 'Do you see
anything out there?' 'Indeed I do.' Miss MacPherson
replied. 'I see a city. I've been told that from here there have
been people who have caught a glimpse of Lyonesse but
I've never seen it before ...' Some years later, Miss
MacPherson saw the visionary city again. This time she was
accompanied by her sister, who saw nothing.

Other Haunted Seascapes

Ghostly forms have been seen on Llanddwyn Island,
Anglesey, near an ancient well used for fortune-telling at
Flynnon Dwynwen. The ruined church there was founded
by St Dwynwen, the Welsh equivalent of St Valentine. He
died in 497 AD and was laid out on a cleft rock facing west
towards sunsets over the Irish sea. Visitors and local people
frequently report ghost monks on Llanddwyn Beach.

The Lleyn Peninsula also has ghostly monk-like figures

walking along the shore where King Arthur's Merlin may
be buried.

The beach at Whitsand Bay, Crafthole, Cornwall, was once
haunted by smugglers – a fact celebrated by an inn named
after one well-known freetrader – and now haunted by a
smuggler who killed a revenue man. The ghost has been
seen and heard in recent years and many visitors still experience the feeling of a desperate struggle here.

The Goodwin Sands off Deal in Kent, a range of
exceedingly dangerous sandbanks and the graveyard of
many vessels, is reputedly haunted by several ghost ships,
the best-known being the *Lady Lovibund*. I met George
Carter who wrote about himself and a fellow watchman on
the North Goodwin Lightship both seeing phantom ships on
the sands.

Part 12

HAUNTED WATERS

A great many ponds and pools and lakes, rivers and running water, have about them an air of mystery and in and around them folklore has always imported monsters and nymphs and water spirits but it is indisputable that there are many areas of water that are haunted. This part on Haunted Waters could have been many times longer for there may well be something about water that is conducive to paranormal activity.

I recall discussing this very subject at some length with Guy Lambert, SPR President 1955–58, and he was utterly convinced that his 'geophysical theory' established that water played a part in all hauntings. The idea dominated Lambert's thoughts during his latter years and he would go to enormous trouble, when a haunting was reported to him, to discover ancient sewers, culverts, tidal water, underground streams and springs, any water in fact that could, he believed, be responsible for strange noises, footsteps, movement of objects and even 'white figures' that were probably no more than drifting mist.

His idea that hauntings were 'place-centred' rather than 'person-centred' was interesting; and it has to be said that he was usually successful in finding water of some kind associated with many haunted stately homes. I remember agreeing that his theory may well serve to explain some hauntings but I, in common with other researchers, could not accept that it was the answer to all ghosts and hauntings. In this part I have sought to explore just a few Haunted Waters that may or may not be ascribed to the geophysical theory.

Berwick-upon-Tweed, Northumberland

The River Tweed runs for nearly a hundred miles and is one of the best salmon rivers in Scotland. The waters of the 'Tweed's fair river broad and deep' rise in the Tweedsmuir Hills. It flows through Selkirk and Roxburgh and forms the boundary between England and Scotland for a time before entering the North Sea at Berwick-upon-Tweed.

These waters that have flowed lazily through Millfield Plain and within sight of Flodden's fateful field, sometimes turn red, if reports are to be believed. This is the result of the awful deaths during the Great Siege of 1296 when the good folk of Berwick were horribly butchered in such numbers and with such ferocity that the streets ran with blood which found its way into the river, giving the peaceful waters a red tinge. Such a spectacle elsewhere has invariably turned out to be the result of natural mineral, organic or structural compounds but such explanations would not seem feasible in this instance. There are many reported examples of indelible bloodstains in haunted houses so perhaps the occasional blood-red river should not be dismissed out of hand.

Certainly the tale of the Tweed having become a 'river of blood' has been circulating for centuries. There were the bloody days before Edward I conquered Berwick in 1302 but there were other equally bloody battles both before and after that one. Witness the series of ramparts that can still be traced surrounding the town, the bell tower (still preserved) from which alarms were given when border raiders were observed and the fact that here were founded the oldest barracks in England, in 1719. Slight remains of the castle can be found but there are no traces of the churches, the monasteries and other principal buildings of the ancient town which perhaps hints at the violence and destruction this place once suffered.

Indeed there is evidence that well within living memory the phenomenon of the waters of the River Tweed turning blood red has been experienced. One visitor in the 1960s, strolling along the riverbank, noticed the quiet waters seemed to be changing to a pinky-red colour rather than the grey-blue shade she had been looking at and soon she was describing the waters as 'glimmering red'. Puzzled by what she had seen, she mentioned the experience to the local vicar who knew all about the legend of Berwick's river of blood and told her what he knew about it.

Even later, in the 1970s, a story is related of a young lad fishing for tiddlers and thinking he had caught something big when his line tightened. He put his hand into the water to see what it was and when he retrieved it, his hand and arm had traces of red upon them. He scooped some water into a jam jar he had with him and found the water therein to be cloudy and reddish. Throwing the water back into the river he walked on some distance downstream and tried again when he found the water clear and normal. One is reminded of many ghosts and ghostly happenings that seem to run down over time, almost like a battery, and perhaps the red river of Berwick is at last running out!

Yet, as recently as 2010 a correspondent informed me that he took a photograph of his wife with the gentle grey-blue Tweed in the foreground but when the photograph was developed the River Tweed had changed to an angry red.

Betws-y-Coed, North Wales

Everyone who visits Wales has to visit Betws-y-Coed and I am no exception. Whenever I visit that beautiful land of myth, legend and ghosts I try to renew acquaintance with one of the most famous – and haunted – spots in Wales. I love its many attractions, among them the Swallow Falls, the Conwy Falls and the Fairy Glen.

Above Betws-y-Coed, when the Gwyde Forest was newly planted, workmen asserted they had encountered dozens of snakes: hoop snakes that moved like bicycle wheels and pursued them before suddenly and completely vanishing. Other people too have reported these strange serpents in the Parc Woods, possibly also the deadly desert sidewinder, probably dumped by a collector, although many people preferred to blame the notorious Sir John Wynne whose spirit was reputed to be imprisoned below the Swallow Falls, still unquiet and unpunished for his many 'foul deeds'. Sir John was a member of Parliament for the county of Caenarton in 1596 and one of the Council of the Marches of Wales but he was notorious for his violent and unrelenting oppression of the 'common' people and by way of vengence his ghost is doomed to linger for ever in the depths of the pool below the Falls but that his evil form ventures onto the road nearby and in the vicinity of these spectacular falls seems indisputable from numerous reports of the indistinct form of a man in sixteenth-century costume lurking among the shadows thereabouts. In this land of waterfalls the Swallow Falls are truly majestic and there is always the possibility of seeing or experiencing something that is not of this world ...

Brimington, Derbyshire

Here, just a couple of miles north-east of Chesterfield, the building of the famous Chesterfield Canal began in 1771 and eventually consisted of nearly fifty miles of waterway with more than sixty locks, overcoming many difficulties including diverting its course because it ran too close to the village of Brimington.

An ancient plague-pit was filled in and used, the site marked by a mound. No one knows for sure how many bodies lie under the mound, victims of the contagious malady that decimated whole communities, but such burial places came to be regarded as holy ground and not to be disturbed. Even today interference of these burial places is frowned upon. So the Chesterfield Canal circumnavigated the mound which, in common with others in this part of the country, has sometimes been the centre of reported strange experiences. In this instance, the close proximity of water, the Chesterfield Canal itself, may provide the requisite conditions for paranormal activity.

In 1993, a local resident, Arthur Skelhorn, prepared to walk his dog along the bank of the canal, as he was in the habit of doing twice a day. It was a cool evening and dusk was falling as he followed his usual route. He noticed a mist hanging over the water and feeling somewhat unexpectedly chilly he hurried his dog along Cow Lane and towards the canal bank, past the mound marking the communal grave.

Suddenly he saw a man standing a short distance ahead of him. A tall man, well over six feet, Skelhorn told himself, and wearing a long dark coat which practically reached the ground. Almost immediately the dog walker felt apprehensive. He had never seen the man before, that he was certain of, and his mode of dress was unusual for the area. When he was about twenty feet from the figure which was facing him, he became more wary. He told himself the man probably required directions to somewhere and he began to slow down as he reached the still and silent figure.

At the same time, he noticed that his dog, a friendly creature that would often run towards strangers, was beginning to hold back and kept close to his side, even touching his leg. But, just before Skelhorn reached the figure, it disappeared.

Skelhorn walked gingerly forward, past the outcrop of land and round the corner expecting to see the man in one direction or the other. There was no sign of anybody anywhere on the embankment. Now Skelhorn was really puzzled. There had been no time for anyone to have disappeared from sight in the few moments that had passed since seeing the figure and reaching the canal. Where on earth could the man have gone?

Back home he told his wife of the strange encounter and said he would find a different route to take the dog in future, after dark. He said he would not go that way again if he could help it. Looking back he felt he had always disliked that particular spot; it felt eerie, even in daylight.

The following year, 1994, Mr Skelhorn heard of another Brimington resident who had seen a very similar figure in the 1970s, an experience he had never forgotten.

As a boy he had been walking towards the canal with a friend one evening when a tall man in a long dark coat and a top hat stepped out of the shadows ahead of them. The boys turned and ran home and told their mothers what had frightened them. Mr Skelhorn talked with one of the mothers who well recalled the distressed condition they were in that evening, the description they gave of the man they had seen, and what they had said. It had all stuck in her mind although twenty years had passed.

The banks of the Chesterfield Canal do seem to be haunted at this spot and there have been several more sightings of the mystery man who disappears, usually at dusk or later and always near the canal. One wonders whether there has been a suicide or accident or sudden death here in the past when perhaps a man lost his life.

One witness said the figure turned towards the canal and seemed to be on the very edge before it disappeared. She thought for a moment that he had gone into the canal although she had heard no splash. In fact, looking back, she realized she had heard no sound at all from the mysterious tall man. Can the combination of a burial pit and slow-moving canal water have any bearing on what has been experienced here, one wonders, and on the expectant and eerie atmosphere of the place?

Edgbaston, Birmingham

The railway line from Barnt Green to Birmingham ran alongside a well-kept stretch of the Worcester to Birmingham canal at Edgbaston, often a place of colourful barges and busy joggers and cyclists.

Just a few miles south, the canal runs through the old and haunted Wasthill Tunnel. One of the longest canal tunnels in England, it was completed in 1797. It is not difficult to find people who have had weird and wonderful experiences inside the tunnel, some very recent, some going back years.

One in the latter category concerns a canal boat owner whose daughter has recalled that her father, working with horse-drawn boats, often related the experience of his friends and himself in the tunnel which has long had the doubtful honour of being haunted by a White or Grey Lady; a similar story being associated with the Tardebigge Tunnel about ten miles to the south.

At both tunnels (where men's lives have been lost) the ghost is indistinct but female. A lady dressed in white or light grey standing near the tunnel entrance has been seen by canal users and the public alike and it is thought that she is waiting for or looking for her husband, drowned in an accident inside the tunnel. She appears to be distraught, wringing her hands and looking up the tunnel and all around her as if pleading for help in finding her husband. Whenever she is approached she gives no indication of being aware of the presence of human beings and she makes no sound but when anyone gets within a few yards of the figure it simply vanishes. An interesting experiment was tried by two young investigators who had learned of the phantom lady and they had planned what to do if ever they saw her.

One day they were lucky. It was late in the afternoon one spring day and they both spotted the figure at the same time and immediately they set their plan in motion. One remained where he was, watching, while the other slowly approached the figure. He said afterwards that the Woman in White seemed to be very distressed and trying to obtain help from anyone but no sound accompanied the apparitional form. He began to feel somewhat apprehensive and colder as he drew nearer, but glancing back he saw his friend still standing watching and indicating that he should proceed, Accordingly, he approached to within two or three yards of the figure, when it suddenly vanished. He looked back to his friend who still waved him on and he proceeded forward, feeling colder by the second as he moved towards the tunnel entrance, and occupying the space where he had seen the ghostly White or Grey Lady.

He went right up to the tunnel entrance, or as far as he could, and then decided he had done all he could and he returned to his waiting friend who said the figure had not vanished from his viewpoint and was in fact still there. His companion looked back and sure enough the ghost had re-appeared where he had seen it originally. His friend told him that the ghost had not vanished at all; he had kept watching and had seen his ghost-hunting partner walk right through the ghost.

I thought this was a very sensible experiment and only wish there could have been a third party to corroborate the story, and photographic evidence from different positions would have been even more interesting but it is easy to be wise after the event. The two friends equipped themselves with cameras and with another friend who, it was agreed, would stand between the other two – but they never saw the ghost again.

A man called Andy related a personal experience at the Wasthill tunnel to Anne Bradford. Apparently, Andy has always been interested in canals and canal boats and even an unnerving experience when he was only fifteen years of age had not deterred him.

He was on a boat with his uncle travelling in convoy to a biannual meeting of a river and canal club. The boat behind them was controlled by a lady who, all the way along, had seemed to be having trouble with an overheating engine and Andy offered to take charge of steering the boat. She jumped at the chance and opted to travel with Andy's uncle on his boat, leaving Andy to deal with the lady's vessel on his own.

Quite familiar with the tunnel, Andy was not too worried as they approached the north entrance and then plunged into darkness since he knew there were vent shafts, about two-thirds of the way through. He suddenly thought he must be approaching another vent except this one was different. It wasn't as bright as he had expected and it seemed smaller than he recalled. He thought perhaps it had become weeded over but as he approached he began to feel distinctly uneasy, for the whiteness he had taken for a vent began to assume the shape of a person!

At this point he was lagging behind as he had to stop and clear the filter on the engine to stop it overheating. When he looked again the misty white shape was definitely that of a person, a woman he decided, dressed in something that hung loosely about her, the sort of thing he remembered seeing in old photographs that his uncle possessed, except that this dress or whatever it was, was more colourful and somehow grander. He was no more than a hundred feet away from the figure that was getting clearer by the moment, when suddenly, as he reached for the reverse lever to avoid any kind of collision, she suddenly faded away and he was left in the complete darkness of the tunnel. He found himself crying, either from fright or relief, and he excited the boat with rather more revs than one should use in a tunnel and he emerged into daylight, as his friends later described it, like a bat out of hell! He was as white as a sheet and badly shaken by the experience, so shaken in fact that he didn't feel able to steer the boat any more and he was helped to sit down for a while to recover. It must have been some experience to so affect a fifteen-year-old boy.

Talking to his uncle afterwards, Andy learned that his uncle tried to avoid the Wasthill canal tunnel and would never go through it on his own. He added that it was well-known that the tunnel was haunted by a Grey Lady ghost. The story was that she had been murdered and her body thrown down the canal tunnel shaft. At all events there were regular reports of her ghost being seen, mainly at night or dusk and usually when the witnesses were alone; 'single handers' managing a boat on their own being the most vulnerable. Andy, I am told, never travelled through that tunnel again and often went out of his way to avoid it. One glimpse of the Grey Lady of Wasthill canal tunnel was enough for him.

Gwithian, Cornwall

Nearby Hell's Mouth with its 275-foot-high cliffs has long been haunted by the sounds of a suicide's cries.

It may be a black-hearted rogue of a man who for some long-forgotten reason, threw himself headlong into the angry waters at the foot of the towering cliffs. It may be a young girl distraught at finding her forthcoming husband in the arms of another, who closed her eyes and jumped at the moment her intended raced towards her with the news that she who was in his arms was his long-lost sister. Whose cries they are no one knows but there is good evidence that human cries have been heard in all kinds of weather and at all times of the year and in daylight and in darkness, echoing from the depths of this dark place.

This wild country was much used by smugglers and doubtless they encouraged the stories of unexplained sounds because the tunnels that run underground at the foot of the cliffs of Hell's Mouth were very useful for hiding smuggled or stolen goods.

There is an old story that one freetrader (whose descendants still live in Cornwall) resided nearby and he and a companion prospered from a nefarious life until his friend was suddenly arrested and taken under escort to Launceston to be hanged. But news travelled fast among the freetraders and neither the prisoner nor his escort reached Launceston, being waylaid and the escort quickly despatched. The two reunited smugglers decided that discretion was called for and they decided to leave the country for a while. One had a new wife but there was nothing for it but a hasty flight and, amid tears and lamentations, they left promising to return one day soon.

A year or two later, during an altercation in the family, the lonely wife was murdered and when, in due course, her husband returned home it was to learn of the tragic circumstances of his wife's death. Driven to distraction by the loss of the one person he had deeply loved, he made his way to the high cliffs by the sea, trying to decide what to do. As he stood with the sea roaring below him and the sound of seagulls in his ears, he became overwhelmed with grief and despair and threw himself into what is aptly called Hell's Mouth. Perhaps it is his anguished cries that haunt this place. At all events it is said that often, but especially when the wind is in the north-west and heavy seas are rolling in, all the way from Labrador, the cries are heard, as they have been time and time again; anguished cries of someone with a broken heart.

Some years ago, some students camped on the rocks below Hell's Mouth and said afterwards they would never again camp there. All night they had been disturbed by fierce shouts, snatches of old sea shanties and awful, heart-rending cries.

Hell's Mouth is an awe-inspiring place. Even on the brightest day the memory of tragic and distressing events that have without doubt taken place here, seems to permeate the whole area and most people are glad to get away from the mouth of hell itself.

Lamberhurst, Kent

Picturesque Scotney Castle sits romantically dreaming above its own reflection in the lily-decorated moat. The rust-coloured tower with its background of sky, trees and ruined mansion amid the steep wilderness of quarry and flowers is breathtakingly beautiful.

I recall being shown over the Old Castle, which is not open to the public, where the Jesuit Father Blount hid in 1598 and, when his hiding place was discovered, he escaped in sensational style by jumping into the moat and evading capture. It has long been thought to be his ghost that haunts these now tranquil waters, because for more than four hundred years there have been periodical reports of a man dripping with water emerging from the moat and making his way to the castle door.

It is known that many years ago a maid drowned in the moat and the coroners of Kent and Sussex were at odds as to who was responsible for an enquiry since Scotney was once in the county of Sussex, the boundary following the original course of the River Bewl which, having been diverted, now flows beside and immediately beyond the castle moat which was formed in the fourteenth century by diverting water from the neighbouring county.

Scotney could well have once been an island at the junction of River Bewl and the small stream that now feeds the moat. This is supported by the name: 'Scot' meaning a payment and 'Ey' meaning an island.

The suspected presence of Father Blount at Scotney gave rise to several searches, with Blount and his faithful servant concealing themselves in a hide adjoining the staircase. During the final search, that lasted ten days, Blount and

Bray were still hiding when they thought the end of Blount's girdle had been seen protruding from the hide. The searchers were intent on battering down the adjacent masonry to find Blount but it was nearly midnight and raining heavily so they decided to postpone further searching until the following morning. Recognizing the danger, Blount and Bray made a dash for it during the night. Bray bursting into the hall where the searchers were resting and giving a false alarm, saying thieves were stealing their horses from the stables. When everyone raced to the stables, Blount made good his escape, clambering over the wall and plunging into the cold waters of the moat. On the other side he was joined by Bray and the two escaped to live another day.

The Darell family were the owners of the castle for many years and one skirmish with revenue officials turned into a life and death struggle and the resident Darell is said to have caused the death of one of the officials. Seeking to hide what he had done he hastily threw the body into the darkness of the moat and it is now thought to be the ghost of the murdered man who has been seen on many occasions emerging from his watery grave, dripping with stagnant water, making its way to the great door of the castle where he repeatedly hammers with his fists, seeking retribution. This gruesome-looking ghost, I have been reliably informed, has been seen on numerous occasions but should the door of the castle be opened, all traces of the figure have disappeared and all is quiet and peaceful in the haunted water of the deeply silent and actively haunted moat at Scotney Castle.

Laugharne, Wales

This small coastal town, full of character and charm, is a place of pilgrimage for being the best-known home of poet and broadcaster Dylan Thomas (1914–53), who was born and brought up in Swansea.

I met the portly Welsh spinner of words when I was with Dents who published his works and several volumes devoted to the imaginative Welshman with a magical voice. Widely regarded as the most outstanding poet of his generation, the magic he worked with words – eventually, for he took hours and hours to get things how he wanted them – will surely be with us for always. The reverse spelling of the name he gave to his fictional town, Llareggub, was perhaps his life philosophy. Already extracts from his poetry comprise nearly a hundred entries in *Chambers Dictionary of Quotations*. Already too we use his words without realizing where they come from: 'And death shall have no dominion', 'As I was young and easy under the apple boughs', 'Though I sang in my chains like the sea', 'Do not go gently into that good night' and 'To begin at the beginning ... a moonless night in the small town, starless and bible-black'. To coin a phrase, he had a way with words. Sadly, the demon drink ruled his life and he died from alcohol abuse in the United States.

But it is not only his poetry that lives on. There are those who swear they have seen the unmistakable figure of Thomas in the vicinity of the Boat House, the famous work-room of his that was really a shed overlooking the River Taf as it flows out to the sea. It is indisputable that he spent many happy hours at the Boat House, but unhappy hours too, worrying about money and the gruelling work, writing, re-writing, revising and polishing until he achieved what he called 'poetic truth'. Has all this been just too much, resulting in 'something' remaining of the happiness and the unhappiness of this unique individual that can sometimes be seen in the vicinity of this haunted water?

I have reports of the clear form of Dylan Thomas being seen in the Boat House; hurrying away from the Boat House (to the pub perhaps!); and on the shore, looking out across the water, striving for inspiration. The witnesses who have become aware of the familiar dumpy figure standing at the water's edge and have gone closer invariably have found the previously seemingly solid figure suddenly disappears.

Incidentally there has been much speculation as to the origin of Milk Wood. An ingenious suggestion has been offered by J. G. Dugdale who refers to the fact that the milkwood tree secretes latex which is used in the manufacture of condoms; certainly Milk Wood in the play is mentioned almost exclusively as a trysting-place for lovers.

It should be remembered that Thomas was rather more than a sponging dipso who died after downing eighteen whiskies; he was also a devoted family man, a crossword and cricket lover, a productive film scriptwriter, a radio performer known for his reliability and, indisputably, a literary perfectionist.

It must be likely that the ghostly form of Dylan Thomas, would probably materialize in the vicinity of his Boat House; in the locality of his house in Laugharne where he and his family lived for a while and, perhaps most likely, at the edge of the creeping 'sloe black, slow, black, crow black, fishing-boat bobbing sea' as he called it but in fact the haunting and haunted waters of his beloved River Taf. (As I write it is reportedly one of the ten cleanest rivers in Britain.)

Llandaff, near Cardiff, South Wales

The banks of the River Taf at Llandaff have several ghosts. My researches suggest that the figure of a distraught young woman has been seen at irregular intervals and at different times of the day near Cloisters Head, seemingly wringing her hands in grief and quite oblivious to any human being in the vicinity. Sometimes she seems to be appealing to passersby for help but no sound accompanies the apparition.

She is said to be the mother of a young boy who was drowned accidentally hereabouts and whose body was never found. Inconsolable in her grief, the young mother fretted herself into an early grave but it has been suggested that her intense feelings and emotion have crossed the barrier of physical death and her form haunts the river bank, still full of unbearable sadness, a pathetic and forlorn figure that affects all those who see her, re-appearing as she does from time to time – just when it is thought that perhaps she has found peace at last.

Another victim of drowning in the River Taf here was Bella, the wife of the landlord of a long-gone public house in Llandaff. After years as joint publican Bella became obsessed with religion and grew to dislike the drinking, the gambling and the less than decent behaviour of those who frequented the premises. One night, after an argument with her husband, she made her way out of the public house, past the cathedral and down to the river which she walked alongside for a while and then, in her distressed and unhappy state of mind, she threw herself into the swirling waters making no attempt to survive as the waters closed over her. But even then, it seems, either she found no peace or the tragic event left an impression on the atmosphere, for there have been many reports over the years of her unhappy figure hastening towards the river late in the evening and there disappearing into the waters with a last dispairing cry.

There have also been reports here of the figure of a Grey Lady, quietly haunting the river bank, apparently waving towards the castle; some say seeking to attract the attention of her love the Duke of Normandy imprisoned in the castle, but if so her efforts must have been in vain for he was blinded by his captors,

There may be other phantom figures here too for in 1984 a local inhabitant reported seeing a very tall man, wearing a helmet, walking towards the castle; a sighting confirmed by other disinterested parties.

Mersea Island, Essex

The ancient causeway connecting Mersea Island with the mainland, known as the Strood, dates from Roman times and was probably built for the convenience of the Roman garrison at nearby Colchester. Appropriately enough, the Strood is haunted by the figure of a Roman soldier, seen here since time immemorial.

The figure has been seen and heard on many occasions as has the formidable figure of a smuggler or wrecker, a huge man armed to the teeth and cursing and slashing at everything as he goes on his way. He seems to be looking for trouble and some frightened witnesses have raced along the Strood fearing he is behind them but when they reach the end and look round there is no sign of him. He seems to favour dark winter nights and the bitter cold.

When Jane Pullen was landlady of the Peldon Rose she heard and saw the ghosts of Roman soldiers on the Strood many times. Once she was on her way to Mersea and heard the steady tramp of a man's footsteps behind her, like a soldier marching. 'He came down off the Barrow Hill,' she said, 'caught up with me and walked alongside me all the way down the Strood. I could see no one on that occasion but the walking feet were so close I felt I could have touched him.' Another time she saw a Roman soldier, 'as plainly as I see you' she said. Other witnesses include John Dening, the Revd Ernest Merryweather, Tommy Frankland, James Wentworth Day and many local people.

No less well-documented locally is the phantom form of a monk that haunts the nearby lanes and borders of the River Blackwater just south of Mersea Island. He is old, white-faced and wrinkled and he glides silently by, harming no one but intent on some long-forgotten errand. Sometimes he seems to emerge from the haunted waters where perhaps his home or his place of worship once stood before the marsh waters buried everything.

Eric Maple, who studied the folklore and alleged hauntings of Essex in some detail stated, categorically, 'a phantom Roman legionary is occasionally seen at dusk moving along the Strood; according to one authority this is the oldest ghost in England.' Well, not the oldest perhaps but old certainly. Possibly the rarefied and individual air of the Essex coast and the unique air of the water that washes over the Strood and has done so for centuries has become impressed for all time with remnants of past happenings in this mysterious part of England.

As I write I learn that Mr H.G. Fulcher of East Mersea claims to have 'often' seen the phantom Roman soldier on the

Strood. In portions of the Strood he sees the figure from the waist upwards. It must be likely that the original level of the causeway has been raised by several feet over the centuries.

Shere, Surrey

Shere, near Guildford in Surrey, can be counted as one of the prettiest villages in the county, a county where, it is said, people have been living for more than 500,000 years. Certainly, at nearby Abinger, the oldest preserved dwelling in Britain was discovered. Hereabouts are perhaps the most beautiful string of villages to be found anywhere: Abinger Hanger with its famous striking clock; Gomshall with its tannery; Friday Street, a lakeside hamlet; Albury with its lovely old houses; and Shere with its spectacular half-timbered properties,

On the outskirts of Shere you will find the romantic Silent Pool, a mysterious and haunted place with a hypnotic attraction for some people. Agatha Christie's deserted car was found nearby in 1926 when the famous detective story writer, suffering from amnesia, disappeared for ten days and was eventually found in a hotel in Harrogate. During the course of the search for her the Pool was dredged. But the Silent Pool yielded no solution to the disappearance although at the time people mentioned the haunted reputation of the Pool.

Legend has mixed with history to shape the best-known story about the Pool and its ghost. There are those who believe that a lovely peasant girl used to bathe in the Pool and one day King John was riding by when he saw her. He drove his horse towards her and she, seeking to escape, fell into deep water and was drowned. Her ghost still haunts the area. The correct name for the pool is Sherborne Ponds for there is another pool nearby but it is neither silent nor haunted.

A writer and poet of sorts, one Martin Tupper, lived nearby at Albury and in 1858 he wrote a volume, *Stephan Langton, a Romance of the Silent Pool* wherein he recounts a similar story but with embellishments. The girl was Emma, the daughter of a woodcutter, and when the king attempts to have his way with the girl she prefers to drown and he rides off in disappointment; Emma's brother is also drowned in trying to save her. Matthew Alexander, the Honorary Remembrancer of Guildford, has looked into the matter and he says there is no historical record of such people as Emma the woodcutter's daughter or her brother – which is not altogether surprising; and he believes we can dismiss other aspects of Tupper's work, although he could well be the source of the name, Silent Pool.

Today we know this small lake just off the A25 originates from springs in the North Downs, a natural process that produces a clear blue-green water that is most attractive and consequently the Silent Pool is a favourite spot for walkers and picnickers in the summer months and not a few of them have reported ghostly experiences.

There is a belief among some folklorists and even some historians that the Pool may once have been the scene of sacred rituals and religious homage, perhaps even unreligious non-Christian rites and ceremonies. All we do know is that the Pool has long been revered and venerated. It is thought to be bottomless and its waters to have healing properties. Bottles of water from the Silent Pool used to be available to patrons and villagers at the Annual Fair that used to be held at Albury.

There are many accounts over the years of a phantom girl

appearing to be on the point of drowning in the middle of the Silent Pool, and her screams of panic echo round the place. After a moment, the phantom girl disappears beneath the calm surface of the water and all is quiet and peaceful again. On other occasions the sound of a screaming girl has been reported but no suggestions of anyone drowning.

Somerton, Cowes, Isle of Wight

It was Gay Baldwin the undisputed expert on Isle of Wight ghosts who first told me that the internationally famous yachting centre with an annual regatta dating from 1814 and the former castle nearby had a haunted reservoir.

Water bailiff Mick Ford thought at first the little lad he saw was fishing on the quiet and trying to get out of paying his fishing-fee. He was on his rounds one August lunch-time and the weather was hot and still. He made his way towards a middle-aged couple who were fishing near the entrance to Somerton Reservoir.

Wondering whether the boy was with them, he asked the couple if they were on their own and the woman, looking around the quiet stretch of water, replied that they seemed to be on their own entirely 'except for the little boy over there in the corner'.

Her husband quickly looked around himself and contra-dicted his wife. 'There's no one here but us,' he said. Mick looked again across the reservoir; it was indeed deserted, apart from the child who now stood motionless. He appeared to be only about six or seven, the bailiff decided, and he was wearing a striped blue and white shirt and white shorts. Without responding to the fishing couple, Mick set off to walk round the edge of the water towards the boy but when he got there the boy had completely disappeared. Convinced now that the boy was trying to avoid paying, Mick thought to himself the little rascal has nipped through the hedge and made his way back to his grandparents or whoever they were.

When he returned to the couple they denied any knowledge of the boy, although they had sometimes seen him. Mick looked back across the still water and there was the little lad, standing exactly where he had been before. Mick hastily asked them to keep an eye on him and shout if they saw him move, then he set off again in the hot sun around the reservoir towards the boy. When he got there the boy had again vanished but neither he nor the couple saw him move. They said he simply vanished for a few seconds and then re-appeared.

Mick looked and there the boy was again, exactly as before. Mick decided that something very strange was going on and he settled down for a little chat with the couple. The husband could not often see the boy at all and he sometimes thought his wife was mad when she said there was a little boy over the other side; but now Mick too ...! But there the boy was standing with his little fishing rod and he and the woman could see him but the man could see nothing.

For the third time Mick set out to speak to the boy and again when he reached the spot where he had seen the boy, there was nothing there. But this time the woman could still see the boy and she shouted across to say Mick was standing right next to the child. Mick didn't know what to think but he began to have goose pimples as he thought he and the woman must be seeing a ghost.

By the time he returned to the couple, the apparition of

the boy had vanished and this time he didn't come back. Making enquiries, Mick learned for the first time of a tragedy that might account for what he and the woman had seen. He learned that a young boy had been drowned while fishing in the reservoir many years before.

The boy was six years old.

Apparently the little ghost boy has been reportedly seen several times since and always on hot and sunny days. This photographic-recording type of ghost may be triggered by a repetition of the exact kind of day the tragedy occurred, at the time it occurred; perhaps strengthened by people seeing him, and the close proximity of water.

Other Haunted Waters

A small stream near Ballater, Scotland, is known as the Spinning Jenny Burn on account of the persistent ghost of a small woman who is always working hard on her spinning wheel, beside the stream. The ghost has been seen for many years. It never interacts with human beings and seems to be an example of a kind of photographic echo of some past event.

A ghost child, a little girl of about eight years of age, has frequently been seen walking near Snuff Mills, Bristol, very close to the river. Usually the child is alone but occasionally it is seen with another child; it has not been established whether the second child, always less distinct, is a boy or a girl. Both vanish in inexplicable circumstances. Dogs are terrified of them.

The vicinity of a footbridge in Vassal Park, Fishponds,

Bristol is haunted by a cowled figure, thought to be the ghost of the Duchess of Beaufort who was often here. The bridge is over the River Frome where the ghost seems to float and always vanishes near the bridge.

Dozmary Pool on Bodmin Moor, Cornwall, is supposed to be the bottomless pool where King Arthur's sword Excalibur was thrown by Sir Bedivere when Arthur was on his deathbed. Now it's the domain of the Lady of the Lake, guardian of the sword, who haunts the lonely place. Visitors have also heard the sound of a pack of hounds and horses' hoofs; some people believe they have seen Excalibur lying just below the surface of the water. Others claim to have seen the phantom form of King Arthur himself. From here he began his journey to Avalon.

The New Forest area in Hampshire is a special place that seems to have a vanishing lake. A friend told me that in 2009 he and his wife came across a shady lake that they decided they would visit one day, but they could not find it again. Some enquiries ascertained that in 1953 a couple from Ilminster and their two children were holidaying in the area when they came upon an attractive lake. They all saw the lake and there was a great boulder in the middle. They were on their way to an arranged dinner with friends but decided to come back to the lake another day. They tried to find the lake several times but could not do so. They tried the following year, and the one after that; in fact since seeing the lake they made about twenty-five visits to the New Forest but they have never seen the lake again.

The River Stour at Longham and at Kinson in Dorset is haunted by a lady in a long white dress wearing an old-fashioned bonnet.

Lovers' Leap, a spot on the River Esk north of Penicuik, Glencorse in Scotland is haunted by a girl disappointed in love who leapt to her death there. She was last seen in 2008.

Kirmond Hall, Ludford in Lincolnshire has a haunted lake. The ghostly figure of a man has been seen to rise out of the lake on many occasions and move slowly with head down towards an old tree where it vanishes. Some witnesses have also heard a sharp cry for help. He always appears at the man-made dam end of the lake.

The old pond, once the fish pond to grand Old Bayham Manor in Kent, long vanished, is haunted by the ghost of Anne West, the last mistress at the manor who loved the place and dreaded dying and leaving it.

Hartley Manditt, new Selborne in Hampshire, has a ghostly coach-and-four, seen and heard, skirting the silent pool beside the little church that has echoed with ghostly music.

Part 13

HAUNTED WOODS AND TREES

The superstitious say 'touch wood' which is supposed to bring good luck, and this is probably a survival of ancient tree-worship although the earliest known reference to the phrase seems to date no earlier than 1805 and there are indications that it may have its origin in a children's chasing game.

Tree-hugging has its adherents, not least among the English royal family, and trees, the oldest living things on the planet, do evoke warm thoughts among many of us and certainly many of them harbour ghosts either individually or as part of woods or forests.

There is something very special about trees. They grow quickly and remain for years. As a schoolboy I was chosen to plant a tree at Letchworth Garden City to commemorate the Silver Jubilee of King George V in 1935. I was astonished at its size when I visited in 2008.

Didn't Browning say, 'You lover of trees – if love remains, your ghost will walk in an English lane.' An old Chinese proverb says that the best time to plant a tree is ten years ago; the second best time is now. So get planting – trees grow on you!

Blandford Forum, Dorset

Two miles out of Blandford, on the B3082 road towards Wimborne, a troop of ghostly horses have been heard careering madly through Down Wood.

Rodney Legg, always passionate and eloquent on all aspects of his beloved Dorset, first told me about the ghostly horde of horsemen that haunted Down Wood, having himself heard sounds that he thought might denote a herd of ghostly horses one night in 1990. He could never quite come to terms with having had such a personal ghostly encounter, although he was adamant that he had heard the loud and alarming sounds that began and ceased suddenly, and he could never find anything to account for what he so plainly heard.

He discovered an account of another person, a man who took a short cut through the trees one evening in the late 1980s, and although he had not heard of the legend of the galloping horsemen of Down Wood, he had no doubt about the sound of frantic galloping horses that he heard approaching his way. Thinking they must be local horses that had broken out of their enclosure and were violently racing towards him, he quickly clambered through a hedge to get out of their path. As he waited for the horses to rush past him, all sound of them suddenly ceased and, more than a little puzzled, he continued on his way, with the story of an experience he willingly related for the rest of his life.

It was only next day, when he related his experience in Down Wood to friends in Blandford that he heard for the first time about the wood being haunted by the sounds of a careering horde of horses, and he made a point of returning that day to the exact place where he had sought to escape from the marauding horde and while he found traces of his own frantic efforts to escape through the hedge, he found no physical trace whatever of any stampede. No trampled bracken or bushes, no broken branches or undergrowth, no trace of a track or path that horses would have made and not a single hoof mark.

Soon after talking with Rodney Legg I was introduced to a young man in Blandford who had been in Down Wood one evening studying maths when he heard the sound of approaching horses. He thought it must be a riding school or a hunt, although it all sounded rather wild and uncontrolled. As the sounds came quickly nearer he picked up his things and made his way into the undergrowth and waited. He was very surprised when, instead of seeing horses racing past, all sounds ceased and the wood was as quiet and peaceful as it had been before he had heard the sounds. He too had no knowledge of the wood being regarded as haunted and he didn't care to investigate. On further excursions to Down Wood he avoided the place where, he was convinced, he heard phantom horses.

Down Wood is the name of the house in the centre of the wood but I have been unable to discover any possible history of the place that could have a bearing on the haunting horses. The wood was almost completely felled in 1971 but by 1986 most of the tree coverage had regenerated – together with the ghostly sounds, it seems.

Brighouse. West Yorkshire

Just north of Brighouse, beyond where the A58 crosses the A641 (a spot long known as Hell Fire Corner, a name recalling the many serious accidents that have occurred here), you will find Judy Woods. (Incidentally such names as Hell Fire Corner often occur at dangerous junctions where there is a history of odd happenings and here, as long as man can recall, there were legends of a spectral horseman and more recently, the appearance and disappearance of a phantom car – both being blamed for causing deaths.)

Judy Woods is haunted and may even be the origin of any crossroads haunting. In 1981 a researcher talked with three witnesses who described 'hideous white shapes' they had seen among the trees, shapes that assumed human forms one minute and indistinct shapes the next, forms that floated in and out of the trees before finally disappearing altogether. Mysterious balls of fire and other sights and sounds that have never been explained have repeatedly been seen and heard in Judy Woods. A spectral horseman used to be seen here and a phantom woman. Andy Roberts, writing in 1992, refers to Judy Woods as being 'plagued by hauntings'.

A nearby wood is associated with Robin Hood, reportedly buried hereabouts, and his ghost and that of another man in green have been seen and heard here. Also, and perhaps less expected, a troop of soldiers in scarlet and white uniforms has been seen marching out of Judy Woods towards the aforementioned crossroads. They disappear in a pall of thick smoke. It has been suggested that the soldiers are thought-forms inasmuch as they may be the result of a psychic person projecting something clearly visible to others; something that has become ingrained into the atmosphere here, to reappear on occasions.

Dinnington, Rotherham, West Yorkshire

In 1862 a barrow, close to Park Avenue Road, was excavated. Eight feet high and a hundred and twenty feet long it was found to contain more than twenty skeletons, men, women and children. Mostly they were buried in a crouching position but one male skeleton was laid out with his head pointing to the north and another in the opposite position, pointing to the south. The lack of articles found in the burial mound suggests that the barrow was of considerable age. Furthermore, the skulls were elongated, probably Neolithic, and those buried could well have been people of the New Stone Age, suggesting the area was inhabited over 4,000 years ago. A hundred or so years after the barrow was excavated houses were built around the site; the barrow itself being shrouded in woodland.

Today this woodland is haunted. Over the years, residents living in the comparatively new houses have repeatedly complained of seeing white figures wandering among the trees at night. And passersby have reported the same thing.

Local and visiting archaeologists have expressed surprise at noticing people dressed in light-coloured clothing walking among the trees in the vicinity of the ancient barrow. The occasional visitor has asked about the figures in the woodland and youngsters, some of them up to no good, have hurriedly left after experiencing a strange atmosphere, feeling they are being watched and seeing silent figures among the trees – figures that are suddenly no longer there.

Nearby Dinnington Hall is comparatively modern, having been built in 1756 but the original Old Hall, a farmhouse on Laughton Road, is regarded as one of the oldest, if not the oldest, building in Dinnington. Some people think parts of it date back to the fifth century and there are certainly traces of a Saxon wall near St Leonard's Church. History is rife here. The Falcon Inn almost certainly takes its name from the fact that a member of the local Athorpe family was Chief Falconer to the Scotsman James I (1566–1625), he took a pride in hunting although he could not ride, and hawks were confined and trained nearby. The Athorpe family owned land here for centuries and their crest of a hawk is still used as a school motif. A number of ghostly incidents have been reported from the ancient building, including the apparition of a tall man wearing a top hat and other incongruous presences, while dogs have been known to lift their heads and apparently follow with their eyes something invisible to their human companions.

In 2007 I met a couple who lived at nearby Laughton-en-le-Morthen, with its outstanding church and spire, and they told me they had seen figures in silvery or cream-coloured clothing flitting among the trees in the vicinity of the ancient barrow; figures that fled and disappeared when they sought to find out who they were. They heard no sound whatever when they saw the figures again in approximately the same place, six weeks later. Each time it had been about ten o'clock at night.

Ganllwyd, near Dolgellau, North Wales

Hidden among winding roads, narrow lanes and wooded Forestry Commission land stands noble Nannau Old Hall, former seat of the Vaughan family. It stands eight hundred feet above sea level and is believed to occupy a higher site than any other mansion in Great Britain – and to have been the scene of an undiscovered murder long, long ago, as I said in my volume devoted to the *Ghosts of Wales* in 1978.

The original mansion belonged to Howel Sele, a first cousin to Owain Glyndwr whom he hated and who hated him. There is a story that the then Abbot Kymmer, hoping to reconcile the cousins, brought the two men together and, at least to his satisfaction, achieved that aim. But all was not what it seemed. The two were out walking together among the nearby trees when Owain saw a doe feeding and drew Howel's attention to it. Howel was always considered to be a very fine archer and Owain challenged Howel to kill the creature at that distance.

Howel immediately took up the challenge. He bent his bow, seeming to take aim at the doe, then suddenly turned and sent the arrow straight towards Owain's chest. Fortunately he was wearing armour beneath his tunic and was not seriously hurt although outraged at the treachery shown to him. He waited for the opportunity to get his own back and did not wait long. One night he set fire to Howel's home and, in all the confusion, he carried off his enemy. The unfortunate Howel Sele was never seen again.

Many years later, on his deathbed, Owain Glyndwr confessed to his faithful companion Madog what had really happened. With Owain dead, Madog hurried to Nannau to inform Howel Sele's ever-hopeful wife that she had in fact been a widow for years and to reveal the whereabouts of her husband's body.

Leading the widow and her kinsmen to a great oak tree in the garden, Madog said the body was inside and they all set about tearing the tree down. Soon they discovered a bleached skeleton which was undoubtedly that of Howel Sele. Notwithstanding full burial rites and family lamentations, the ghost of the murdered lord of Nannau was restless and there were many stories of the appearance of Sele's ghost and of mournful sighs and weird sounds attributed to the ghost, invariably in the locality of the fateful tree. All sorts of people stated they had seen the unmistakable form of Howel Sele where he had been murdered and where his body had remained hidden for so long. Something of the unquiet spirit of Howel Sele lingers still at Nannau or so I was told when I was there.

On the lawn there used to be a sundial bearing an inscription on a brass plate, referring to the incident, and the representation of an oak tree, marking the spot where the tree had long stood – a tree that had hidden the crime of Owain Glyndwr for over forty years. The owner of Nannau when I visited was Mr E.A. Morrison who informed me that it was common knowledge that on certain nights a great oak tree stood again in the garden at Nannau and for a few short moments the air was filled with hate and menace and the harsh breathing of an exhausted man, almost as though he was struggling to hide a heavy burden within the confines of the gigantic tree; then suddenly all would be quiet again, silent and still. The tree would have disappeared and in its place the sundial for all to see and wonder at before that too vanished.

The 'mythical sundial' was for years an essential part of

the house and garden, Mr Morrison told me, but today it is all a memory and Nannau slumbers with its unusual ghost story. But very occasionally the ghost of Howel Sele returns.

Hyde Park, London

There is a haunted tree in London's Hyde Park. This iconic and popular location belonged to the Abbey of Westminster until Henry VII used it to extend his deer hunting grounds. In 1619 some deer-stealers were executed at Hyde Park Gate, together with a labourer who had merely held their dogs. In Charles I's time it was well-known for its races, by foot and on horseback; and in Cromwell's time it was known for its coach races. In 1625 Queen Henrietta Maria, barefoot and in sackcloth, is said to have walked across Hyde Park to Tyburn Gallows where she prayed for the executed martyrs. Charles I opened the park to the public. Mrs Carlyle, wife of the famous Thomas, died in 1866 while driving in Hyde Park and the coachman, entirely unaware of the circumstances, continued his progress around the Ring Road. For over two hundred years Hyde Park was the most popular and fashionable place for duels, Sunday being the favourite day. In the duel in 1712 between the Duke of Hamilton and Lord Mohun, both men were killed. In fact so many violent deaths have occurred in the park through duels, murders and suicides that many people came to believe that ghosts of the departed were accustomed to appear in Hyde Park at night. 'To some extent this belief persists to the present day,' says George Cunningham writing in 1927. He goes on, 'Dick Turpin and his mare Bess are said to have been seen here and also the ghosts of Jack the Ripper and the girl murdered in the Serpentine.'

There is one particularly haunted tree here and in its vicinity, even on the brightest summer day, there is in the air a strange feeling of expectancy as though something sad is about to happen and the sensation of sadness is often apparent in the shady walks and among some of the gnarled and ancient trees.

This tree has long had a bad reputation. Layabouts never slumber beneath its twisted branches, lovers are never to be found lingering in its shade and even birds seem to shun its twisted branches. I have talked with several park attendants over the years and they are well aware of the reputation the tree has acquired and two of them, independently, told me they sometimes heard voices that they could have sworn emanated from the tree itself.

They both said there seemed to be at least two distinct voices, one the harsh and loud tones of an angry man that suddenly cease as you try to catch some of the words, and sometimes there is a low, shrewd and artful laugh that sends a chill through the person hearing it. This is followed by a mournful groaning sound as of someone in agony, mortal pain and utter despair. The sounds, seemingly close at hand and certainly objective, dissolve and cease within seconds and the hearer finds himself looking about the empty space around him, quite unable to find any practical reason for what he has heard.

This one tree in Hyde Park is a favourite one for suicides and many people can discern an almost overwhelming sense of gloom and despair and sadness in the immediate vicinity of the 'tree of death' as it has been called.

Similar stories and associations circulate about a certain tree in Green Park, once the scene of numerous robberies, murders ands duels – the ghostly sound of one duel is still said to be heard at dawn on the anniversary of the fatal fight.

North Benfleet, Essex

Here, near Basildon, a haunted wood adjoining Fanton Hall is known as Shrieking Boy Wood, a reminder of a murder and of the victim's ghostly appearance.

For some long-forgotten reason – perhaps it was an accident –a ploughman caused the death of a plough boy as he led the plough horses, a dangerous occupation at the best of times and more especially so in the event of extreme weather, or bad temper, or restive horses. Whatever the cause the boy was killed by the plough and his screams or those of his ghost have haunted the area ever since.

Jessie K. Payne traced an entry in the church registers referring to a murder on the farm belonging to Fanton Hall in 1734 and it may be that this terrible event is the basis of the present haunting. Alternatively, she suggests a more colourful event could be responsible for it is said that in a fit of temper a woodsman attacked the boy helping him because he was not working hard enough. And the attack, at the end of Kingsley Lane, ended with the boy's head being separated from his body. In a panic the woodsman hid the boy's remains inside the nearby wood, in a hollow tree, and spread a story about the boy having run away.

But the man's conscience troubled him and he found he was afflicted more and more by the dying screams of the innocent boy, screams that seemed to be forever coursing through his head. He was in the habit of frequenting The

Hart public house at nearby Thundersley and whenever the missing boy was mentioned the woodcutter found himself confused and so violently agitated that he had to make a hasty exit

Meanwhile, the boy's ghost was reportedly seen, time after time, sitting on a gate that gave entrance to the wood, where his body had been dragged and hidden from sight, and the sound of the boy's screams was supposed to be heard by scores of people passing the wood. Those who ventured inside, among the trees, might encounter the form of a headless boy with arms outstretched as though trying to find his way out of the wood and back to places familiar to him.

The screaming figure has been reported extensively. Once, two boys decided to see whether there really was anything in the story of a ghost in the wood; but they didn't get as far as exploring among the trees for as they were about to enter the wood they both saw the ghost boy sitting on the gate, and they quickly fled.

Another witness was a local farmer who knew the boy and he went to the place where people said they saw his ghost. He saw nothing but the sudden and awful screams that he heard haunted him for the rest of his life.

In recent years there have been only occasional reports of the appearance of the ghost, usually silent and quickly disappearing when seen. Perhaps whatever power or energy that is necessary for its appearance is finally diminishing and will soon be so weak that the appearance of the Shrieking Boy will be no more – although within the wood unearthly shrieks are still sometimes heard.

Northampton

Situated about seven miles south of Northampton, Salcey Forest, one of three really ancient forests in the county used to form part of the boundary between Northamptonshire and Buckinghamshire. This line of demarcation led to a notorious episode in the history of prizefighting and perhaps to one of several ghosts associated with this small but once royal forest.

In the days when bare-fist prizefighting continued until one fighter was beaten and sometimes died there was a remarkable fight in July 1830 when Alex McKay 'the Highland Hercules' was matched with local man Simon Byrne. The fight was scheduled to take place at Handlope in Buckinghamshire, but when the Bucks authorities tried to stop the fight, the pugilists and their followers crossed into the adjoining county and there battled for forty-seven rounds at Salcey Green on the edge of the forest before McKay had received such a mauling and beating that he had to be carried back to the Watts Arms where he died the following day. Byrne was tried for murder but gained an acquittal amid great acclaim from his supporters.

The grim sounds of this bruising battle have been heard at the forest edge; a sickening sound of blow after blow amid the grunts and groans and faint cheers that must have been heard here that fateful day all those years ago. Some witnesses aver that they have glimpsed two men, stripped to the waist, slugging away at each other but the 'vision' soon fades and only the sounds remain.

Here too there are ghostly forms known as 'the Spectres of Salcey Forest' that never seem to have been identified although several ideas have been floated. An exceptionally tall figure is sometimes confused with the figure of a monk who glides at great speed among the trees of the forest. This ghostly monk is reportedly a frequent and regular visitor to Salcey Forest. Ghost hunter Joan Forman told me that when she was researching one of her books in 1973 she discovered that Salcey Forest had had a reputation for being haunted for as long as many of the local people could remember and their parents and grandparents seemed to take the matter for granted. The ghost monk, in particular, was quoted as one frequent phantom form that haunted the forest and she said she had spoken to four people who had seen it.

There is a tradition that, after being restored to the throne, Charles II used a house nearby to accommodate his favourite mistress, Nell Gwynne. Salcey Lawn, an isolated property in the middle of the forest was not to Nell's liking when her royal lover was away and she is thought to have acquired a local lover, much to Charles's displeasure and the king, so runs the story, had the luckless man murdered and ever since the ghost of the distressed man is seen hurrying through the forest for some unknown reason. Perhaps this is a kind of 'forethought form' of what the man should have done before the king's men caught him.

Another apparition in the forest is said to be the unmistakable form of Nell Gwynne herself. She is an active ghost, reputedly haunting Salisbury Hall in Hertfordshire, which she certainly knew, and the Gargoyle Club in London, formerly her Soho house. The flamboyant figure has been seen at the king's Salcey Forest retreat, sitting idly in the orchard or strolling in the garden or wandering in the adjacent woods, where the sounds of a horse and carriage have been heard on occasions.

Pengrugla, Cornwall

In September 2011 I visited a haunted tree. My good friend Michael Williams, author, publisher, and President of the renowned Paranormal Investigation organization took me to meet the owner of the oak tree and the land about it, delightful Wayne Edwards.

We duly arrived at Pengrugla in the parish of St Ewe. It was as well that Michael, who has himself written about the tree, told me we were there for Pengrugla consists of no more then half a dozen houses, off the Mevagissey road at the Heligan bend. There is no mention of Pengrugla in most of the dozens of publications that exist on Cornwall, nor is it included in the AA's excellent *Gazetteer and Touring Guide* (circa 1952) or Oliver Mason's two-volume *Gazetteer of England* (1972).

Today, situated beneath the sprawling great tree there is a post box, a reminder of the prosaic and everyday alongside the world of fable, legend and mystery. So we arrived at Pengrugla – which some people have it is an old Cornish word for the head of the gibbet – and here was the Hangman's Tree.

Just beyond the tree there is a curiously overgrown but not forsaken piece of land, that I found strangely silent and full of atmosphere; it is not difficult to accept that here, after being hanged the bodies were buried.

The late Maisie Herring of Heligan House was one person who did explore the history of this ancient spot. She said that people posting their letters in the post box today often didn't realize that in the past a body could well have dangled immediately above their heads!

According to Dr James Whetter, gibbets were usually

located at parish boundaries and Pengrugla stands on such a boundary. Maisie Herring, writing in 1996, refers to a moonlit night, a swaying body, the grieving relatives and 'the unhallowed internment'. That last turn of phrase, Michael Williams has pointed out, reflects a local theory that the hanged were indeed buried in the small unsanctified area behind the haunted tree.

Michael is of the opinion that digging there might well reveal traces and perhaps skeletons to confirm the distinct likelihood of the spot being a burial place, and I agree with him. The Revd Brian Coombes, a mine of information on all things Cornish, has suggested that had there been regular hangings here there should be records and personally he suspects that any hangings here may have been matters of setting examples rather than a regular occurrence.

In any case, some sort of excavation could not but be interesting but the owner of the tree and the adjoining land told us no excavations had taken place there and he had no plans for any to take place. There is about that small area a distinct air of mystery and a feeling of expectation. But what exactly is enshrouded in the curiously ambient air with a definite and inexplicable sense of the past is uncertain.

The tree itself – certainly five hundred years old one would think – is perhaps a shadow of the majestic oak it once was but is full of character and individuality and, as Thomas Pakenham puts it in his *Meetings with Remarkable Trees* (1996), 'To visit these trees, to step beneath their domes and vaults, is to pay homage at a mysterious shrine. But tread lightly. Even these giants have delicate roots. And be warned that this may be your farewell visit. No one can say if this prodigious trunk will survive the next storm or outlive us all by centuries.'

There are vague stories of vague forms being seen hereabouts and no one visiting the ominously named Hanging

Tree with an open mind will deny the strange, fascinating and completely inexplicable effect that this haunted tree has on many people.

Tarrant Gunville, Dorset

Here Cranborne Chase really is a haunted place with some well-authenticated sightings of ghosts to prove the point. What remains of the old woodland at Bussey Stool beyond the village of Tarrant Gunville is bordered by a track that continues straight ahead where the road turns into a farmyard, towards Bloody Shard Gate, the meeting place of several paths. Rodney Legg believed the individual name preserved the memory of past events.

A violent engagement took place between poachers and gamekeepers here at the end of the eighteenth century when deer stealing was a serious offence. Leading the poachers that night was an Army major and he lost a hand in the affray – which was buried in nearby Pimperne churchyard. The brawl happened in the vicinity of a coppice known as Bloodway Coppice and the adjoining field, to where the fight spread, is still called Bloody Field. Both are reputedly haunted by the one-armed soldier; some people think he is looking for his lost hand. In those days it was considered to be 'highly ill-advised' for a body to be buried that was not complete. The phantom form of a soldier in old-fashioned uniform has repeatedly been seen wandering about the coppice, his handless arm swinging beside him.

The area is also haunted by a prehistoric man. The grandson of Dr R.C.C. Clay himself told me of the remarkable sighting. At the time his grandfather was a

Fellow of the Society of Antiquaries and was in charge of some excavations being carried out at Pokesdown near Bournemouth and every afternoon he would drive down to the site from his home near Salisbury and return at dusk.

One evening, motoring along the straight road over the open downland between Cranborne and Sixpenny Handley he reached a spot where there was a clump of beech trees on the east side and a pinewood on the west. Just there the road goes down into a dip before rising to cross the old Roman road from Badbury Rings. Straightaway he saw on his right-hand side near the trees a horseman travelling in the Sixpenny Handley direction, that is in the same direction as himself. Suddenly the rider turned his horse's head and he galloped off as though trying to reach the road ahead first. Dr Clay was so interested that he slowed the car down so that they would in fact meet and he would get a closer look at the man.

However, as he again almost drew level, the rider turned his horse in a northern direction and galloped along almost parallel with Dr Clay and about fifty yards from the present road. Now the archaeologist could see that the rider was no ordinary horseman as he had suspected, perhaps from the nearby riding stables at Nine Yews. Far from it. This rider had bare legs and wore a long, loose cloak while the horse, with long mane and tail, seemed to have no bridle and the man's feet were not in any stirrups. Although the man looked towards him, Dr Clay found difficulty in distinguishing any features but the man assumed a threatening attitude, brandishing in his right hand some implement or weapon and waving it above his head.

The astonished motorist now realized that he was looking at a prehistoric man and he tried to identify the weapon being waved about so that he might be able to date it. Then, after travelling alongside the car for about a hundred yards, the horse and rider suddenly vanished. They did not turn into the trees; one moment they were racing alongside the motorist, the next moment there was nothing there. Dr Clay immediately pulled up and established that there was no sign of the horse or its rider and nowhere in the trees or anywhere else it could have gone. He carefully noted the exact spot, for he had already decided he would look further into the matter next day in full daylight.

Accordingly next day, driving along the road he found the spot and noticed for the first time that where the horseman had disappeared there was a low, round barrow. Over the following weeks, time and time again, in all weathers, at different times of the day, and when he was weary and when he was alert, he hoped to see the horseman again but he never did. He also looked carefully for any bush or other natural object that his brain, tired at the end of the day, might have mistaken for a horseman, but there was nothing.

Making enquiries in the district he talked with an iron craftsman from Ebbesbourne Wake near Salisbury who himself made enquiries and met one old shepherd who immediately said, 'Do you mean the man that comes out of the opening in the pinewood?' Apparently he and others knew all about a ghost horseman that haunted the area.

There the matter rested until a couple of years later Dr Clay heard from an archaeologist friend to whom he had related his experience, He wrote, 'Your horseman has turned up again. Two girls, cycling from Handley to a dance at Cranborne one night recently, have complained to the police that a man on horseback followed them over the downs and frightened them . . .'

Obviously, these sightings are most important. First, the apparition is vouched for by a highly qualified and respected witness; there is evidence of some sort that the same form has been seen in the same place before, a fact of which Dr Clay was not aware; and later the same form was reportedly seen by two independent witnesses and there would appear to have been other people who have seen the same apparitional form.

Two significant points emerge from all this: the man and his horse suddenly vanish near a 'low, round barrow'; and the old shepherd who seemed to be quite familiar with a ghostly horseman being seen there said it 'came out of the opening in the pinewood'.

It has been deduced that the horseman may have been badly, perhaps mortally, wounded while in the pinewood, where enemies and wild animals might well dwell and there must exist the possibility that the man lies buried with his horse, in the low, round barrow. If these suppositions are correct the spectral ride from the wood to the barrow would signify the man's last living journey on earth.

Dorset is particularly rich in prehistoric barrows. In fact there are upwards of two thousand ancient burial mounds in the county but only about forty have been excavated and explored. There is no doubt that men of the Bronze Age (Dr Clay was of the opinion that the figure he saw could well have dated from 1,000 to 2,000 BC) especially men of importance, were often buried with their horses in barrows and it is fascinating to speculate on whether, if the 'low, round barrow' was excavated, it might well contain the remains, not only of the prehistoric man but also his horse. The barrow in question is numbered 'Wimborne St Giles 35' in Leslie Grinsell's authoritative *Dorset Barrows* (1959) and lies beside the B3081 road and Bottlebush Down, 1,200 yards south-east of Handley Cross. The scenery at this point has changed little in 3,500 years and if ghosts have survived from such a distant age, here is where they might be expected to appear. Grinsell concludes: 'Within the last thirty years there have been other reports, from shepherds and others, of apparitions having been seen in the vicinity of Bottlebush Down.' And I am sure there have been other sightings of the ghost from the haunted pinewood since Grinsell wrote that and that there will be many more in the years that lie ahead, as long as the pinewood remains intact.

Watton, Norfolk

Some twelve miles north of Thetford, near to Watton, Wayland Wood is said to harbour the ghosts of two lost children who might be the original Babes in the Wood.

An old Elizabethan Hall at Merton, or possibly Griston Hall, in the same parish, was once the home of 'the wicked uncle' and the nearby Wayland Wood is where he is supposed to have lured the children and there left them to die. Centuries later this oak and ash wood came under the protection of the Norfolk Naturalists Trust.

The story goes that the widowed father of the children was a Norfolk man and when he was dying he bequeathed his children to the care of his brother but he was a cruel man, despite his name, Arthur Truelove, and he sought to dispose of the children, a boy and a girl, in order to gain their inheritance. Hand in hand they tried to find a way out of the wood but, wandering in circles in the dark forest, they at last lay down exhausted and died from cold and hunger. Legend has it that a robin covered their dead bodies with moss and leaves.

The forms of two young children have reportedly been seen here, ever since the sixteenth century, and the cries and wails of the lost children have not infrequently been heard.

Cynics say the cries are those of gulls flying over the nearby fields.

However, sightings have been numerous over many years including one in 2008 and another in 2010. An old ballad tells the story:

> Thus wandered these poor innocents
> Til death did end their grief
> In one another's arms they died
> As wanting due relief.
> No burial this pretty pair
> Of any man receives
> Til Robin Red-breast piously
> Did cover them with leaves.

According to some accounts, fate punished the uncle severely for his evil deeds with his barns being fired, his land becoming barren, his cattle dying, his two sons being drowned while on a voyage to Portugal, and in the end he came to extreme poverty and misery and died in jail.

As for the ghosts: especially it would seem on dark and stormy nights you may see the ghost children and hear their wailing, sounds that gave this wood its local name of Wailing Wood.

Windsor Great Park, Berkshire

This ancient forest is the setting for one of England's most famous ghosts: Herne the Hunter galloping on horseback across Windsor Park. The story seems to be almost as ancient as the forest and the origin of the tale is lost in the mists of time. Herne has even been described as a 'wood-spirit metamorphosed into a ghost' and the story was old in Shakespeare's day for the immortal bard mentions it in his *Merry Wives of Windsor*, written about 1598 where he says:

> There is an old tale that Herne the Hunter
> Sometime a keeper here in Windsor forest,
> Doth all the winter-time at still midnight,
> Walk round about an oak, with great ragg'd horns;
> And there he blasts the tree and takes the cattle
> And makes milch kine yield blood and shakes a chain
> In a most hideous and dreadful manner.

Shakespeare has used the legend that Rycharde Herne, a forest warden in the service of Richard II (1367–1400) who hanged himself on an oak tree, that was then old. The stories of Herne the Hunter, clad in deerskins and wearing a helmet with antlers, speeding silently through the forest with his pack of spectral hounds, are numerous and range over the past three hundred years. Henry VIII was only one who claimed to see the ghost and witnesses come thick and fast right up to the present day. Lord Burton saw the arresting spectacle just before the First World War; a Justice of the Peace witnessed the phenomenon in 1926; other wit-nesses include a respected Army man in 1941; a local doctor in 1958; a Coldstream guardsman in 1976; a servant at Windsor Castle in 1984; a couple and their two children (all said they saw the phantom horseman) in 2001; a promi-nent historian in 2004, and I have additional reports dated 2006 and 2010.

This ghost would appear to be of very ancient lineage, possibly representing Odin the Norse god who rode the

Wild Hunt; maybe the horned god of primitive man, representative of some nature spirit. It has been suggested that Cernunnos, the Celtic god of the underworld and worshipped in pre-Roman Britain might be a candidate, suggested by the stag's antlers. Possibly it had its origin in terms of folk memory of some pre-Christian sanctuary in the forest where the priests wore some kind of antlered head-dress.

At all events, Harrison Ainsworth (1805–82) used the story in his romance *Windsor Castle*, published on 1843 and George Cruikshank (Dickens's illustrator) pictured it as 'a wild, spectral object, possessing a slight resemblance to a human being, clad in the skin of a deer and wearing on its head a sort of helmet, formed of the skull of a stag, from which branched a large pair of antlers.'

As to the tree itself: for many years a tree stood in Windsor Park that was said to be Herne's Oak, but this has long disappeared. It is said that when the tree was cut down in the 1860s, Queen Victoria, notoriously superstitious, reserved some of the logs for her own fire to help to lay the ghost, for appearances of Herne the Hunter were said to be disadvantageous to the royal family. In 1838 John Claudius Loudon in his monumental *Arboretum et Fruticetum Britannicum* listed two possible Herne's Oaks in Windsor Park, both long gone. One is tempted to think that it would be a phenomenon of the highest order if a fifteenth century or earlier tree existed today. However, there is an extremely old oak tree in Windsor Forest – some say even older than Herne's Oak, the so-called William the Conqueror's Oak, still standing opposite the pink lodge at Cranborne Gate, its hollow trunk some twenty-seven feet in circumference and now jealousy guarded by the Crown Estate Commissioners who are well aware that it too has a haunted reputation. A strange-looking, silent, motionless figure has been seen by many witnesses, standing close to the ancient rotting trunk, a figure that seems to merge and disappear into the tree itself when approached.

Wootton Rivers, Wiltshire

To the east stretches Severnake Forest, south of Marlborough, long reputed to heavily haunted; it is easy to feel the other world is closer than you think in this atmospheric place, still regarded as one of the loneliest counties of England. This ancient and celebrated forest, once one of the largest areas of virgin tracts of wooded land anywhere in England has been progressively curtailed by government and other officialdom.

Long owned by the Seymour family whose best known member was Lady Jane Seymour who became the third wife of Henry VIII, after being a lady-in-waiting to both Catherine of Aragon and Anne Boleyn and who died shortly after giving birth to a son who became Edward VI.

Many are the stories of strange happenings in Severnake Forest, including various apparitions from silent but fearsome-looking horsemen to half-glimpsed prehistoric human forms. Here, where the past and the present seem to blend and become blurred, all too often the array of reported ghostly appearances is quite bewildering.

My records include many instances of paranormal noises: running footsteps, heavy marching feet, the thunder of horses' hooves, the sound of weeping and wailing, rattling chains, horns blowing and even the sound of sweet voices singing. Apparitions and phantom forms that have been reported here include fierce-looking horsemen on fiery steeds, a solitary soldier in ancient, possibly Roman, costume, a phantom cottage, a spectral coach and horses, a crying child seeking comfort (who disappears when approached), a dreadful-looking animal with horns that may be a type of wild boar, a huge half-human form that looks like a prehistoric man, a young girl who seems to be searching for someone or something and a hooded form that could be a monk or a nun – the list seems endless. Horses have frequently been known to shy here for no apparent reason.

More than one researcher into Britain's ghostly population has concluded that Severnake Forest is abundantly haunted for those with eyes to see and ears that can hear. Not a few amateur investigators have fled the forest, even in daylight, because of what they feel there and these feelings and impressions of the forest being inhabited by beings not of this world are enhanced when night falls.

Little is known of the woodland phantom forms that apparently dwell here, remnants of past events and people and animals that once frequented and knew this forest of antiquity. One persistent legend has a headless woman riding a white horse along one of the avenues between some very old trees; another story tells of a murderer and his victim appearing deep in the forest where a murder once took place. The headless woman is said to be a girl who was riding through the forest when her horse bolted and she was decapitated as it took her through overhanging branches in the course of taking part in a royal hunting party long ago. I have seen no record of a murder but it is not unlikely.

The headless girl was seen by a picnic party in 1969 and Marc Alexander tells he received a letter in 1988 from a family then living in Reading who were visiting Severnake Forest for the first time and while resting and enjoying the peace and quiet one very still and sunny summer day, they were suddenly surprised to hear the sound of a horse approaching them at speed. Three of the party saw the shadowy form of a woman on horseback race past them but she appeared to have no head; the remaining member of the party heard the sound of horses' hooves approaching fast, heard the sound of them passing quite close and heard them fade away into the distance, but she saw nothing.

In 2010, a ghostly black dog was added to the list of phantoms reported here. Interestingly enough, such an animal has long been said to haunt the vicinity of Severnake Forest Hotel and Deane Water Bottom, a very lonely spot, although this information was not known, to my knowledge, to the latest percipient of paranormal activity at persistently haunted Severnake Forest.

Other Haunted Woods and Trees

There is or was a tree on Ladder Lane in Swindon where a groom in the employ of Colonel Colley died and where no grass would grow, where the form of a manservant has been seen on occasions, and where the exposed earth formed the shape of a cross.

At Brading Harbour, Isle of Wight (there are remains of a Roman villa nearby) there was once a great oak forest where our pagan ancestors cremated human sacrifices. The smell of burning human flesh is still experienced here.

The woods at Stapleton near Bristol are haunted by a somewhat mystifying phantom. People walking in the woods have been approached by a man who appears as if to speak to them. He seems quite normal but when right in front of the witnesses, he suddenly disappears. No one seems to know who he is or why he haunts.

At Eccles near Aylesford in Kent, the site of an excavated Roman fortress bordering a wood is haunted by the figure of a Roman centurion who appears out of the wood.

Monks Wood at Stevenage in Hertfordshire may have been the site of an ancient monastery. A headless monk is said to walk here in the vicinity of a pond deep inside the wood. I talked with several witnesses who said the monk's cowl seemed to be empty which may be why he is reputed to be headless.

At Lackford on the edge of the Fens, between West Stow and Icklingham east of Mildenhall in Suffolk, there is a strip of fir trees known as Icklingham Belt, trees that predate the nearby Forestry Commission plantation. Here on a stretch of the Icknield Way there are reports of a ghostly horseman who could be an Archbishop of Sudbury, murdered here by the followers of Wat Tyler.

The Heddon Oak is a haunted tree situated at a crossroads in the West Country, some fifty miles west of Sedgemoor where legend has it some of Monmouth's men were caught by Royalist soldiers who summarily hanged them on the oak tree. The area has long been haunted by the sound of running footsteps and frantic panting and choking sounds suggesting strangulation. Unclear figures have been seen around the tree.

In Shropshire, not far from Newport, tall trees bordering the road are known locally as the Windy Oaks, trees that are haunted by a suicide. Richard Tauber is among witnesses.

Select Bibliography

Adams, Paul, Eddie Brazil and Peter Underwood *Shadows in the Nave* 2011

Alexander, Marc *Haunted Castles* 1974

Alexander, Matthew *Tales of Old Surrey* 1985

Bell, David *Ghosts and Legends of Staffordshire* 1994

Baring-Gould, S. *Cliff Castles & Cave Dwellings of Europe* 1911

Bradford, Anne *The Haunted Midlands* 2006

Broadhurst, Paul *The Secret Land* 2009

Caidin, Martin *Ghosts of the Air* 1991

Coventry, Martin *Haunted Places of Scotland* 1999

Day, James W. *A Ghost Hunter's Game Bookbook* 1958

———, *Essex Ghosts* 1973

Dyer, James *Prehistoric England and Wales* 1981

Fisher, Graham *Historic Britain* n.d.

Forman, Joan *The Haunted South* 1978

Fraser, John *Ghost Hunting* 2010

Fox, Ian *Haunted Places of Hampshire* 1993

Haliday, Ron *Paranormal Scotland* 2000

Hall, Mike *Haunted Places of Middlesex* 2004

Halpenny, Bruce B. *Ghost Stations* 1986–1995

Holder, Geoff *Mysterious Perthshire* 2007

Home, Gordon *Through East Anglia* 1925

Legg, Penny *Haunted Southampton* 2011

Legg, Rodney *Mysterious Dorset* 1987

Lockley, Steve *Ghosts of South Wales* 1996

Maple, Eric *The Dark World of Witches* 1962

Maple, Eric *The Realm of Ghosts* 1964

Newland, R.J. and M.J. North *Dark Dorset* 2002

Owen, Andy *Yorkshire Stories of the Supernatural* 1999

Payne, Jessie K. *Ghost Hunter's Guide to Essex* 1987

Pugh, Jane *Welsh Ghostly Encounters* 1990

Puttick, Betty *Ghosts of Essex* 1997
Rackham, John *Brighton Ghosts, Hove Hauntings* 2001
Robertson, James *Scottish Ghost Stories* 1996
Seafield, Lily *Scottish Ghosts* 1999
Underwood, Peter *Gazetteer of British Ghosts* 1971
——, *Gazetteer of Scottish & Irish Ghosts* 1973
——, *Ghostly Encounters* 1992
——, *Ghosts of Cornwall* 1983, 1998
——, *Ghosts of Wales* 1978, 2010
——, *Haunted Gardens* 2009
——, *Haunted London* 1973, 2010
——, *Nights in Haunted Houses* 1994
Toulson, Shirley *Walking the Ley Lines* 1979
Wallace, Graham *R.A.F. Biggin Hill* 1957
Williams, Michael *Cornish Mysteries* 1980
——, *Supernatural in the West* 1996
——, *Supernatural Investigation* 1993
——, *Supernatural Search in Cornwall* 1991
Wood, Alan C. *Military Ghosts* 2010
Wood, Dave and Nicky Sewell *Haunted Swindon* 2008

Index

Abbot Kymmer, 382
Abbots Langley, Hertfordshire, 165–168
Abbotsbury Hill, Dieset, 52, 222
Aberdeen, Scotland, 189, 244
Aberystwyh, Wales, 4, 148, 151
Abinger, Surrey, 367
Abinger Hanger, Surrey, 367
Adams, Norman, 114
African High Commissioner, 24
Agincourt, 169
Ainsworth, Harrison, 399
Airports Ltd, 42
Alan, A.J., 122–123
Alan, River, Cornwall, 122–123
Albury, Surrey, 367, 368
Alexandria, Egypt, 285
Alexander, Marc, 291–292, 401
Alexander, Matthew, 242, 368
Alexander I, King, 158
Alleged Haunting of B- House, The, 140
Allen, Susan, 219–220
Allison, Mrs J., 303
Alperton, Thomas, Mrs., 26
Alton, Hampshire, 279
Alton, Inspector Leslie, 25–26
Ambresbury Bank, Essex, 47
An Adventure, 344
Andrews, Muriel, 270–271
Anglesey, 72, 178, 345
Anglian Paranormal Investigation
    Society, 64
Angus, Scotland, 108
Ann Seymour House, Abbots Langley,
    Herts., 168
Annan, Dumfriesshire, Scotland,
    197–200
Arbor Low, Derbyshire, 72
Arboretum et Fruticetum Britannicum,
    399
Argyll, Duke of, 100
Argyll, Scotland, 86–88, 324–326
Arizona, U.S.A., 223
Arthur, King, 52, 66, 72, 73, 74,
    123–124, 227–229, 312, 346, 372
Arthur, Lieutenant Desmond L., 32–36
Arundel, Earls of, 289, 290
Arundel, Sir John, 103
Ashhie, Loch, Scotland, 107
Aspel, Michael, 126
Assembly Rooms, Bath, 202, 205

Athenaeum Club, London, 36
Athorpe family, 381
Attrill, Ft.Lieutenant John, 37–38
Audley End, Essex 127
Audley End House, Essex 127
Augustiune, Saint 55–56
Australia, 42, 147, 322, 338, 340
Avalon, 372
Avebury, Wiltshire, 48–52
Aviation Ghosts, 43
Aylesford, Kent, 200–202, 403
Aylmerton, Norfolk, 69–71
Azimghir Barracks, Wiltshire, 19

BOAC, 18
Babes in the Wood, 396–397
Badbury Rings, Dorset, 52–54, 393
Baddesley Clinton, Warwickshire,
    133–136
Baker, Claire, 24–25
Bakewell, Derbyshire, 185–186
Balcarres, Lord, 91
Baldock, Hertfordshire, 62
Baldwin, Gay, 369
Balfour, Lord, 33
Balfour, Sir William, 84
Balgonie Castle, Scotland, 161
Ballater, Scotland, 222, 371
Bellinsallock, Scotland, 111–112
Ballindallock Castle, Moray, Scotland,
    162
Balmoral, Scotland 244
Bamburgh, Northumberland, 326
Bankes, Lady, 114
Baring-Gould, Sabine, 228–229
Barnato-Hasssan Special car, 230
Barnt Green, Birmingham, 354
Barnwell Castle, Northamptonshire, 311
Baron, Stanley, 343
Barracuda aircraft, 39
Barrow Gurney, Somerset, 223
Barrow Hill, Essex, 366
Barton, Mr and Mrs, 249–250
Basing, Hampshire, 93–96
Basingstoke, Hampshire, 279
Bassingbourne, Cambridgeshire, 42–43
Basingstoke, Hampshire, 279
Bastwick Place, Norfolk, 121
Bath, Somerset, 19, 202–206
Bath Road, Bedford Park, London,
    266–267

Battle of Britain, 34, 36–37, 38, 93
Battlefield House, St. Albans,
  Hertfordshire, 98–99
Battlefields, haunted, 77–108
Baxter, Mrs Frances, 321
Baxter, Willie, 265–266
Bayham Abbey, Kent, 310–311
Beachy Head, East Sussex, 315–318
Beaker people, 298
Beaminster, Dorset, 170, 206–207
Beaminster Manor House, Dorset, 207
Beaufighters aircraft, 18
Beaufort, Duchess of, 372
Beaulieu, Hampshire, 135–140, 303
Bedford Park, London, 266–267
Bedfordshire, 99
Bedivere, Sir, 372
Beeleigh Abbey, Essex, 271
Beer, Peter, 171–172
Beeston Regis, Norfolk, 70
Belgium, 35, 156
Bell, David, 173, 174, 176
Bell Tout Lighthouse, 315, 318
Bella (publician), 364–365
Bellars, Commander Bill, 306
Bellechin, Perthshire, Scotland, 140–141
Benfleet, Essex, 232
Bennett Street, Bath, 203
Bentley, Hampshire, 154
Bere Regis, Dorset, 276, 277
Berkeley Castle, Gloucestershire,
  290–291
Berkshire, 121, 397–400, 401
Berkshire, Earl of, 290
Berlin, Germany, 13
Berry Pomeroy, Devon, 312
Berwick Castle, Northumberland, 285,
  286
Berwick Railway Station,
  Northumberland, 286
Berwick-upon-Tweed, Northumberland,
  88–90, 285–286, 326, 349–351
Bethleham, 310
Betjeman, John, 107
Betws-y-Coed, North Wales, 351–352
Bewl, River, Kent, 360
Biggin Hill, 11–13
Binnie, Ann, 34–35
Binns, The, West Lothian, Scotland, 162
Bira, Prince, 230
Bircham Newton, Norfolk, 13–18
Birling Gap, Beachy Head, East Sussexz,
  317
Birmingham, 352–358
Bishop's Stortford, Hertfordshire, 192

Bishopsbourne, Kent, 250
Black dog (ghost) 118
Black Magic, 161, 168
Black Prince (Edward, Prince of Wales)
  289
Blackheath, London, 247, 248
Blackwater, River, Essex, 271, 366
Blackwell Tunnel, London, 247
Blaker, Sir Reginald, 291
Blandford Forum, Dorset, 118, 377–378
Blenheim aircraft, 18
Bletchley, Buckinghamshire, 43
Bloodway Coppice, Dorset, 392
Bloody Assizes, 171
Bloody Field, Dorset, 392
Bloody Shard Gate, Dorset, 392–393
Blount, Father (Jesuit), 360–361
Blur Bell Hill, Kent, 200, 201, 202
Bluebell Line, East Susex, 281
Bluestones (at Stonehenge), 71, 72
Boat House, (Dylan Thomas's), 362–363
Bodmin, Cornwall, 22, 60–61, 103, 372
Bognor Regis, West Sussex, 139
Boleyn, Anne, 119, 120, 155, 400
Boleyn, Sir Thomas, 119
Bonham Carter, Lieutenant-Colonel,
  143–144
Bonnie Prince Charlie: see Steward
  family
Bordean House, Langrish, Hampshire,
  141–143
Borley Rectory, Essex, 206
Borough House, Bossiney, Cornwall, 228
Boscastle, Cornwall, 66, 67, 227,
  319–323
Boscombe Down, Wiltshire, 43
Bossiney, Cornwall, 66, 68, 73, 227–229
Bossiney Books, 227
Bossiney House Hotel, Cornwall, 227
Bossiney Mound, Cornwall, 66, 73,
  227–229
Boswell, James, 158
Bottlebush Down, Dorset, 395, 396
Bottreaux family, 66, 228
Boudicca, Queen, 47–48, 292
Boulogne, France, 305
Bourne, Doreathea St Hill, 85, 156–157
Bournemouth, Hampshire, 393
Brabazon, Lord, 231
Braddock Down, Cornwall, 107–108
Bradford, Anne, 85, 356
Brading, Isle of Wight, 402
Bradwell, Essex, 304
Braemar, Scotland, 244
Bramshott Grange, Hampshire, 240

Brancaster, Norfolk, 289, 304
Bray (Blount's servant), 360–361
Breakspear, Nicholas, 165
Brecklands, Norfolk, 58–60
Breconshire, Wales, 65
Brede Place, East Sussex, 127
Brest, France, 289
'Bride's Walk', Canvey Island, Essex, 233
Bridge House, Beaminster, Dorset, 170
Bridge of Avon, Scotland, 111–112
Bridge of Orchy, Scotland, 112–114
Bridge Street Station, Glasgow, Scotland, 265
Bridgwater, Somerset, 100, 101
Bridport, Dorset, 280
Brighouse, West Yorkshire, 379–380
Brighton, West Sussex, 253–256
Brighton and South Coast Railway, 268
Brimington, Derbyshire, 352–354
Bristol, Somerset, 18, 101, 219, 223, 250, 330, 371, 372, 403
British Airport Authority, 41–42
British Museum, London, 59, 61, 325
Brittany, Duke of, 289
Broadhurst, Paul, 66, 67–68, 71–72, 123–124, 228–229
Bronze Age, 47, 53, 79, 90, 395
Brooklands, Surrey, 230–231
Broome family, 133–134
Broomhead, Corporal Roderick, 38
Brotherhood of the North, 327
Broughall, Tony, 99
'Brown of Priesthill', 91–92
Brown, Raymond Lamont, 85
Browning, Robert, 375
Bruce, Lucy, 336
Bruce, Robert, 89
Brussels, Belgium, 156
Brychan, King, 65
Bryn Celli Ddu, Anglesey, 72
Buckinghamshire, 60, 388
Buckland, Mrs Florence, 168
Bude, Cornwall, 103, 106
Burgh Castle, Suffolk, 304
Buriton Manor, Hampshire, 143–146
Burks, Eddie, 95–96
Burton, Lord, 398
Burtonwood, Lincolnshire, 42
Bury, Lancashire, 256–259
Bury St Edmunds, Suffolk, 311–312
Bussey Stool, Dorset, 392
Byng, Admiral, 246
Byrne, Simon, 388
Byron, Lord, 148

Cadbury, Somerset, 73–74, 108
Caernarfon, Wales, 178, 180, 351
Caerphilly, Wales, 286–288
Caidin, Martin, 48
Camborne, Cornwall, 207–209
'Camborne Hill' (song), 209
Cambridgeshire, 42–43
Camelot, (King Arthur's) 73–74
Cameron, Janet, 317
Cameron clan, 90
Camlam, Battle of, 124
Cammeringham, Lincolnshire, 48
Campbell, Marie, 4
Campbell clan, 87–88
Camulodunum (Colchester). 292
Canada, 21, 28, 29, 246, 359
Canewdon, Essex, 168–170
Canterbury, Archbishop of, 55
Canterbury, Kent, 55, 309, 310
Canvey Island, Essex, 232–233
Cape St Vincent, 176
Cape Wrath, Sandwood Bay, Scotland, 334–339
Capland Road Station, Glasgow, Scotland, 264
Carausius, Marcus A., 305
Cardiff, South Wales, 364
Cardington, Bedfordshire, 43
Careeleon, Wales, 312
Carew, Lady Evelyn Montefiore, 121–122
Carew Castle, Wales, 312
Carlton, Notttinghamshire, 74
Carlyle, Thomas, 384
Carn Brea hill, Camborne, Cornwall, 209
Carroll, Lewis, 307
Carter, George, 346
Casey, Micheal, 241–242
Castle Rising, Norfolk, 289–292
Catherine, Saint, 55
Catherine of Aragon, Queen, 119, 400
Cave of the Nativity, Bethleham, 310
Celts, 58, 221, 298, 327, 399
Cerne Abbas, Dorset, 55–58
Cernunnos, 58, 399
Chambers Dictionary of Quotations, 362
Charing Cross Hospital, London, 141
Charles I, King, 84, 86, 94–96, 114, 185, 384
Charles II, King, 100, 114, 222, 389
Charlton, London, 247
Charlton House, Greenwich, London, 247
Charmouth, Dorset, 222–223
Chartwell, Kent, 12

Cheadle Road, Leek, Staffordshire, 175
Chequer Street, St Albans, Hertfordshire
98–99
Cheshire, 43, 214–216
Chesterfield Canel, Derbyshire, 352–354
Chewton, Somerset, 250
Chiddesden, Hampshire, 279
Chiddingfold, Surrey, 250
Childe's Tomb, Dartmoor, Devon, 237
Chiuna, 375
Christ of the Trade (medieval painting),
61
Christie, Agatha, 367
Chudleigh, Sir George, 103
Chudleigh, Sir John, 103
Church Parade, Canvey Island, Essex, 232
Churchill, Winston, 12
Cistercians, 136–137, 300, 303, 307
Civil Wars, 83, 93, 95, 96–7, 103, 105,
108, 192, 288, 293, 296
Claridge, Colonel Frances (and family),
152–153
Clark, Peter, 14, 15
Claverhouse's Stone, Pass of
Killiecrankie, Scotland, 90
Clay, Dr R.C.C., 392–395
Clay, Rachel, 299
Cleaves, Stephen, 102
Cley Hill, Warminster, Wiltshire, 74
Cloisters Head, Llandaff, Wales, 364
Clwyd, North Wales, 210–212
Clydec River, Scotland, 266
Cobb, John, 230
Colchester, Essex, 223, 292–293, 365
Colerne, Wiltshire, 18–21
Colinburgh Castle, Scotland, 91
Colley, Colonel, 402
Connah's Quay, Wales, 210, 211
Conwy Castle, North Wales, 294–295
Conwy Falls, Wales, 351
Coombes, Revd. Brian, 391
Corbett, Tom, 138, 144
Corfe Castle, Dorset, 114–116, 290,
295–6, 332
Corfe Mullen, Dorset, 54
Cornwall, 21–24, 60–61, 65–69, 73,
74, 103–107, 108, 123–124, 128
146–148, 159–161, 180–185,
192–193, 207–209, 210, 227–229,
312, 319–323, 342–345, 346,
358–360, 372, 380–382, 390–392
Cosford, Shropshire, 43
Court of the Saxon Shore, 304
Covent Garden Underground Station,
London, 280

Coiw Lane, Brimington, Derbyshire, 352
Cowes, Isle of Wight, 280–281, 369–371
Cowloe Rocks, Sennen Cove, Cornwall,
342–343
Cox, Peter, 207
Coxe, Anthony Hippisley, 335
Crafthole, Cornwall, 346
Cranborne, Dorset, 393, 394, 396
Cranborne Gate, Windsor Great Park,
399
Cranham, Greater London, 216
Cranmere Pool, Dartmoor, Devon, 237
Crawford, O.G.S., 53
Creswell Crags, Derbyshire, 74
Crich Nunnery, Essex, 188
Crighton, Abraham, 189–191
Crimean War, 301–302
Critchill, Somerset, 223
Cromwell, Oliver, 93, 108, 189, 327, 384
Crowley, Aleister, 315
Crown Estate Commissioners, 399
Croydon, London, 43
Cruikshank, George, 399
Crusades, 63
Crying Boy Lane, Leigh-on-Sea, Essex,
224
Culliford, Lady Jane, 221–222
Culloden Moor, Scotland, 79–83
Cumberland, Duke of, 79–83
Cumhaill, Fionn mac, 107
Cunningham, Georege, 384–385
Curse of Scotland, (nine of diamonds),
87
Cwmdonkin Park, Wales, 234–236
Cyclical ghosts, 88, 92, 94, 96, 101, 104,
119–120, 121–123, 169, 180, 227, 228

DC3 aircraft, 25, 26
D'Arcy family, 189
Dalrymple, Sir John, 87
Dalyell, General Tam, 162
Daniel, Hannah, 172
Daniel, James, 170–173
Daniel's Knowle, Dorset, 170–173
Dapifer, Eudo, 61
Darell family, 361
Darlington, Durham and Teeside,
259–262
Darnley, Lord, 158
Dartmoor, Devon, 109, 236–240
Dartmouth, Devon, 19
Daventry, Northamptonshire, 94–96
Davidstow, Cornwall, 21–2
Davidstow Airfield and Cornwall at War
Museum, 21–24

Davies, Sergeant Arthur, 244–245
Dawkins, Christopher, 201
Day, James Wentworth, 298, 366
Day, Kevin, 14–15
de Clare, Gilbert, ('the Red Earl') 287, 288
de Clare, Walter, 307
de Culwin, Dorothea, 250
de Manio, Jack, 17
de Tremur, Ralph, 161
Deabill, Eleanor, 28
Deal, Kent, 346
Deane Water Bottom, Wiltshire, 402
Decline and Fall of the Roman Empire, 143
Deeside, 211
Defiant aircraft, 18
'Demon's Bridge'. Sheffield, 129
Denbigh Road, Haslemere, Surrey, 250
Denham, Matthew, 122
Dening, Revd. John, 366
Denmark and the Danes, 35, 186, 304, 311–312, 325, 328
Densham, Denny, 14–17
Densham, Revd. Frederick William, 159–161
Deptford, london, 247
Derby-Miller cars, 230
Derbyshire, 72, 74, 80, 185–186, 215, 352–354
Dering, Lady, 192
Desmond, Kevin, 43
Devereux, Robert, Earl of Essex, 84
Devil Stone, Carlton, Nottinghamshire, 74
Devil's Chimney, Beachy Head, East Sussex, 315, 316
Devil's Punch Bowl, Hindhead, Surrey, 241, 242
Devil's Staircase, Glencoe, Scotland, 86
Devon, 19, 54, 72, 103, 109, 212–214, 236–240, 312
Devonshire, Flight Lieutenant Len, 39–40
Devoran, Cornwall, 106
Dickens, Charles, 399
Dickson, Thomas, 116–117
Dinnnington, Rotherhasm,, West Yorkshire, 380–381
Dinnington Hall, West Yorkshire, 38
Dolgellau, Wales, 382
Domesday Book, 289
Don, Kaye, 230
Doncaster, West Yorkshire, 280
Dorchester, Dorset, 52, 220–222, 298
Dorking, Surrey, 249–250

Dorset, 1, 49, 52–54, 55–58, 96–97, 100, 108, 114–116, 117–118, 152–153, 170–173, 206–207, 214, 220–223, 276–279, 280, 295–296, 298–299, 332–334, 372, 377, 392–396
Dorset Barrows, 395–396
Dover, Kent, 304
Down Wood, Dorset, 377–378
Downton, Wiltshire, 152
Doyle, Sir Arthur Conan, 138, 307
Dozmary Pool, Bodmin Moor, Cornwall, 372
Drake, Sir Francis, 228
Drem, Scotland, 43
Druids and Druidism, 60–61, 68
Drummossie Muir, Scotland, 79, 81
Dryburgh Abbey Hotel, Scotland, 116–117
Dudley, Captain, 86
Dugdale, J.G., 362
Dumfries and Galloway, Scotland, 189–191
Dumnonia, Kingdom of, 65
Dundee, Scotland, 92, 279
Dundee, Viscount ('Bonnie Dundee') 90–93
Dunhail, Scotland, 262–263
Dunkeld, Scotland, 91
Dunn, Miss J.M., 50–51
Dunvegan, Scotland, 223
Durdle Door, Dorset, 334
Durer, Albrecht, 156
Durham, Co. Durham, 326
Durham, James, 259–261
Durness, Scotland, 339
Durweston Bridge, Dorset, 117, 118
Dyer, James, 53
Dymond, Carolyn, 321

East Kirby, Lincolnshire, 43
East Lothian, Scotland, 162
Eastbourne, East Sussex, 315
Eastbourne Herald, 317
Eastertime, 56
Easters, Private, 39
Ebbesbourne Wake, Wiltshire, 394
Ebbingford Manor, Bude, Cornwall, 106
Eccles, near Aylesford, Kent, 403
Eden, River, Kent, 119
Edgbaston, Birmingham, 354–358
Edgehill, Battle of, Warwickshire, 83–86
Edgehill 1642, 85
Edinburgh, Scotland, 245–246, 337, 338
Edmund (Saint), King of East Anglia, 311–312

Edmund's Hollow, Wales, 210–212
Edward, Earl of Oxford, 290
Edward the Confessor, 310
Edward, 'the Martyr', 295–296
Edward I, King, 349
Edward II, King, 288, 290–291
Edward III, King, 88–89, 289, 290, 291, 298
Edward VI, King, 400
'Edwardian' (architecture) 288
Edwards, Wayne, 390
Eleanor, Queen, 63
Eleanor of Castile, 294
Elizabeth I, Queen, 115, 156, 189, 206, 212, 246, 290, 295, 396
Elsie, Lilly, 128
Emma, of the Silent Pool, 368
English Heritage, 299
Epping Forest, Essex, 47
Erasmus, Desiderius, 310
Eric, Sir William, 240
Ermine Sytreet, (Roman road), 48, 61
Esk, River, Scotland, 373
Essex, 36–38, 47, 48, 168–170, 187–189, 193, 206, 223, 224, 232–233, 270–272, 297–298, 304, 365–367, 386–387
Ethlebert, 55
Euston, London, 266
Evans, David, 277
Evans, Gruffydd, 150
Everard, Kathlen, 68
Exeter, Devon, 103

Fairfax, Robert, 192
Fairfax, Sir Thomas, 93–94
Fairies, King of the, 74
Fairy Glen, Wales, 351
Falcon Inn, Dinnington, West Yorkshire, 381
Falkirk, Scotland, 79
Fanton Hall, Essex, 386
Fareham, Hampshire, 304
Farnborough, Hampshire, 31
Farrs, Beaminster, Dorset, 207
Fawkes, Guy, 133, 205
Felix Hall, Essex, 272
Felixstowe, Suffolk, 304
Ferguharson, Alexander, 245
Ferrers, Major Thomas, 135
Fife, Scotland, 161
First World War, 13, 22, 38, 165, 230, 268–270, 299, 398
Fishponds, Bristol, 371–372
Fiskerton, Nottinghamshire, 275–276
Fitzgibbon, Constantine, 235

Flamsteed House, Greenwich, London, 248
Flemish (Belgian), 212
Flint, North Wales, 210–212
Flodden, Northumberland, 349
Flowers Barrow, Dorset, 332
Flying Fortress aircraft, 21
Flynnon Dwynwen, Wales, 345
Fobbing, Essex, 298
Foggin, Major Cyril, 32
Fogging Quarry, Dartmoor, Devon, 237–240
Folklore Society, 247
Ford, Mick, 369–371
Forestry Commission, 58, 383, 403
Forman, Joan, 49–50, 70, 141, 389
Forres, Scotland, 262
Fort William, Scotland, 87
Fosse Way, 19
Fox, Ian, 305–306
Fox Tor, Dartmoor, Devon, 237
Foyle, Christina, 271
France, 18, 21–22, 35, 82, 222, 268, 288, 289, 296, 305, 315, 344
Francis, Maggie, 106
Frankland, Tommy, 324–325, 366
Fraser, John, 335, 339–341
Frewin, Roger, 127
Friday Street, Surrey, 367
Frithweld, King, 187
Frome, River, Dorset, 332
Frome, Somerset, 223
Fulcher, H.G., 366–367
Fulmar aircraft, 39
Furse, Bishop Michael, 167

Gairnshiel Lodge, Scotland, 222
Ganllwyd, near Dolgellan, North Wales, 382–384
Gargoyle Club, London, 389
Garry, River, Scotland, 90, 91
Gatwick Airport, 41–42
Gaveston, Piers, 290
Gazetteer and Touring Guide, 390
Gazetteer of England, 390
Geare, Bengie, 237
General's Tomb, Kent, 201
George V, King, 61, 158, 375
George Street, Bath, 203
Georgian period, 177
Gessoriacum (Boulogne), France, 305
Gatty, J.Paul, 155–157
Germany, 15, 35, 36–38, 269
Ghost Club (Society), 60, 68, 101–02, 121, 141–142, 154, 168, 175, 192, 242, 247, 250, 256, 307, 328

Ghost Club – A History, The, 142
Ghost Stations books, 43
Ghost Train, The, 251
Ghosts of Cornwall, 124, 147
Ghosts of Kent, 11
Ghosts of the Broads, 121
Ghosts of Wales, 382
Giant hill, Cerne Abbas, Dorset, 56–58
Giant's Coffin, Camborne, Cornwall, 209
Giant's Cradle, Comborne, Cornwall, 209
Giant's Hand, Camborne, Cornwall, 209
Giant's Heart, Camborne, Cornwall, 209
Giant's Wheel, Camborne, Cornwall, 209
Gibbet Hill, Hindhead, Surrey, 240–242
Gibbon, Edward, 143, 144
Gittings, Mrs, 203–204
Gladstone, William, 307
Glamorgan, Lord of, 287
Glasgow, Scotland, 263–266, 340
Glasgow Central Station, Scotland, 266
Glasson, Mr, 182
Glastonbury, Somerset, 64
Glemoreston, Laird of, 90
Glen of the Fairies, 243, 246
Glen Orchy, Scotland, 112–114
Glencoe, Scotland, 86–88
Glencorse, Scotland, 373
Glenshee, Perthshire, Scotland, 243–246
Glossop, Cheshire, 214
Gloucestershire, 205, 287, 290, 291, 403
Gog and Magog, 58
Gomshall, Surrey, 367
Goodwin Sands, off Deal, Kent, 346
Goos Wood, Castle Rising, Norfolk, 289
Gore-Browne, Colonel Robert, 138–139
Goss, David, 216
Govan, Scotland, 264–265
Gower peninsula, Wales, 329
Grange Hill, Dorset, 332
Grant, General James, 111, 162
Great Eastern inn, Maldon, Essex, 271
Great North Road, 259
Great Siege (Berwick) 349
Green, Andrew, 70, 188–189, 199
Green Park, London, 385–386
Green Park Underground Station, London, 280
Greenwich, London, 246–249
Gregory, Tom, 319
Grenville, Sir Bevill, 106
Gretna Green, Scotland, 207
Griffiths, William, 148
Grim (supernatural giant) 60
Grime's Graves, Weeting, Norfolk, 58–60

Grinsell, Leslie, 395–396
Griston Hall, Norfolk, 396
Groaning Bridge, Brede Place, East Sussex, 127
Guildford, Surrey, 155, 241, 242, 367, 368
Gulval, Cornwall, 182
Gunn, Sandy, 335–336
Gunpowder Plot, 133
Gwithian, Cornwall, 358–360
Gwyde Forest, Wales, 351
Gwyn ap Nudd, 66
Gwynne, Nell, 389

Hadleigh, Essex, 297–298
Hadleigh Castle, Essex, 297–298
Hadrian's Wall, (Roman), Northumberland, 285
Hague, The, Holland, 100
Haining, Peter, 70
Halidon Hill, Northumberland, 88–90
Halifax, Lord, 307
Halifax aircraft, 21, 28, 29
Hallness, George, 122
Halpenny, Bruce Barrymore, 4, 28, 34, 39, 43, 256–259
Hamilton, Bill, 264
Hamilton, Duke of, 384
Hammersmith, London, 266–267
Hammond, Carol, 27–28
Hampden aircraft, 28
Hampshire, 31, 136–140, 141–146, 154, 186–187, 192, 240, 241, 242, 267–8, 279, 301–306, 312, 372, 373
Hampstead, London, 162
Handley, Dorset, 394, 395
Handley Page aircraft, 13–14, 28
Handlope, Buckinghamshire, 388
Hangman's Tree, 390–392
Hardy, Revd R.W., 246
Hardy, Thomas, 170, 206, 333
Harlow, Essex, 193
Harper, Tom, 201–202
Harridence, Alan, 29–30
Harrier aircraft, 39
Harris, Eric, 25
Harris, 'Tiny', 41
Harrison, Mrs., 203
Harrogate, West Yorkshire, 29, 367
Hart inn, Thundersley, Essex, 386–387
Hartley Manditt, Hampshire, 373
Haslemere, Surrey, 240, 242, 250
Haslitt, Sir Godfrey, 121
Hastings, East Sussex, 315
Hastings aircraft 20–21

Hastings, Battle of, 93
Hattonn, Sir Christopher, 115, 295
Haunted Gardens, 147
Haunted London, 246
Hawker, Colonel, 321
Hawker, R.W. (vicar), 105
Hay, Will, 279
Hayle, Cornwall, 183
Hayling Billy Line, 267
Hayling Island, Hampshire, 267–268
Hawley, Lieutenant-General Henry, 79
Hearst, William Randolph, 156
Heathrow Airport, London, 24–28
Heaton, Howard, 135–136
Hecht, Ernest, 4
Heddon Oak, 403
Heligan, Cornwall, 146–148, 390
Heligan House, Cornwall, 390–391
Hell Fire Corner, near Brighouse, West
    Yorkshire, 379
Hell's Mouth, Cornwall, 358–359
Helmshore, Lancashire, 256, 257
Hendon, London, 43
Henrietta Maria, Queen, 384
Henry II, King, 63, 308
Henry III, King, 303
Henry V, King, 169
Henry VII, King, 310, 384
Henry VIII, King, 115, 118, 155, 156,
    189, 246, 289, 310, 317, 398
Herbert, Benson, 152
Hercules, 58
Heme, Rycharde 398
Heme the Hunter, 397–400
Herring, Maisie, 390–391
Hertfordshire, 60, 61–65, 97–99,
    165–168, 192, 375, 389, 403
Herthill, Mr., 133–134
Hever Castle, Kent, 118–120
Hewitt, Mrs Katrina, 126
Higham Ferrers, Northamptonshire,
    42–43
Higham Special car, 230
Highland Railway Line, 262–263
Hill figures, 56–58, 75, 83
Hill of Christie, Glencoe, Scotland, 245,
    246
Hill of Death, 201
Hillhead Station, Scotland, 264
Hindhead, Surrey, 240–242
Hindley, Peter, 31
Hints Road, Hopwas, Staffordshire, 173
History of Nanteos, 148
Hoath, R, 272–273
Hod Hill, Dorset, 118

Holbein, Hans, 156
Hole, Christina, 70
Hole Haven Road, Canvey Island, Essex,
    233
Holehaven Creek, Essex, 298
Holland, 35, 232
Holy Island (Lindisfarne), 326–328
Honington, Lincolnshire, 43
Honiton, Devon, 212–214
Hopkins, General Matthew, (witchfinder)
    293
Hopkins, Margaret, 235–236
Hopton, Sir Ralph, 106
Hopwas, Staffordshire, 173–177
Horisi, (or Hsris), 289
Horsa, (Jutish leader), 201
Horsemen, phantom, 51, 74, 85, 111,
    118, 162, 311, 379, 385, 393–396,
    397–401, 403
Hounslow, London, 25
House of Lords, 94
Howard, Henry, Earl of Northampton,
    290
Howard, Thomas, Earl of Arundel, 290
Howard, Thomas, Earl of Berkshire, 290
Howard, Thomas, Duke of Norfolk,
    289–290
Howley, Yorkshire, 108
Hsris, (or Horisi), 289
Hughes, John Vivian, 300
Hughes, Sergeant Bernard, 37
Hunt, Robert, 65
Huntingdonshire, 38–40, 108, 303
Hurricane aircraft, 12, 18, 21, 35
Hussey, Christopher and Elizabeth,
    154–155
Hyde, Cheshire, 214
Hyde Park, London, 384–386

Iceni tribe, 47–48
Icklingham, Suffolk, 403
Icknield Way, (Roman road), 61, 403
Ilminster, Somerset, 372
Imperial War Museum, 36
Indianapolis Duesenberta cars, 230
Ingro Tunnel, Keighley, West Yorkshire,
    279–280
Innerleithen, Scotland, 158
Inverness, Scotland, 79–83
Iona Community, 324
Iona Cross, Glencoe, Scotland, 86
Ireland (and Irish), 324, 342, 345
Ireton, General, 93–95
Irish Sea, 178, 180
Iron Age, 47, 54, 58, 59, 209

Irving, Sir Henry, 69
Isobella, Queen, 289, 290, 291
Isfield, East Sussex, 268–270
Isle of Iona, Scotland, 324–326
Isle of Wight, 280–281, 301, 315, 369–371, 402
Isles of Scilly, 34

Jack the Ripper, 217–220, 385
Jackson, Revd A.W., 327
Jacobite Risings, 222
James I, King, 381
James II, King, 87, 91, 100–101
James VI, King, 158
Japan, 35
Jill's Pool, Bossiney, Cornwall, 228
Job, The, 25
Joel, Janet, 4, 148–149
John, King, 136–137, 296, 303, 367–368
Johnson, Samuel, 158
Jordan, Debbie, 320
Judy Wood, near Brighouse, West Yorkshire, 379
Jurassic Coast, Dorset, 332

Keat's House, Hampstead, London, 162
Keighley, West Yorkshire, 279–280
Keighley and Worth Valley Railway, 279
Keiller, A., 53
Kelstern Moor, Lincolnshire, 43
Kelvedon, Essex, 272
Kelvinbridge Station, Glasgow, Scotland 264
Kendel, Revd Henry, 261
Kent, 11–13, 55–56, 74, 118–120, 127–128, 154–155, 192, 200–202, 249, 304, 310–311, 346, 360–361, 373, 403
Kenward, Trevor, 102, 341
Ketch, Jack, 100
Kiernander, Stewart, 175–176, 268
Killiecrankie, Pass of, Scotland, 2, 90–93
Kineton, Warwickshire, 83–86
King, Mrs M.A., 207–209
King's Mound, Stirling Castle, Scotland, 74
Kings Lynn, Norfolk, 289–292
Kingshouse Hotel, Glencoe, Scotland, 112–114
Kingsley, Charles, 210
Kingsley Lane, Benfleet, Essex, 386
Kingston, Surrey, 242
Kingston Lacy House, Dorset, 52
Kinlochbervie, Scotland, 337, 339
Kinson, Dorset, 372

Kirmond Hall, Ludford, Lincolnshire, 373
Kit's Coty House, Kent, 200–201
Kinghts Templar, 63
Knightswish Farm, Canvey Island, Essex, 233
Knowle Farm, Beaminster, Dorset, 171–172
Knowlton, Wiltshire, 128–129

Labrador, Newfoundland, Canada, 359
Lackford, Suffolk, 403
Ladder Lane, Swindon, 402
Lady Lovibund, 346
Lady of the Lake, 372
Lake District, 108
Lakenheath, Suffolk 42
Lamberhurst, Kent, 154–155, 310–311, 360–361
Lambert, Guy W., 240, 347–348
Lambert, Percy, 231
Lancashire, 42, 256–259
Lancaster aircraft, 21
Lancia cars, 230
'Land of the Mermaids', 335
Land's End, Cornwall, 342–345
Landseer, Sir Edwin, 156
Langham, Dorset, 372
Langhorne, Sir William, 247
Langport, Somerset, 101
Langrish, Hampshire, 141–143
Langrish, Roger, 141
Laugharne, Wales, 235, 362–363
Laughton-en-le-Morthern, West Yorkshire, 381
Launceston, Cornwall, 103, 359
Lavender Line, Sussex, 268–270
Le Maine, Marie, 311
Lee, Laurie, 290–291
Leek, Staffordshire, 175–176
Leeming, Yorkshire, 28–31
Legg, Rodney, 52–53, 96, 118, 377, 378, 392
Leicestershire, 48
Leigh-on-Sea, Essex, 224
Letchworth Garden City, Hertfordshire, 375
Lethbridge, Tom, 240
Lewes Road, Brighton, 254
Lewis, Gwyneth, 4
Ley Lines, 49, 107
Leyland-Thomas cars, 230
Liberator aircraft, 21
Lichfield, Staffordshire, 42, 107
Lightning aircraft, 18, 39

Lincolnshire, 43, 48
Lindisfarne, Northumberland, 326–328
Linkinhorne, Cornwall, 61
Llanbadarn Fawr, Wales, 150
Llandaff, near Cardiff, South Wales, 364–365
Llanddwyn Island, Anglesey, Wales, 345
Llanfaglan, Wales, 178–180
Llannddwyn Island, Wales, 178
Llewelyn the Younger, 288
Lleyn Peninsula, Wales, 345–346
Lobster Smack Inn, Canvey Island, Essex, 233
Loch Laidon, Sclotland, 112–114
London, 24–28, 43, 69, 100, 121, 133, 156, 162, 192, 216–220, 234, 246–249, 266, 267, 276, 280, 291, 292, 299, 308, 327, 384–386, 389
London Fire Service, 22
London Hospital, Whitechapel, London, 219
London Road, St Albans, Hertfordshire, 98
London Underground railway, 280
Lonegan, Edward, 241–242
Longfellow, Henry Wadsworth, 3
Lord Halifax's Ghost Book, 307
Lost Bells of Lyonesse, 343
Lost Gardens of Heligan, Cornwall, 146–148
Lostwithiel, Cornwall, 107–108
Loudon, John Claudius, 399
Louis XVIII of France, 63
Lourdes, Grotto of, 310
Lovatt, Lance-Corporal Steve, 38
Lovers' Leap, River Esk, Scotland, 373
Ludford, Lincolnshire, 373
Ludgvan, Cornwall, 180–185
Lulworth Castle, Dorset, 333–334
Lulworth Cove, Dorset, 332–334
Lutyens, Sir Edwin, 127, 327
Lyme Regis, Dorset, 100, 101
Lyonesse, off Cornwall, 343–345

Macaulay, Rose, 154
MacDonald, Alexander, 245–246
MacDonald, Robertson, 335, 340
MacDonald clan 80, 86–88, 223
McDonald, John, 262
MacHardie, Isobel, 245–246
MacMillan, John, 324–325
MacPherson, Alexander, 245–246
MacPherson, Miss, 345
MacPherson clan, 80
Madog (of Nannau Old Hall), 382–383

Maiden Castle, Dorset, 108, 298–299
Maidstone, Kent, 200
Malcolm, Earl of Lennox, 89
Malldon, Essex, 270–272
Malet, Baldwin, 96–97
Malet, Sir Thomas, 97
Manchester, Greater, 280
Manningtree, Essex, 223
Mansfield, Nottinghamshire, 272
Maple, Eric, 70, 77, 168, 206, 247, 366
Marches of Wales, The, 351
Margam, South Wales, 300
Margam Abbey and Castle, South Wales, 300
Margaret, Countess of Salisbury, 192
Margaret, Lady, 312
Margate Grotto, Kent, 74
Marlpits Hill, Honiton, Devon, 212–214
Marshall, James, 241–242
Marston Moor, Yorkshire, 108, 327
Mary, Queen, 158
Mary Queen of Scots, 158
Marypark, Moray, Scotland, 112
Masefield, Sir Peter, 36
Maserati cars, 230
Mason, Oliver, 390
Maximinus, Emperor, 305
Maxwell, Donna, 200
Maxwell-Hyslop, Rachel, 299
May Day, 55, 56
Mayfield Station, Greater Manchester, 280
McCue, Peter, 199
McKay, Alex, 388
McKay, George, 335–336
Meaykin, Tom, 176–177
Medlycott family, 152–153
Meetings with Remarkable Trees, 391
Melbourne Street, Royston, Hertfordshire, 62
Melrose, Scotland, 116
Merlin, (King Arthur's magician), 72, 346
Merlin engine, 12
Merry Wives of Windsor, 398
Merryweather, Revd Ernest, 366
Mersea Island, Essez, 365–367
Merton Hall, Norfolk, 396
Mevagissey, Cornwall, 146, 390
Middleham Castle, near Richmond, Yorkshire, 311
Midland Railway, 272
Midsummer Eve and Day, 55, 56, 73, 227, 228, 229,
Mildenhall, Suffolk, 403

Mildenhall, Wiltshire, 43
Milford, Surrey, 241
Military Ghosts, 43
Milky Way (Trackway) 310
Miller, Garson and Maria, 200
Miller, Mrs Pat, 41
Miller-Stirling, Mr and Mrs., 144–145
Millfield Plain, Scotland, 349
Ministry of Defence, 19, 85
Moffram, Cheshire, 214–216
Mohammedans, 309
Mohun, Lord, 384
Molesworth Arms, Wadebridge, Cornwall, 128
Monks Walk, Stevenage, Hertfordshire, 403
Monmouth, Duke of, 100–101
Monmouth Rebellion, 170, 171, 212–214, 403
Montagu, Lord, 138–140
Montagu Motor Museum, 139
Monte Point, Devon, 72
Montefiore, Mrs Cynthia, 203
Montrose, Scotland, 31–36
Monyash, Derbyshire, 185–186
Moot Hall, Maldon, Essex, 271
Moray, Scotland, 162
Morley, Mr and Mrs A., 186–187
Morrison, E.A., 383–384
Mortimer, Roger, 289, 290, 291
Morton, H.V., 136
Morwenstow, Cornwall, 105–106
Mosquitoe aircraft, 18, 21
Most Amazing Haunted Places . . . 206
Mother Goddess, 299
Moulsecoomb Station, Brighton, Sussex, 253–256
Mount's Bay, Cornwall, 184
Mountain Circuit, Brooklands, Surrey, 230
Mousehill, near Milford, Surrey, 241
Mumbles, The, near Swansea, Wales, 328–331
Murphy, Theresa, 276
Murray, Lord George, 80–82
Mustang aircraft, 39

Nannau Old Hall, Wales, 382–384
Nanteos Mansion, Wales, 148–152
Napier cars, 230
Napier Railton cars, 230
Napoleon, Bonaparte, 332–333
Naseby, Northamptonshire, 93–96
National Gallery, London, 266
National Trust 54, 240

Nazareth, 309
Neath, Wales, 331
Nechtanesmere, Scotland, 108
Nectan or Nudd (Celtic river god), 66, 67
Nelson, Kord, 148, 176
Neolithic age, 58, 59, 209, 298, 299,380
Netley Abbey, Southampton, Hampshire 301–304
New Forest, Hampshire, 372
New Year's Eve, 262
Newark, Nottinghamshire, 272
Newlands, Dorset, 222–223
Newport, Isle of Wight, 280–281
Newport, Shropshire, 404
Newton Road, The Mumbles, Wales, 329
Nicholson family, 141–143
Nightingale, Florence, 301
Nine Yews Riding Stables, Dorset, 393
Noon, Joseph Patrick, 266
Norfolk, 13–18, 47, 56–60, 69–71, 120–123, 289–292, 304, 309–310
Norfolk, Dukes of, 290
Norfolk Naturalist Trust, 396
Norman (architecture, etc.) 285, 290, 292, 295, 304
Norman, Barry and Diana, 138
Normandy, Duke of, 365
North Benfleet, Essex, 386–387
North Goodwin Lightship, 346
North Hessary, Dartmoor, Devon, 237
North Sea, 349
North Weald, Essex, 36–38
North Weald Bassett, Essex, 36–38
Northampton, 388–389
Northsampton, Earl of, 290
Northamptonshire, 43, 93–96, 311, 388–389
Northumberland, 88–90, 108, 285–286, 326–328, 347–351
Norton motorcycles, 250
Norway, 324
Nottingham Castle, 291
Nottinghamshire, 74, 247, 272–276, 291
Nugent, Lord, 84–85
Nunnery, Somerset, 223
Nun's Wood, St Osyth, Essex, 188

Observatory Hill, Greenwich Park, London, 247–249
O'Dell, Damien, 64
Odiham, Hampshire, 312
Odin, (or Woden), Norse god, 59, 398–399
O'Donnell, Elliott, 92, 147, 219, 328
Oh! Mr Porter, 279

Okehampton, Devon, 237
Old Bayham Manor, Kent, 373
Old Chatham Road, Kent, 200
Old Hall, Laughton Road, Dinnington, Yorkshire, 381
Old Mill, Boscastle, Cornwall, 319
Old Post Office, Royston, Hertfordshire, 63–64
Old Priest's Track, Dorset, 222
Oliver, Edith, 50, 344–345
Osborne House, Isle of Wight, 301
Ossian (Galic bard), 86
Osyth, daughter of Frithwald, 187–189
Oughtibridge, Sheffied, Yorkshire, 129
Oundle, Northamptonshire, 311
Our Lady of Welsingham (shrine), 309–310
Outer Circuit, Brooklands, Surrey, 230
Outer Hebrides, Scotland, 75
Owain Glyndwr, 288, 383
Owen, Elizabeth and William, 149–150
Oxford, 84, 86
Oysterfleet, Essex, 232
Osystermouth Castle, The Mumbles, Wales, 329

Pakenham, Thomas, 391
Palaeolithic age, 59
Palmer, Parsenal, 27
Paranormal Essex, 48
Paranormal Investigation (organization), 104–107, 159, 227, 390
Paraphysical Laboratory, 152
Pare Woods, Wales, 351
Park Avenue Road, Dinnington, Yorkshire, 380–381
Parnell, Geoff, 42–43
Parnelll, James, 293
Parrish, Mrs Eileen, 205
Paulet, Sir Wiliam, 303
Payne, Anthony, 103, 106
Payne, Jessie, 233
Payne, Jessie K., 386
Pearce-Higgins, Revd John, 327–328
Pease, Edward, 261
Peddlers Way (trackway), 289
Peldon Rose inn, 366
Penally Hill, Boscastle, Cornwall, 321–322, 323
Penally House, Boscastle, Cornwall, 321–322
Pendulum dowsing, 106–107
Pengrula, Cornwall, 390–392
Penkaet Castle, East Lothian, Scotland, 162

Penzance, Cornwall, 180, 183, 192,
Pepper, Prudence, 22–24
Percy, Thomas, 123
Perry, Bill, 302–303
Perrymead, Bath, 205
Perth, Duke of, 81
Perthshire, Scotland, 90–93, 140–141, 243–246
Peterborough, Huntingdon, 303
Petersfield, Hampshire, 242
Photography of Ghosts (lecture), 202
Pimperne, Dorset, 392
Piskeys, Cornish, 181, 182
Pissarro, Camille, 266
Pitlochry, Scotland, 90, 92
Pluckley, Kent, 192
Plume and Feathers, Princetown, Devon, 238
Pokesdown, Bournemouth, Hampshire, 393
Poland, 18, 21, 335
Polgrain family, 182–184,
Polin, Scotland, 335
Pope Adrian IV, 165
Pope, Gregory, 55
Porchester, near Fareham, Hampshire, 304–306
Port Talnot, Wales, 300
Portland Place, Bath, 203
Portsmouth, Hampshire, 186–187, 241, 304–305,
Portsmouth Cathedral, 186
Portugal, 397
Potter Heigham, Norfolk, 120–123
Powell family, 150, 151
Powerstock Station, Dorset, 280
Powles, Revd Robert, 137
Poyntington, Dorset, 96–97
Price, Harry, 2
Priestley, J.B. 228
Princetown, Devon, 237
Prior Park Road, Bath, 205
Proust, Marcel, 3
Public Records Office, 85
Pugh, Jane, 178–180, 211–212
Pullen, Jane, 366
Purbeck Hills, Dorset, 114, 332–334
Puttick, Betty, 68, 70, 271

Quakers 185–186, 203, 293
Queen Charlton, Somerset, 250
Queen's House, Greenwich, London, 246

Rackham, John 4
Railway Straight, Brooklands, Surrey, 231

Rake, Hampshire, 242
Rannoch Moor, Scotland, 112
Rapier missile, 22
Readers Digest, 54, 206, 292
Reading, Berkshire, 401
Reculver, Kent, 304
Red Earl, see de Clare, Gilbert
Red Horse (hill figure) 83
Red Lion Inn, Avebury, Wiltshire, 51
Red Lion inn, Thursley, Surrey, 241
Red River, Camborne, Cornwall, 208
Relics (True Cross, etc.), 310
Reynolds, Sir Joshua, 156
Rhydyfelin, Wales, 148
Richard, EArl of Cornwall, 228
Richard II, King, 398
Richard III, King, 298
Richard Coeur de Lion, 63, 310
Richards, Lady 309
Richards, Parson, 209
Richborough, Kent, 304
Richmond, Yorkshire, 311
Ridgeway Hill, Dorset, 52, 222
Rillaton, Cornwall, 60–61
Rillaton Barrow, Cornwall, 61
Risina (later Rising), 289
Rivers, Brian, 303–304
Robert, Earl of Mortoun, 227
Robert the Bruce, 310
Roberts, Andy, 379
Robin Hood, 379
Roche Rock, Cornwall, 74
Rocky Valley Maze, Cornwall, 65
Rogers, Carmen, 26
Rohesia, (later Royston) 61
Rolleston, Nottinghamshire, 272–276
Roman (architecture etc.) 286, 304–305, 312, 393, 402
Roman Camp, Norfolk, 69
Roman ghosts, 1, 51–52, 53, 54, 107, 108, 221, 222, 292, 299, 305, 332, 365–367, 403
Roman Heights, Corfe Mullen, Dorset, 54
Roman occupation, 289, 292, 298–299, 304, 401, 403
Rome, Italy, 82, 310
Romney, George, 156
Romney Marsh, Kent, 304
Rose Cottage, Beaminster, Dorset, 170
Ross, Donald, 114
Rotherham, Yorkshire, 380–381
Roxburgh, Scotland, 349
Royal, Margaret, 202, 203, 204, 205
Royal Aero Club, 36

Royal Air Force 11, 12, 14, 16, 17, 18–21, 22, 29, 31, 34, 41–43, 48
Royal Corps of Transport, 41
Royal Enfield motorcycles, 250
Royal Flying Corps, 11, 31–33, 36
Royal Maritime Auxiliary Servuce, 19
Royal Naval College, Greenwich, London, 246
Royal Navy, 39
Royal Photographic Society, 202
Royal Society of Antiquaries, 62
Royal Victoria Country Park, Southampton, Hampshire, 303
Royal Victoria Hospital, Netley, Hampshire, 301–304
Royston Cave, Hertfordshire, 61–65
Royston Community, Hertfordshire, 63–64
Runavey, Scotland, 243
Rupert, Prince, 85, 93–95
Rushton Spencer, Staffordshire, 176
Russell Street, Bath, 203
Rye, East Sussdex, 193
Ryedale Windy Pits, Yorkshire, 75

Sacred Wells, 55, 56, 61
Sage, Richard, 216
St Aidan, 326
St Algan, (martyr), 98
St Albans, Hertfordshire, 97–99, 192
St Albans Abbey, Hertfordshire, 192
St Augustine, 310
St Austell, Cornwall, 106
St Catherine the Martyr, 63
St Catherine's Day, 55
St Cedd, 304
St Chads, Hopwas, Staffordshire, 173, 174
St Christopher, 63
St Columba and Columban, 324, 326
St Cuthbert, 326–328
'St Cuthbert's Beads', 327
St Dwynan, 178
St Dwynwen, Wales, 345
St Enochs Station, Glasgow, Scotland. 265
St Ewe, Cornwall, 390
St John the Baptist, 63
St John the Evangelist church, Wotton, Surrey, 249
St John's church, Hopwas, Staffordshire, 173, 174–175
St Lawrence church, Abbots Langley, Hertfordshire, 165–168
St Leonard's church, Dinnington, Yorkshire, 381

St Leonard's church, Rushton Spencer, Staffordshire. 177
St Levan, near Penzance, Cornwall, 192–193
St Mary's church, Beaminster, Dorset, 170, 172
St Mary's Lane, Uprainster/Cranham, London, 216
St Mary's church, Latton, Harlow, Essex, 193
St Melor, 61
St Michael's church, Bishops Stortford, Hertfordshire, 192
St Michael's church, Honiton, Devon, 212
St Nectan's Glen, Cornwall, 65–69
St Nicholas church, Aberdeen, Scotland, 191
St Nicholas church, Pluckley, Kent, 192
St Osyth Priory, Essex, 187–189
St Osyth's Well, St Osyth, Essex, 188
St Peter's church, Ythancaestir, Essex 304
St Peter and St Paul church, St Osyth, Essex, 188
St Peter's church, Rome, Italy, 310
St Thomas a Becket, 63, 310
St Thomas's church, Portsmouth, Hampshire, 186
St Valentine, 345
Saffron Walden, Essex, 127
Salcey Forest, Northampton, 388–389
Salcey Lawn, Salcey Forest, Northampton, 389
Salisbury, Wiltshire, 49–53, 344, 393, 394
Salisbury Hall, Hertfordshire, 389
Sandford Orcas, Dorset, 152–153
Sandwood Bay, Sutherland, Scotland, 334–343
Sangster, Paul, 139–140
Sanquhar, Scotland, 189–191
Saville Road, Bath, 203, 205
Saxons, 237, 304, 305, 381
Scampton, Lincolnshire, 43
Scandinavia, 59, 60
Scarry, Mrs Jean, 193
Scotland, 31–36, 43, 45, 74, 75, 79–83, 86–88, 89, 90–93, 107, 108, 111–114, 116–117, 140–141, 158–159, 161, 162, 189–191, 197–200, 207, 222, 223, 243–246, 262–266, 279, 285, 310, 324–326, 334–343, 349, 371, 373
Scotney Castle, Kent, 154–155, 360–361
Scott, James, Duke of Monmouth, 100–101

Scott, R, 247–248
Scott, Sir Walter, 158, 325–326, 328
Scottish Highland Folklore, 340
Seafield, Lily, 189
Seaford, East Sussex, 315
Seafire aircraft, 39
Seagrave, Henry, 230
Second World War, 12, 14, 15, 16, 18, 22, 28, 30, 33–36, 38–40, 42, 43, 127, 137, 141, 247–248, 250, 277, 301
Secret Land, The, 66–67, 71
'Sedgemoor, Battle of, 100–102, 171, 212–214, 403
Sedgemoor, Westonzoyland, Somerset, 100–102
Sedgwick, Michael, 139
Selborne, Hampshire, 373
Sele, Howel, 382–384
Selkirk, Scotland, 349
Sennen Cove, Cornwall, 342–345
Serpent's Stone, Glenshee, Scotland, 243
Severnake Forest, Wiltshire, 400–402
Severnake Forest Hotel, Wiltshire, 402
Seymour, Lady Jane, 400
Shakespeare, William, 398
Sharpe, Ian, 201
Shaw, William, 244
Sheffield, Yorkshire, 129
Sherborne, Dorest, 96–97, 152
Sherborne Park, Surrey, 368
Shere, Surrey, 367–369
Sheridan, Claire, 127
Sherrick, Gerry, 162
Shields Road Station, Glasgow, Scotland, 265
Ship Tavern, Greenwich, London, 247
Shirley aircraft, 42
Shortwell, Nottinghamshire, 272
Shrieking Boy Wood, Essex, 386–387
Shrieking Pits, Aylmerton, Norfolk, 69–71
Shropshire, 43, 404
Siam (Thailand), 230
Sicily, Mediterranean, 315
Sidgwick, Professor Henry, 261
Sigghere, King, 187–188
Signal Rock, Glencoe, Scotland, 86
Sil, King, 51–52
Silbury Hill, Wiltshire, 51–52
Silent Pool, Shere, Surrey, 367–369
Simnel, Lambert, 310
Simpson, Dr Charles, 121–122
Simpson, Eric, 34
Singleton Bank, Wales, 235
Sixpenny Handley, Dorset, 393

Skelhorn, Arthur, 352–354
Skye, Isle of, Scotland 223
Slaughter Bridge, Cornwall, 123–124
Slaughter Stone, Stonehenge, 71
Slaybrook Hall, Kent, 127–128
Slogatt, William, 321–322
Smalley, John, 272–273
Smit, Tom, 146
Smith, Becky, 174
Smith, Gladys, 174
Smith, James MacRory, 340
Smith-Rownsley, Pamela, 106
Snuff Mills, Bristol, 371
Society for Psychical Research, (SPR), 140, 199, 201, 219, 240, 247, 250, 261, 307, 335, 347
Society of Antiquaries, 393
Society Of Apothecaries, 121
Soho, London, 389
Soldier's Leap, Pass of Killicrankie, Scotland, 90
Solihull, Warwickshire, 133
Somerset, 73–74, 75, 96, 100–102, 108, 202–206, 223, 250, 372
Sopwith Camel aircraft, 35
Souter Fell, Lake District, 108
South Wales Echo, 287
Southampton, Hampshire, 301–304
Southern Evening Echo, 302–303
Southwark Cathedral, London, 327
Southhwell Racecourse, Nottinghamshire, 274
Spain, 176, 199, 294
'Spectres of Salcey Forest', 388–389
Spinning Jenny Burn, Scotland, 371
Spiritualist Association of Great Britain, 26
Spitfire aircraft, 11, 12, 21, 37
Spittalgate Airfield, near Gratham, Lincolnshire, 41
Stafford, Earl of, 94, 96
Staffordshire, 42, 107, 173–177
Stamford, Earl of, 103, 106
Stamford Hill, Cornwall, 103–107
Stopleton near Bristol, Gloucestershire, 403
Stately Ghosts of England, The, 138
Statfall, Romney Marsh, Kent, 304
Steadlands, Surrey, 250
Stephan Langton, A Romance of the Silent Pool, 368
Stephenson, George (1781–1848), 285–286
Stepniak, (Russian anarchist), 266–267
Stevenage, Hertfordshire, 403

Stewart family, including 'Bonnie Prince Charlie', 79–83, 158–159
Stewart, Gwenda, 230
Stirling Castle, Scotland, 74, 79
Stockbridge, Yorkshire, 125–127
Stockton and Darlington Railway, 259
Stone, Staffordshire, 176
Stone Age (and New Stone Age), 69, 298, 380
Stone Tape, The, 3
Stonehenge, Wiltshire, 47, 49, 71–73, 75
Stones of Clava, Scotland, 79
Stour, River, 117–118, 128–129, 223, 372
Stourpaine, Dorset, 117–118
Straight, Whitney, 230
Strange, Baron and Baroness, 94
Strange But True, 126
Stratton, Cornwall, 103, 106
Strood, The, Mersea Island, Essex, 365–367
Stubbins Junction, Lancashire, 256, 257
Sudbury, Archbishop of, 403
Sue Rider Home, 141
Suffolk, 42, 47, 223, 304, 311–312, 403
Sugar Hill, Dorset, 277–279
Summerleaze Downs, Bude, Cornwall, 103
Supernatural England, 70, 206
Surrey, 155–158, 230–231, 240–242, 249–250, 367–369
Sussex, 127, 139, 193, 253–256, 291, 268–270, 281, 304, 315–318, 360
Sussex Paranormal Investigation Society, 253
Sutherland, Scotland, 334–343
Sutton Place, Surrey, 155–158
Swallow Falls, Wales, 351, 352
Swanage, Dorset, 52, 222, 276–279
Swanage, Wales, 234, 235, 328–331, 362
Swansea and Mumbles Railway, 330
Swinburne, Algernon Charles, 148
Swindon, Wiltshire, 402
Symes, Ann, 207

Taf, River, Wales, 362–363
Talbot cars, 230
Taliesin stone, Wales, 4
Tamworth, Staffordshire, 173,174
Tarbarwith, Cornwall, 322
Tardebigge Canal Tunnel, Worcestershire, 355
Tarrrant Gunville, Dorset, 392–396
Tauber, Richard, 404
Taunton, Somerset, 101

Tay, River, Scotland, 279
Tay Bridge, Dundee, Scotland, 279
Tayock Caravan Site, Montrose,
    Scotland, 34
Tennyson, Lord, 307
Terig, Mr and Mrs Duncan, 245, 246
Tess of the D'Urbervilles, 206
Thames, River, 58, 232, 246, 298
Thatcher, Margaret, 155
The Times, 299
Thetford, Norfolk, 396
Thomas, Dylan, 234, 236, 362–363
Thundersley, Essex, 387
Thurne, River, Norfolk, 122
Thursley, Surrey, 241, 242
Tihidy Hospital, Camborne, Cornwall,
    208
Tihidy Road, Camborne, Cornwall, 208
Tintagel, Cornwall, 66, 123, 227, 229,
    312
Tintern Abbey, Monmouthshire, 307–309
Tintern Parva, Monmouthshire, 307–309
Tintoretto, Jacopo, 156
Titchbourne Street, The Mumbles, Wales,
    330–331
Tobutt, Victor and Solange, 319
Tock, Mary, 16–17
Tolbooth, Edinburgh, Scotland, 245–246
Tower of London, 100, 156, 192
Trafalgar Road, Greenwich, London, 247
Traquair, Earl of, 158
Traquair House, Scotland, 158–159
Treble, Mary Anne, 165–167
Tree Inn, Stratton, Cornwall, 103, 106
Tregony, Cornwall, 181
Trent Valley, Staffordshire, 176
Trerice, Cornwall, 103
Trewarnan Bridge, Cornwall, 128
Trooper's Den, Killicrankie, Scotland, 90
Truelove, Arthur, 396
Truro, Cornwall, 181
Tulip Staircase, Queen's House,
    Greenwich, London, 246
Tupper, Martin, 368
Turner, J.M.W., 307
Twain, Mark, 307
Tweed, River, 286, 349–351
Tweedsmuir Hills, Scotland, 349
Twm Celwydd Teg, Wales, 300
Two Haunted Counties, 99
Tyburn, London, 291, 384
Tyler, Wat, 403
Tysoe, Dr., 192

Under Milk Wood, 363

United States of America, 223, 263, 362
University of Brighton, 253, 255
Upminster, London, 216–217
USAAF, 18, 21, 39, 42
Utrecht University, 3

Vassal Park, Fishponds, Bristol, 371–372
Valley, Island of, Scotland, 75
Valley of Death, (Glencoe), Scotland,
    86–88
Vatican, The, Brooklands, Surrey, 231
Vaughan family, 382
Vauxhall cars, 230
Versailles, France, 344
Verulamium, (St Albans), 98
Vespasian, (Roman emperor), 52
Victoria, Queen (and Victorian times),
    70, 173, 179, 200, 218–220, 244, 248,
    272, 300, 301, 307, 329, 331, 399
Victoria Gardens, Neath, Wales, 331
Vikings, 271, 324–325, 326, 328
Vincent, Admiral St., 176
Virgin Mary (vision), 309

WAAF, 14, 16, 17, 39–40
Waddon-Martyn, David, 322–333
Wadebridge, Cornwall, 128
Wagner, Richard, 148
Wailing Wood, Norfolk, 397
Wales, 45, 65, 72, 148–152, 178–180,
    210–212, 234–236, 286–288,
    294–295, 300, 307, 312, 345–346,
    351–352, 362–363, 364–365,
    382–384
Wales, National Poet of, 4
Walker, Stewart, 92
Walpole, Sir Robert, 80
Walsingham, Norfolk, 309–310
Walter, Mrs R., 149
Walton Castle, Suffolk, 304
War of the Roses, 98–99
War Office, 301
Warbarrow Bay, Dorset, 332
Warblington church, Hampshire, 192
Wareham, Dorset, 276
Warleggan, Cornwall, 159–161
Warminster, Wiltshire, 74
Warwickshire, 48, 83–86, 133–136
Wasthill Canal Tunnel, 354–358
Waterloo (battle), 136
Waterside Farm, Canvey Island, Essex,
    232
Watton, Norfolk, 396–397
Watts Arms, Northhampton, 388
Waugh, Neil, 173–174

Waugh, Mrs Pat, 173–174
Wayland Wood, Norfolk, 396
Wellington aircraft, 21
Wellington Hotel, Boscastle, Cornwall, 319–321
Wells, healing, 55, 56, 310
Wells of the Dead, Scotland, 83
Welsh Ghostly Encounters, 178, 211
Wentworth, Lady Henrietta, 100
Wesleyan Methodism, 185
West, Ann, 373
Westr Kirby, Cheshire, 43
West Lothian, Scotland, 162
West Stow, Suffolk, 403
Westminster Abbey, 310, 384
Weston, Sir Richard, 155
Westonzoyland, Somerset, 100–102
Weybourne, Norfolk, 70
Weymouth, Dorset, 52, 222
Wheatsheaf Hotel, Daventry, Northamptonshire, 94–96
Wheeler, Sir Mortimer, 298, 299
Whetter, Dr James, 390–391
Whirlwinds aircraft, 18
Whitaker, Terence, 114
White Funnel paddle steamer, 330
White Horse (hill carving) Wiltshire, 75
White Mill Bridge, Knowlton, Wiltshire, 128–129
White Sands, Isle of Iona, Scotland, 324–325
Whitechapel, London, 217–220
Whitchurch Canonicorum, Dorset, 222–223
Whitehead, Bill, 256–259
Whitley aircraft, 21, 28
Whitsand Bay, Crafthole, Cornwall, 346
Wickenby, Lincolnshire, 43
Widdale Fell, Yorkshire, 28–29
Wiley, an airman, 15
Wilkins, Henry, 267
William of Malmesbury, 56
William of Orange, 87, 91
William the Conqueror, 61, 227, 399
Williams, Mr and Mrs John, 248–249
Williams, Michael, 4, 68, 104–107, 159, 227–229, 343–344, 390–391
Willis, Iris, 276–279
Willis, Richard, 277–278
Wilton, Wiltshire, 344
Wiltshire, 18–21, 43, 47, 48–52, 60,
71–73, 74, 75, 108, 128–129, 152, 344, 394, 400–402
Wimborne Minster, Dorset, 52, 222, 377
Wincanton, Somerset, 96
Windsor, Berkshire, 121
Windsor Castle, 399
Windsor Castle, Berkshire, 398
Windsor, Duke of, 157
Windsor Great Park, Berkshire, 397–400
Windy Oaks, Shropshire, 404
Winter, Lieutenant-Colonel Patrick, 38
Winterborne Monkton, Dorset, 52
Winterbourne Abbas, Dorset, 220–222
Wintergarden, Canvey Island, essex, 232
Witchcraft, 168–169, 243, 247, 288, 293, 315, 368
Wittering, Huntingdonshire, 38–40
Woden, (or Odin) Norse god, 59
Wolfe, General, 249
Wolsey, Thomas, 119
Women's Institute, 173–174
Wong Lane, Tickhill, Dorset, 280
Wood, Alan C., 4, 43, 48
Wood, Charles Lindley (Lord Halifax), 307
Woodcroft, Peterborough, Huntingdonshire, 108
Woodham-Smith, C, 301
Wookey hole, Somerset, 75
Woolmanton, Wiltshire, 108
Wootton Rivers, Wiltshire, 400–402
Worcester, 354, 355
Wordsworth, William, 307
Worthing, West Sussex, 328
Wotton, Surrey, 249–250
Wright, Basil, 19
WRNS, 141
Wye, River, Monmouthshire, 307
Wynne, Sir John, 351

Yates Jackie 320
Yorkshire, 28–31, 75, 108, 125–127, 129, 279–280, 311, 367, 379–381
Yorkshire, Jack, 182, 185
Young, Brigadier Peter, 77, 79, 85
Young Dracula films, 288
Ythancaestir, Essex, 304

Zuccaro, Federigo, 156